FEDERAL RULES OF BANKRUPTCY PROCEDURE
2025 Edition
Updated through January 1, 2025

Michigan Legal Publishing Ltd.
QUICK DESK REFERENCE SERIES™

WE WELCOME YOUR FEEDBACK: info@michlp.com

ISBN-13: 978-1-64002-162-4

Table of Contents

Federal Rules of Bankruptcy Procedure

Rule 1001. Scope; Title; Citations; References to a Specific Form

(a) **In General**. These rules, together with the Official Bankruptcy Forms, govern the procedure in cases under the Bankruptcy Code, Title 11 of the United States Code. They must be construed, administered, and employed by both the court and the parties to secure the just, speedy, and inexpensive determination of every case and proceeding.

(b) **Titles**. These rules should be referred to as the Federal Rules of Bankruptcy Procedure and the forms as the Official Bankruptcy Forms.

(c) **Citations**. In these rules, the Bankruptcy Code is cited with a section sign and number (§101). A rule is cited with "Rule" followed by the rule number (Rule 1001(a)).

(d) **References to a Specific Form**. A reference to a "Form" followed by a number is a reference to an Official Bankruptcy Form.

(As amended Mar. 30, 1987, eff. Aug. 1, 1987; Apr. 30, 1991, eff. Aug. 1, 1991; Apr. 27, 2017, eff. Dec. 1, 2017; Apr. 2, 2024, eff. Dec. 1, 2024.)

Part I—Commencing a Bankruptcy Case; The Petition, the Order for Relief, and Related Matters

Rule 1002. Commencing a Bankruptcy Case

(a) **In General**. A bankruptcy case is commenced by filing a petition with the clerk.

(b) **Copy to the United States Trustee**. The clerk must promptly send a copy of the petition to the United States trustee.

(As amended Mar. 30, 1987, eff. Aug. 1, 1987; Apr. 30, 1991, eff. Aug. 1, 1991; Apr. 2, 2024, eff. Dec. 1, 2024.)

Rule 1003. Involuntary Petition: Transferred Claims; Joining Other Creditors; Additional Time to Join

(a) **Transferred Claims**. An entity that has transferred or acquired a claim for the purpose of commencing an involuntary case under Chapter 7 or Chapter 11 is not a qualified petitioner. A petitioner that has transferred or acquired a claim must attach to the petition and to any copy:

    (1) all documents evidencing the transfer, whether it was unconditional, for security, or otherwise; and

    (2) a signed statement that:

        (A) affirms that the claim was not transferred for the purpose of commencing the case; and

        (B) sets forth the consideration for the transfer and its terms.

(b) **Joining Other Creditors After Filing**. If an involuntary petition is filed by fewer than 3 creditors and the debtor's answer alleges the existence of 12 or more creditors as provided in §303(b), the debtor must attach to the answer:
  (1) the names and addresses of all creditors; and
  (2) a brief statement of the nature and amount of each creditor's claim.

(c) **Additional Time to Join**. If there appear to be 12 or more creditors, the court must allow a reasonable time for other creditors to join the petition before holding a hearing on it.

(As amended Mar. 30, 1987, eff. Aug. 1, 1987; Apr. 2, 2024, eff. Dec. 1, 2024.)

Rule 1004. Involuntary Petition Against a Partnership

A petitioner who files an involuntary petition against a partnership under §303(b)(3) must promptly send a copy of the petition to—or serve a copy on—each general partner who is not a petitioner. The clerk must promptly issue a summons for service on any general partner who is not a petitioner. Rule 1010 governs the form and service of the summons.

(As amended Apr. 29, 2002, eff. Dec. 1, 2002; Apr. 2, 2024, eff. Dec. 1, 2024.)

Rule 1004.1. Voluntary Petition on Behalf of an Infant or Incompetent Person

(a) **Represented Infant or Incompetent Person**. If an infant or an incompetent person has a representative—such as a general guardian, committee, conservator, or similar fiduciary—the representative may file a voluntary petition on behalf of the infant or incompetent person.

(b) **Unrepresented Infant or Incompetent Person**. If an infant or an incompetent person does not have a representative:
  (1) a next friend or guardian ad litem may file the petition; and
  (2) the court must appoint a guardian ad litem or issue any other order needed to protect the interests of the infant debtor or incompetent debtor.

(Added Apr. 29, 2002, eff. Dec. 1, 2002; amended Apr. 2, 2024, eff. Dec. 1, 2024.)

Rule 1004.2. Petition in a Chapter 15 Case

(a) **Designating the Center of Main Interests**. A petition under Chapter 15 for recognition of a foreign proceeding must:
  (1) designate the country where the debtor has its center of main interests; and
  (2) identify each country in which a foreign proceeding against, by, or regarding the debtor is pending.

(b) **Challenging the Designation**. The United States trustee or a party in interest may file a motion challenging the designation. If the motion is filed by a party in interest, a copy must be sent to the United States trustee. Unless the court orders otherwise, the motion must be filed at least 7 days before the date set for the hearing on the petition. The motion must be served on:

- the debtor;
- all persons or bodies authorized to administer the debtor's foreign proceedings;
- all entities against whom provisional relief is sought under §1519;
- all parties to litigation pending in the United States in which the debtor was a party when the petition was filed; and
- any other entity as the court orders.

(Added Apr. 26, 2011, eff. Dec. 1, 2011; amended Apr. 2, 2024, eff. Dec. 1, 2024.)

Rule 1005. Caption of a Petition; Title of the Case

(a) **Caption and Title; Required Information**. A petition's caption must contain the name of the court, the title of the case, and the case number (if known). The title must include the following information about the debtor:

(1) name;

(2) employer-identification number;

(3) the last 4 digits of the social-security number or individual taxpayer-identification number;

(4) any other federal taxpayer-identification number; and

(5) all other names the debtor has used within 8 years before the petition was filed.

(b) **Petition Not Filed by the Debtor**. A petition not filed by the debtor must include all names that the petitioner knows have been used by the debtor.

(As amended Mar. 30, 1987, eff. Aug. 1, 1987; Mar. 27, 2003, eff. Dec. 1, 2003; Apr. 23, 2008, eff. Dec. 1, 2008; Apr. 2, 2024, eff. Dec. 1, 2024.)

Rule 1006. Filing Fee

(a) **In General**. Unless (b) or (c) applies, every petition must be accompanied by the filing fee. In this rule 1 "filing fee" means:

(1) the filing fee required by 28 U.S.C. §1930(a)(1)–(5); and

(2) any other fee that the Judicial Conference of the United States requires under 28 U.S.C. §1930(b) to be paid upon filing.

(b) **Paying by Installment**.

(1) *Application to Pay by Installment*. The clerk must accept for filing an individual's voluntary petition, regardless of whether any part of the filing fee is paid, if it is accompanied by a completed and signed application to pay in installments (Form 103A).

(2) *Court Decision on Installments*. Before the meeting of creditors, the court may order payment of the entire filing fee or may order the debtor to pay it in installments, designating the number of installments (not to exceed 4), the amount of each one, and payment dates. All payments must be made within 120 days after the petition is filed. The court may, for cause, extend the time to pay an installment, but the last one must be paid within 180 days after the petition is filed.

(3) *Postponing Other Payments*. Until the filing fee has been paid in full, the debtor or Chapter 13 trustee must not make any further payment to an attorney or any other person who provides services to the debtor in connection with the case.

(c) **Waiving the Filing Fee**. The clerk must accept for filing an individual's voluntary Chapter 7 petition if it is accompanied by a completed and signed application to waive the filing fee (Form 103B).

(As amended Mar. 30, 1987, eff. Aug. 1, 1987; Apr. 23, 1996, eff. Dec. 1, 1996; Apr. 23, 2008, eff. Dec. 1, 2008; Apr. 27, 2017, eff. Dec. 1, 2017; Apr. 2, 2024, eff. Dec. 1, 2024.)

Rule 1007. Lists, Schedules, Statements, and Other Documents; Time to File

(a) **Lists of Names and Addresses**.

(1) *Voluntary Case*. In a voluntary case, the debtor must file with the petition a list containing the name and address of each entity included or to be included on Schedules D, E/F, G, and H of the Official Forms. Unless it is a governmental unit, a corporate debtor must:

(A) include a corporate-ownership statement containing the information described in Rule 7007.1; and

(B) promptly file a supplemental statement if changed circumstances make the original statement inaccurate.

(2) *Involuntary Case*. Within 7 days after the order for relief has been entered in an involuntary case, the debtor must file a list containing the name and address of each entity included or to be included on Schedules D, E/F, G, and H of the Official Forms.

(3) *Chapter 11—List of Equity Security Holders*. Unless the court orders otherwise, a Chapter 11 debtor must, within 14 days after the order for relief is entered, file a list of the debtor's equity security holders by class. The list must show the number and type of interests registered in each holder's name, along with the holder's last known address or place of business

(4) *Chapter 15—Information Required from a Foreign Representative*. If a foreign representative files a petition under Chapter 15 for recognition of a foreign proceeding, the representative must—in addition to the documents required by §1515—include with the petition:

      (A) a corporate-ownership statement containing the information described in Rule 7007.1; and

      (B) unless the court orders otherwise, a list containing the names and addresses of:

          (i) all persons or bodies authorized to administer the debtor's foreign proceedings;

          (ii) all entities against whom provisional relief is sought under §1519; and

          (iii) all parties to litigation pending in the United States in which the debtor was a party when the petition was filed.

  (5) *Extending the Time to File.* On motion and for cause, the court may extend the time to file any list required by this Rule 1007(a). Notice of the motion must be given to:

    • the United States trustee;

    • any trustee;

    • any committee elected under §705 or appointed under §1102; and

    • any other party as the court orders.

(b) Schedules, Statements, and Other Documents.

  (1) *In General.* Except in a Chapter 9 case or when the court orders otherwise, the debtor must file—prepared as prescribed by the appropriate Official Form, if any—

    (A) schedules of assets and liabilities;

    (B) a schedule of current income and expenditures;

    (C) a schedule of executory contracts and unexpired leases;

    (D) a statement of financial affairs;

    (E) copies of all payment advices or other evidence of payment that the debtor received from any employer within 60 days before the petition was filed—with all but the last 4 digits of the debtor's social-security number or individual taxpayer-identification number deleted; and

    (F) a record of the debtor's interest, if any, in an account or program of the type specified in §521(c).

  (2) *Statement of Intention.* In a Chapter 7 case, an individual debtor must:

    (A) file the statement of intention required by §521(a) (Form 108); and

    (B) before or upon filing, serve a copy on the trustee and the creditors named in the statement.

  (3) *Credit-Counseling Statement.* Unless the United States trustee has determined that the requirement to file a credit-counseling statement under §109(h) does not apply in the district, an individual debtor must file a statement of compliance (included in Form 101). The debtor must include one of the following:

    (A) a certificate and any debt-repayment plan required by §521(b);

(B) a statement that the debtor has received the credit-counseling briefing required by §109(h)(1), but does not have a §521(b) certificate;

(C) a certification under §109(h)(3); or

(D) a request for a court determination under §109(h)(4).

(4) *Current Monthly Income—Chapter 7.* Unless §707(b)(2)(D) applies, an individual debtor in a Chapter 7 case must:

(A) file a statement of current monthly income (Form 122A–1); and

(B) if that income exceeds the median family income for the debtor's state and household size, file the Chapter 7 means-test calculation (Form 122A–2).

(5) *Current Monthly Income—Chapter 11.* An individual debtor in a Chapter 11 case (unless under Subchapter V) must file a statement of current monthly income (Form 122B).

(6) *Current Monthly Income—Chapter 13.* A debtor in a Chapter 13 case must:

(A) file a statement of current monthly income (Form 122C–1); and

(B) if that income exceeds the median family income for the debtor's state and household size, file the Chapter 13 calculation of disposable income (Form 122C-2).

(7) *Personal Financial-Management Course.* Unless an approved provider has notified the court that the debtor has completed a course in personal financial management after filing the petition or the debtor is not required to complete one as a condition to discharge, an individual debtor in a Chapter 7 or Chapter 13 case—or in a Chapter 11 case in which §1141(d)(3) applies—must file a certificate of course completion issued by the provider.

(8) *Limitation on a Homestead Exemption.* This Rule 1007(b)(8) applies if an individual debtor in a Chapter 11, 12, or 13 case claims an exemption under §522(b)(3)(A) in property of the type described in §522(p)(1) and the property value exceeds the amount specified in §522(q)(1). The debtor must file a statement about any pending proceeding in which the debtor may be found:

(A) guilty of the type of felony described in §522(q)(1)(A); or

(B) liable for the type of debt described in §522(q)(1)(B).

(c) **Time to File.**

(1) *Voluntary Case—Various Documents.* Unless (d), (e), (f), or (h) provides otherwise, the debtor in a voluntary case must file the documents required by (b)(1), (b)(4), (b)(5), and (b)(6) with the petition or within 14 days after it is filed.

(2) *Involuntary Case—Various Documents.* In an involuntary case, the debtor must file the documents required by (b)(1) within 14 days after the order for relief is entered.

(3) *Credit-Counseling Documents.* In a voluntary case, the documents required by (b)(3)(A), (C), or (D) must be filed with the petition. Unless the court orders otherwise, a debtor who has filed a statement under (b)(3)(B) must file the documents required by (b)(3)(A) within 14 days after the order for relief is entered.

(4) *Financial-Management Course.* Unless the court extends the time to file, an individual debtor must file the certificate required by (b)(7) as follows

    (A) in a Chapter 7 case, within 60 days after the first date set for the meeting of creditors under §341; and

    (B) in a Chapter 11 or Chapter 13 case, no later than the date the last payment is made under the plan or the date a motion for a discharge is filed under §1141(d)(5)(B) or §1328(b).

(5) *Limitation on Homestead Exemption.* The debtor must file the statement required by (b)(8) no earlier than the date of the last payment made under the plan or the date a motion for a discharge is filed under §1141(d)(5)(B), 1228(b), or 1328(b).

(6) *Documents in a Converted Case.* Unless the court orders otherwise, a document filed before a case is converted to another chapter is considered filed in the converted case.

(7) *Extending the Time to File.* Except as §1116(3) provides otherwise, the court, on motion and for cause, may extend the time to file a document under this rule. The movant must give notice of the motion to:

- the United States trustee;
- any committee elected under §705 or appointed under §1102; and
- any trustee, examiner, and other party as the court orders.

If the motion is granted, notice must be given to the United States trustee and to any committee, trustee, and other party as the court orders.

(d) **List of the 20 Largest Unsecured Creditors in a Chapter 9 or Chapter 11 Case.** In addition to the lists required by (a), a debtor in a Chapter 9 case or in a voluntary Chapter 11 case must file with the petition a list containing the names, addresses, and claims of the creditors that hold the 20 largest unsecured claims, excluding insiders, as prescribed by the appropriate Official Form (Form 104 or 204). In an involuntary Chapter 11 case, the debtor must file the list within 2 days after the order for relief is entered under §303(h).

(e) **Chapter 9 Lists.** In a Chapter 9 case, the court must set the time for the debtor to file the list required by (a). If a proposed plan requires real estate assessments to be revised so that the proportion of special assessments or special taxes for some property will be different from the proportion in effect when the petition is filed, the debtor must also file a list that shows— for each adversely affected property—the name and address of each known holder of title, both legal and equitable. On motion and for cause, the court may modify the requirements of this Rule 1007(e) and those of (a).

(f) **Social-Security Number**. In a voluntary case, an individual debtor must submit with the petition a verified statement that gives the debtor's social-security number or states that the debtor does not have one (Form 121). In an involuntary case, the debtor must submit the statement within 14 days after the order for relief is entered.

(g) **Partnership Case**. The general partners of a debtor partnership must file for the partnership the list required by (a) and the documents required by (b)(1)(A)–(D). The court may order any general partner to file a statement of personal assets and liabilities and may set the deadline for doing so.

(h) **Interests in Property Acquired or Arising After a Petition Is Filed**. After the petition is filed in a Chapter 7, 11, 12, or 13 case, if the debtor acquires—or becomes entitled to acquire—an interest in property described in §541(a)(5), the debtor must file a supplemental schedule and include any claimed exemption. Unless the court allows additional time, the debtor must file the schedule within 14 days after learning about the property interest. This duty continues even after the case is closed but does not apply to property acquired after an order is entered:

  (1) confirming a Chapter 11 plan (other than one confirmed under §1191(b)); or

  (2) discharging the debtor in a Chapter 12 case, a Chapter 13 case, or a case under Subchapter V of Chapter 11 in which the plan is confirmed under §1191(b).

(i) **Security Holders Known to Others**. After notice and a hearing and for cause, the court may direct an entity other than the debtor or trustee to:

  (1) disclose any list of the debtor's security holders in its possession or under its control by:

    (A) producing the list or a copy of it;

    (B) allowing inspection or copying; or

    (C) making any other disclosure; and

  (2) indicate the name, address, and security held by each listed holder.

(j) **Impounding Lists**. On a party in interest's motion and for cause, the court may impound any list filed under this rule and may refuse inspection. But the court may permit a party in interest to inspect or use an impounded list on terms prescribed by the court.

(k) **Debtor's Failure to File a Required Document**. If a debtor fails to properly prepare and file a list, schedule, or statement (other than a statement of intention) as required by this rule, the court may order:

  (1) that the trustee, a petitioning creditor, a committee, or other party do so within the time set by the court; and

  (2) that the cost incurred be reimbursed as an administrative expense.

(l) **Copies to the United States Trustee**. The clerk must promptly send to the United States trustee a copy of every list, schedule, or statement filed under (a)(1), (a)(2), (b), (d), or (h).

(m) **Infant or Incompetent Person**. If a debtor knows that a person named in a list of creditors or in a schedule is an infant or is incompetent, the debtor must also include the name, address, and legal relationship of anyone on whom process would be served in an adversary proceeding against that person under Rule 7004(b)(2).

(As amended Mar. 30, 1987, eff. Aug. 1, 1987; Apr. 30, 1991, eff. Aug. 1, 1991; Apr. 23, 1996, eff. Dec. 1, 1996; Apr. 23, 2001, eff. Dec. 1, 2001; Mar. 27, 2003, eff. Dec. 1, 2003; Apr. 25, 2005, eff. Dec. 1, 2005; Apr. 23, 2008, eff. Dec. 1, 2008; Mar. 26, 2009, eff. Dec. 1, 2009; Apr. 28, 2010, eff. Dec. 1, 2010; Apr. 23, 2012, eff. Dec. 1, 2012; Apr. 16, 2013, eff. Dec. 1, 2013; Apr. 29, 2015, eff. Dec. 1, 2015; Apr. 11, 2022, eff. Dec. 1, 2022; Apr. 2, 2024, eff. Dec. 1, 2024.)

Rule 1008. Requirement to Verify Petitions and Accompanying Documents

A petition, list, schedule, statement, and any amendment must be verified or must contain an unsworn declaration under 28 U.S.C. §1746.

(As amended Apr. 30, 1991, eff. Aug. 1, 1991; Apr. 2, 2024, eff. Dec. 1, 2024.)

Rule 1009. Amending a Voluntary Petition, List, Schedule, or Statement

(a) **In General**.

   (1) *By a Debtor*. A debtor may amend a voluntary petition, list, schedule, or statement at any time before the case is closed. The debtor must give notice of the amendment to the trustee and any affected entity.

   (2) *By a Party in Interest*. On a party in interest's motion and after notice and a hearing, the court may order a voluntary petition, list, schedule, or statement to be amended. The clerk must give notice of the amendment to entities that the court designates.

(b) **Amending a Statement of Intention**. A debtor may amend a statement of intention at any time before the time provided in §521(a)(2) expires. The debtor must give notice of the amendment to the trustee and any affected entity.

(c) **Amending a Statement of Social-Security Number**. If a debtor learns that a social-security number shown on the statement submitted under Rule 1007(f) is incorrect, the debtor must:

   (1) promptly submit an amended verified statement with the correct number (Form 121); and

   (2) give notice of the amendment to all entities required to be listed under Rule 1007(a)(1) or (a)(2).

(d) **Copy to the United States Trustee**. The clerk must promptly send a copy of every amendment filed under this rule to the United States trustee.

(As amended Mar. 30, 1987, eff. Aug. 1, 1987; Apr. 30, 1991, eff. Aug. 1, 1991; Apr. 12, 2006, eff. Dec. 1, 2006; Apr. 23, 2008, eff. Dec. 1, 2008; Apr. 2, 2024, eff. Dec. 1, 2024.)

Rule 1010. Serving an Involuntary Petition and Summons

(a) **In General**. After an involuntary petition has been filed, the clerk must promptly issue a summons for service on the debtor. The summons must be served with a copy of the petition in the manner that Rule 7004(a) and (b) provide for service of a summons and complaint. If service cannot be so made, the court may order service by mail to the debtor's last known address, and by at least one publication as the court orders. Service may be made anywhere. Rule 7004(e) and Fed. R. Civ. P. 4(l) govern service under this rule.

(b) **Corporate-Ownership Statement**. A corporation that files an involuntary petition must file and serve with the petition a corporate-ownership statement containing the information described in Rule 7007.1.

(As amended Mar. 30, 1987, eff. Aug. 1, 1987; Apr. 30, 1991, eff. Aug. 1, 1991; Apr. 22, 1993, eff. Aug. 1, 1993; Apr. 11, 1997, eff. Dec. 1, 1997; Apr. 23, 2008, eff. Dec. 1, 2008; Apr. 28, 2016, eff. Dec. 1, 2016; Apr. 2, 2024, eff. Dec. 1, 2024.)

Rule 1011. Responsive Pleading in an Involuntary Case; Effect of a Motion

(a) **Who May Contest a Petition**. A debtor may contest an involuntary petition filed against it. In a partnership case under Rule 1004, a nonpetitioning general partner—or a person who is alleged to be a general partner but denies the allegation—may contest the petition.

(b) **Defenses and Objections; Time to File**. A defense or objection to the petition must be presented as prescribed by Fed. R. Civ. P. 12. It must be filed and served within 21 days after the summons is served. But if service is made by publication on a party or partner who does not reside in—or cannot be found in—the state where the court sits, the court must set the time to file and serve the answer.

(c) **Effect of a Motion**. Serving a motion under Fed. R. Civ. P. 12(b) extends the time to file and serve an answer as Fed. R. Civ. P. 12(a) permits.

(d) **Limitation on Asserting a Debtor's Claim Against a Petitioning Creditor**. A debtor's answer must not assert a claim against a petitioning creditor except to defeat the petition.

(e) **Limit on Pleadings**. No pleading other than an answer to the petition is allowed, but the court may order a reply to an answer and set the time for filing and service.

(f) **Corporate-Ownership Statement**. A corporation that responds to the petition must file a corporate-ownership statement containing the information described in Rule 7007.1. The corporation must do so with its first appearance, pleading, motion, or response, or other first request to the court.

(As amended Mar. 30, 1987, eff. Aug. 1, 1987; Apr. 26, 2004, eff. Dec. 1, 2004; Apr. 23, 2008, eff. Dec. 1, 2008; Mar. 26, 2009, eff. Dec. 1, 2009; Apr. 28, 2016, eff. Dec. 1, 2016; Apr. 2, 2024, eff. Dec. 1, 2024.)

Rule 1012. Contesting a Petition in a Chapter 15 Case

(a) **Who May Contest the Petition**. A debtor or a party in interest may contest a Chapter 15 petition for recognition of a foreign proceeding.

(b) **Time to File a Response**. Unless the court sets a different time, a response to the petition must be filed at least 7 days before the date set for a hearing on the petition.

(c) **Corporate-Ownership Statement**. A corporation that responds to the petition must file a corporate-ownership statement containing the information described in Rule 7007.1. The corporation must do so with its first appearance, pleading, motion, or response, or other first request to the court.

(Added Apr. 28, 2016, eff. Dec. 1, 2016; amended Apr. 2, 2024, eff. Dec. 1, 2024.)

Rule 1013. Contested Petition in an Involuntary Case; Default

(a) **Hearing and Disposition**. When a petition in an involuntary case is contested, the court must:

    (1) rule on the issues presented at the earliest practicable time; and

    (2) promptly issue an order for relief, dismiss the petition, or issue any other appropriate order.

(b) **Default**. If the petition is not contested within the time allowed by Rule 1011, the court must issue the order for relief on the next day or as soon as practicable.

(As amended Apr. 30, 1991, eff. Aug. 1, 1991; Apr. 22, 1993, eff. Aug. 1, 1993; Apr. 2, 2024, eff. Dec. 1, 2024.)

Rule 1014. Transferring a Case to Another District; Dismissing a Case Improperly Filed

(a) **Dismissal or Transfer**.

    (1) *Petition Filed in the Proper District*. If a petition is filed in the proper district, the court may transfer the case to another district in the interest of justice or for the convenience of the parties. The court may do so:

        (A) on its own or on a party in interest's timely motion; and

    (B) only after a hearing on notice to the petitioner, United States trustee, and other entities as the court orders.

  (2) *Petition Filed in an Improper District.* If a petition is filed in an improper district, the court may dismiss the case or may transfer it to another district on the same grounds and under the same procedures as stated in (1).

(b) **Petitions Involving the Same or Related Debtors Filed in Different Districts.**

  (1) *Scope.* This Rule 1014(b) applies if petitions commencing cases or seeking recognition under Chapter 15 are filed in different districts by, regarding, or against:

    (A) the same debtor;

    (B) a partnership and one or more of its general partners;

    (C) two or more general partners; or

    (D) a debtor and an affiliate.

  (2) *Court Action.* The court in the district where the first petition is filed may determine the district or districts in which the cases should proceed in the interest of justice or for the convenience of the parties. The court may do so on timely motion and after a hearing on notice to:

- the United States trustee;
- entities entitled to notice under Rule 2002(a); and
- other entities as the court orders.

  (3) *Later-Filed Petitions.* The court in the district where the first petition is filed may order the parties to the later-filed cases not to proceed further until the motion is decided.

(As amended Mar. 30, 1987, eff. Aug. 1, 1987; Apr. 30, 1991, eff. Aug. 1, 1991; Apr. 30, 2007, eff. Dec. 1, 2007; Apr. 28, 2010, eff. Dec. 1, 2010; Apr. 25, 2014, eff. Dec. 1, 2014; Apr. 2, 2024, eff. Dec. 1, 2024.)

Rule 1015. Consolidating or Jointly Administering Cases Pending in the Same District

(a) **Consolidating Cases Involving the Same Debtor**. The court may consolidate two or more cases that are regarding or brought by or against the same debtor and that are pending in its district.

(b) **Jointly Administering Cases Involving Related Debtors; Exemptions of Spouses; Protective Orders to Avoid Conflicts of Interest**.

  (1) *In General.* The court may order joint administration of the estates in a joint case or in two or more cases pending in the court if they are brought by or against:

    (A) spouses;

    (B) a partnership and one or more of its general partners;

    (C) two or more general partners; or

    (D) a debtor and an affiliate.

   (2) *Potential Conflicts of Interest.* Before issuing a joint-administration order, the court must consider how to protect the creditors of different estates against potential conflicts of interest.

   (3) *Exemptions in Cases Involving Spouses.* If spouses have filed separate petitions—with one electing exemptions under §522(b)(2) and the other under §522(b)(3)—and the court orders joint administration, that order must:

      (A) set a reasonable time for the debtors to elect the same exemptions; and

      (B) advise the debtors that if they fail to do so, they will be considered to have elected exemptions under §522(b)(2).

(c) **Protective Orders to Avoid Unnecessary Costs and Delay**. When cases are consolidated or jointly administered, the court may issue orders to avoid unnecessary costs and delay while still protecting the parties' rights under the Code.

(As amended Mar. 30, 1987, eff. Aug. 1, 1987; Apr. 23, 2008, eff. Dec. 1, 2008; Apr. 28, 2010, eff. Dec. 1, 2010; Apr. 27, 2017, eff. Dec. 1, 2017; Apr. 2, 2024, eff. Dec. 1, 2024.)

Rule 1016. Death or Incompetency of a Debtor

(a) **Chapter 7 Case**. In a Chapter 7 case, the debtor's death or incompetency does not abate the case. The case continues, as far as possible, as though the death or incompetency had not occurred.

(b) **Chapter 11, 12, or 13 Case**. Upon the debtor's death or incompetency in a Chapter 11, 12, or 13 case, the court may dismiss the case or may permit it to continue if further administration is possible and is in the parties' best interests. If the case continues, it must proceed and be concluded in the same manner as though the death or incompetency had not occurred.

(As amended Apr. 30, 1991, eff. Aug. 1, 1991; Apr. 2, 2024, eff. Dec. 1, 2024.)

Rule 1017. Dismissing a Case; Suspending Proceedings; Converting a Case to Another Chapter

(a) **Dismissing a Case—In General**. Except as provided in §707(a)(3), 707(b), 1208(b), or 1307(b), or in Rule 1017(b), (c), or (e), the court must conduct a hearing on notice under Rule 2002 before dismissing a case on the petitioner's motion, for want of prosecution or other cause, or by the parties' consent. For the purpose of the notice, a debtor who has not already filed a list of creditors and their addresses must do so before the deadline set by the court. If the debtor fails to timely file the list, the court may order the debtor or another entity to do so.

(b) **Dismissing a Case for Failure to Pay an Installment Toward the Filing Fee**. If the debtor fails to pay any installment toward the filing fee, the court may dismiss the case after a hearing on notice to the debtor and trustee. If the court dismisses or closes the case without full payment of the filing fee, previous installment payments must be distributed as if full payment had been made.

(c) **Dismissing a Voluntary Chapter 7 or Chapter 13 Case for Failure to File a Document on Time**. On motion of the United States trustee, the court may dismiss a voluntary Chapter 7 case under §707(a)(3), or a Chapter 13 case under §1307(c)(9), for a failure to timely file the information required by §521(a)(1). But the court may do so only after a hearing on notice served by the United States trustee on the debtor, trustee, and any other entity as the court orders.

(d) **Dismissing a Case or Suspending Proceedings Under §305**. The court may dismiss a case or suspend proceedings under §305 only after a hearing on notice under Rule 2002(a).

(e) **Dismissing an Individual Debtor's Chapter 7 Case for Abuse or Converting it to Chapter 11 or 13**.

(1) *In General*. On motion under §707(b), the court may dismiss an individual debtor's Chapter 7 case for abuse or, with the debtor's consent, convert it to Chapter 11 or 13. The court may do so only after a hearing on notice to:

- the debtor;
- the trustee;
- the United States trustee; and
- any other entity as the court orders.

(2) *Time to File a Motion; Content*. Except as §704(b)(2) provides otherwise, a motion to dismiss a case for abuse under §707(b) or (c) must be filed within 60 days after the first date set for the meeting of creditors under §341(a). On request made within the 60-day period, the court may, for cause, extend the time to file. The motion must:

(A) set forth all matters to be considered at the hearing; and

(B) if made under §707(b)(1) and (3), state with particularity the circumstances alleged to constitute abuse.

(3) *Hearing on the Court's Own Motion; Serving Notice*. If the hearing is set on the court's own motion, the clerk must serve notice on the debtor within 60 days after the first date set for the meeting of creditors under §341(a). The notice must set forth all matters to be considered at the hearing.

(f) **Procedures for Dismissing, Suspending, or Converting a Case**.

(1) *In General*. Rule 9014 governs a proceeding to dismiss or suspend a case or to convert it to another chapter—except under §706(a), 1112(a), 1208(a) or (b), or 1307(a) or (b).

(2) *Cases Requiring a Motion*. Dismissing or converting a case under §706(a), 1112(a), 1208(b), or 1307(b) requires a motion filed and served as required by Rule 9013.

(3) *Conversion in a Chapter 12 or 13 Case.* If the debtor files a conversion notice under §1208(a) or §1307(a), the case will be converted without court order. The notice date becomes the date of the conversion order in applying §348(c) or Rule 1019. The clerk must promptly send a copy of the notice to the United States trustee.

(As amended Mar. 30, 1987, eff. Aug. 1, 1987; Apr. 30, 1991, eff. Aug. 1, 1991; Apr. 22, 1993, eff. Aug. 1, 1993; Apr. 26, 1999, eff. Dec. 1, 1999; Apr. 17, 2000, eff. Dec. 1, 2000; Apr. 23, 2008, eff. Dec. 1, 2008; Apr. 2, 2024, eff. Dec. 1, 2024.)

Rule 1018. Contesting a Petition in an Involuntary or Chapter 15 Case; Vacating an Order for Relief; Applying Part VII Rules

(a) **Applying Part VII Rules.** Unless the court orders or a Part I rule provides otherwise, Rules 7005, 7008–10, 7015–16, 7024–26, 7028–37, 7052, 7054, 7056, and 7062—together with any other Part VII rules as the court may order—apply to the following:
   (1) a proceeding that contests either an involuntary petition or a Chapter 15 petition for recognition; and
   (2) a proceeding to vacate an order for relief.
(b) **References to an "Adversary Proceeding."** Any reference to an "adversary proceeding" in the rules listed in (a) is a reference to the proceedings listed in (a)(1)–(2).
(c) **"Complaint" Means "Petition."** For the proceedings described in (a), a reference to the "complaint" in the Federal Rules of Civil Procedure must be read as a reference to the petition.

(As amended Mar. 30, 1987, eff. Aug. 1, 1987; Apr. 28, 2010, eff. Dec. 1, 2010; Apr. 2, 2024, eff. Dec. 1, 2024.)

Rule 1019. Converting or Reconverting a Chapter 11, 12, or 13 Case to Chapter 7

(a) **Filing Various Documents; Filing a Statement of Intention.**
   (1) *Lists, Inventories, Schedules, Statements of Financial Affairs.* Unless the court orders otherwise, when a Chapter 11, 12, or 13 case is converted or reconverted to Chapter 7, the lists, inventories, schedules, and statements of financial affairs previously filed are considered filed in the Chapter 7 case. If they have not been previously filed, the debtor must comply with Rule 1007 as if an order for relief had been entered on an involuntary petition on the same date as the order directing that the case continue under Chapter 7.
   (2) *Statement of Intention.* A statement of intention, if required, must be filed within 30 days after the conversion order is entered or before the first date set for the meeting of creditors, whichever is earlier. The court may, for cause, extend the time to file only on motion filed—or

on oral request made during a hearing—before the time has expired. Notice of an extension must be given to the United States trustee and to any committee, trustee, or other party as the court orders.

(b) **New Time to File a §707(b) or (c) Motion, a Proof of Claim, a Complaint Objecting to Discharge, or a Complaint to Determine Dischargeability**.

  (1) *When a New Time Begins*. When a case is converted to Chapter 7, a new time begins under Rule 1017, 3002, 4004, or 4007 to file:

  (A) a motion under §707(b) or (c);

  (B) a proof of claim;

  (C) a complaint objecting to discharge; or

  (D) a complaint to determine whether a specific debt may be discharged.

  (2) *When a New Time Does Not Begin*. No new time to file begins when a case is reconverted to Chapter 7 after a previous conversion to Chapter 11, 12, or 13 if the time to file in the original Chapter 7 case has expired.

  (3) *New Time to Object to a Claimed Exemption*. When a case is converted to Chapter 7, a new time begins under Rule 4003(b) to object to a claimed exemption unless:

  (A) more than 1 year has elapsed since the court issued the first order confirming a plan under Chapter 11, 12, or 13; or

  (B) the case was previously pending in Chapter 7 and time has expired to object to a claimed exemption in the original Chapter 7 case.

(c) **Proof of Claim Filed Before Conversion**. A proof of claim filed by a creditor before conversion is considered filed in the Chapter 7 case.

(d) **Turning Over Documents and Property**. Unless the court orders otherwise, after a trustee in the Chapter 7 case qualifies or assumes duties, the debtor in possession— or the previously acting trustee—must promptly turn over to the Chapter 7 trustee all documents and property of the estate that are in its possession or control.

(e) **Final Report and Account; Schedule of Unpaid Postpetition Debts**.

  (1) *In a Chapter 11 or Chapter 12 Case*. Unless the court orders otherwise, when a Chapter 11 or 12 case is converted to Chapter 7, the debtor in possession or, if the debtor is not a debtor in possession, the trustee serving at the time of conversion must:

  (A) within 14 days after conversion, file a schedule of unpaid debts incurred after the petition was filed but before conversion and include the name and address of each claim holder; and

  (B) within 30 days after conversion, file and send to the United States trustee a final report and account.

  (2) *In a Chapter 13 Case*. Unless the court orders otherwise, when a Chapter 13 case is converted to Chapter 7:

(A) within 14 days after conversion, the debtor must file a schedule of unpaid debts incurred after the petition was filed but before conversion and include the name and address of each claim holder; and

(B) within 30 days after conversion, the trustee must file and send to the United States trustee a final report and account.

(3) *Converting a Case to Chapter 7 After a Plan Has Been Confirmed.* Unless the court orders otherwise, if a case under Chapter 11, 12, or 13 is converted to a case under Chapter 7 after a plan is confirmed, the debtor must file:

(A) a schedule of property that was acquired after the petition was filed but before conversion and was not listed in the final report and account, except when a Chapter 13 case is converted to Chapter 7 and §348(f)(2) does not apply;

(B) a schedule of unpaid debts that were incurred after confirmation but before conversion and were not listed in the final report and account; and

(C) a schedule of executory contracts and unexpired leases that were entered into or assumed after the petition was filed but before conversion.

(4) *Copy to the United States Trustee.* The clerk must promptly send to the United States trustee a copy of any schedule filed under this Rule 1019(e).

(f) **Preconversion Administrative Expenses; Postpetition Claims.**

(1) *Request to Pay an Administrative Expense; Time to File.* A request to pay an administrative expense incurred before conversion is timely filed under §503(a) if it is filed before conversion or within a time set by the court. Such a request by a governmental unit is timely if it is filed:

(A) before conversion; or

(B) within 180 days after conversion or within a time set by the court, whichever is later.

(2) *Proof of Claim Against the Debtor or the Estate.* A proof of claim under §348(d) against either the debtor or the estate may be filed as specified in Rules 3001(a)–(d) and 3002.

(3) *Giving Notice of Certain Time Limits.* After the filing of a schedule of debts incurred after the case was commenced but before conversion, the clerk, or the court's designee, must notify the entities listed on the schedule of:

(A) the time to request payment of an administrative expense; and

(B) the time to file a proof of claim under §348(d), unless a notice of insufficient assets to pay a dividend has been mailed under Rule 2002(e).

(As amended Mar. 30, 1987, eff. Aug. 1, 1987; Apr. 30, 1991, eff. Aug. 1, 1991; Apr. 23, 1996, eff. Dec. 1, 1996; Apr. 11, 1997, eff. Dec. 1, 1997; Apr. 26, 1999, eff. Dec. 1, 1999; Apr. 23, 2008, eff. Dec. 1, 2008; Mar. 26, 2009, eff. Dec. 1, 2009; Apr. 28, 2010, eff. Dec. 1, 2010; Apr. 2, 2024, eff. Dec. 1, 2024.)

Rule 1020. Designating a Chapter 11 Debtor as a Small Business Debtor

(a) **In General**. In a voluntary Chapter 11 case, the debtor must state in the petition whether the debtor is a small business debtor and, if so, whether the debtor elects to have Subchapter V of Chapter 11 apply. In an involuntary Chapter 11 case, the debtor must provide the same information in a statement filed within 14 days after the order for relief. The case must proceed in accordance with the debtor's statement, unless and until the court issues an order finding that the statement is incorrect.

(b) **Objecting to the Designation**. The United States trustee or a party in interest may object to the debtor's designation. The objection must be filed within 30 days after the conclusion of the meeting of creditors held under §341(a) or within 30 days after an amendment to the designation is filed, whichever is later.

(c) **Procedure; Service**. An objection or request under this rule is governed by Rule 9014 and must be served on:
- the debtor;
- the debtor's attorney;
- the United States trustee;
- the trustee;
- the creditors included on the list filed under Rule 1007(d)—or if a committee has been appointed under §1102(a)(3), the committee or its authorized agent; and
- any other entity as the court orders.

(Added Apr. 11, 1997, eff. Dec. 1, 1997; amended Apr. 23, 2008, eff. Dec. 1, 2008; Mar. 26, 2009, eff. Dec. 1, 2009; Apr. 11, 2022, eff. Dec. 1, 2022; Apr. 2, 2024, eff. Dec. 1, 2024.)

Rule 1021. Designating a Chapter 7, 9, or 11 Case as a Health Care Business Case

(a) **In General**. If a petition in a Chapter 7, 9, or 11 case designates the debtor as a health care business, the case must proceed in accordance with the designation unless the court orders otherwise.

(b) **Seeking a Court Determination**. The United States trustee or a party in interest may move the court to determine whether the debtor is a health care business. Proceedings on the motion are governed by Rule 9014. If the motion is filed by a party in interest, a copy must be sent to the United States trustee. The motion must be served on:

- the debtor;
- the trustee;
- any committee elected under §705 or appointed under §1102, or its authorized agent;
- in a Chapter 9 or Chapter 11 case in which an unsecured creditors' committee has not been appointed under §1102, the creditors on the list filed under Rule 1007(d); and
- any other entity as the court orders.

(Added Apr. 23, 2008, eff. Dec. 1, 2008; amended Apr. 2, 2024, eff. Dec. 1, 2024.)

Part II—Officers and Administration; Notices; Meetings; Examinations; Elections and Appointments; Final Report; Compensation

Rule 2001. Appointing an Interim Trustee Before the Order for Relief in an Involuntary Chapter 7 Case

(a) **Appointing an Interim Trustee**. After an involuntary Chapter 7 case commences but before an order for relief, the court may, on a party in interest's motion, order the United States trustee to appoint an interim trustee under §303(g). The motion must set forth the need for the appointment and may be granted only after a hearing on notice to:
- the debtor;
- the petitioning creditors;
- the United States trustee; and
- other parties in interest as the court orders.

(b) **Bond Required**. An interim trustee may be appointed only if the movant furnishes a bond, in an amount that the court approves, to indemnify the debtor for any costs, attorney's fees, expenses, and damages allowable under §303(i).

(c) **The Order's Content**. The court's order must state the reason the appointment is needed and specify the trustee's duties.

(d) **The Interim Trustee's Final Report**. Unless the court orders otherwise, after the qualification of a trustee selected under §702, the interim trustee must:
(1) promptly deliver to the trustee all the records and property of the estate that are in the interim trustee's possession or under its control; and
(2) within 30 days after the trustee qualifies, file a final report and account.

(As amended Mar. 30, 1987, eff. Aug. 1, 1987; Apr. 30, 1991, eff. Aug. 1, 1991; Apr. 2, 2024, eff. Dec. 1, 2024.)

Rule 2002. Notices

(a) **21-Day Notices to the Debtor, Trustee, Creditors, and Indenture Trustees**. Except as (h), (i), (l), (p), and (q) provide otherwise, the clerk or the court's designee must give the debtor, the trustee, all creditors, and all indenture trustees at least 21 days' notice by mail of:
(1) the meeting of creditors under §341 or §1104(b), which notice—unless the court orders otherwise—must include the debtor's:
(A) employer-identification number;
(B) social-security number; and
(C) any other federal taxpayer-identification number;

(2) a proposal to use, sell, or lease property of the estate other than in the ordinary course of business—unless the court, for cause, shortens the time or orders another method of giving notice;

(3) a hearing to approve a compromise or settlement other than an agreement under Rule 4001(d)—unless the court, for cause, orders that notice not be given;

(4) a hearing on a motion to dismiss a Chapter 7, 11, or 12 case or to convert it to another chapter—unless the hearing is under §707(a)(3) or §707(b) or is on a motion to dismiss the case for failure to pay the filing fee;

(5) the time to accept or reject a proposed modification to a plan;

(6) a hearing on a request for compensation or for reimbursement of expenses, if the request exceeds $1,000;

(7) the time to file a proof of claim under Rule 3003(c);

(8) the time to file an objection to—and the time of the hearing to consider whether to confirm—a Chapter 12 plan; and

(9) the time to object to confirming a Chapter 13 plan.

(b) **28-Day Notices to the Debtor, Trustee, Creditors, and Indenture Trustees**. Except as (l) provides otherwise, the clerk or the court's designee must give the debtor, trustee, all creditors, and all indenture trustees at least 28 days' notice by mail of:

(1) the time to file an objection and the time of the hearing to:

(A) consider approving a disclosure statement; or

(B) determine under §1125(f) whether a plan includes adequate information to make a separate disclosure statement unnecessary;

(2) the time to file an objection to—and the time of the hearing to consider whether to confirm—a Chapter 9 or 11 plan; and

(3) the time of the hearing to consider whether to confirm a Chapter 13 plan.

(c) **Content of a Notice**.

(1) *Proposed Use, Sale, or Lease of Property*. Subject to Rule 6004, a notice of a proposed use, sale, or lease of property under (a)(2) must include:

(A) a general description of the property;

(B) the time and place of any public sale;

(C) the terms and conditions of any private sale;

(D) the time to file objections; and

(E) for a proposed sale or lease of personally identifiable information under §363(b)(1), a statement whether the sale is consistent with any policy that prohibits transferring the information.

(2) *Hearing on an Application for Compensation or Reimbursement*. A notice under (a)(6) of a hearing on a request for compensation or for reimbursement of expenses must identify the applicant and the amounts requested.

(3) *Hearing on Confirming a Plan That Proposes an Injunction*. If a plan proposes an injunction against conduct not otherwise enjoined under the Code, the notice under (b)(2) must:

    (A) state in conspicuous language (bold, italic, or underlined text) that the plan proposes an injunction;

    (B) describe briefly the nature of the injunction; and

    (C) identify the entities that would be subject to it.

(d) **Notice to Equity Security Holders in a Chapter 11 Case**. Unless the court orders otherwise, in a Chapter 11 case the clerk or the court's designee must give notice as the court orders to the equity security holders of:

    (1) the order for relief;

    (2) a meeting of equity security holders under §341;

    (3) a hearing on a proposed sale of all, or substantially all, the debtor's assets;

    (4) a hearing on a motion to dismiss a case or convert it to another chapter;

    (5) the time to file an objection to—and the time of the hearing to consider whether to approve—a disclosure statement;

    (6) the time to file an objection to—and the time of the hearing to consider whether to confirm—a Chapter 11 plan; and

    (7) the time to accept or reject a proposal to modify a plan.

(e) **Giving Notice of No Dividend in a Chapter 7 Case**. In a Chapter 7 case, if it appears from the schedules that there are no assets from which to pay a dividend, the notice of the meeting of creditors may state:

    (1) that fact;

    (2) that filing proofs of claim is unnecessary; and

    (3) that further notice of the time to file proofs of claim will be given if enough assets become available to pay a dividend.

(f) **Other Notices.**

    (1) *Various Notices to the Debtor, Creditors, and Indenture Trustees*. Except as (l) provides otherwise, the clerk, or some other person as the court 1 may direct, must give the debtor, creditors, and indenture trustees notice by mail of:

    (A) the order for relief;

    (B) a case's dismissal or conversion to another chapter;

    (C) a suspension of proceedings under §305;

    (D) the time to file a proof of claim under Rule 3002;

    (E) the time to file a complaint to object to the debtor's discharge under §727, as Rule 4004 provides;

    (F) the time to file a complaint to determine whether a debt is dischargeable under §523, as Rule 4007 provides;

    (G) a waiver, denial, or revocation of a discharge, as Rule 4006 provides;

    (H) entry of an order confirming a plan in a Chapter 9, 11, 12 or 13 case;

     (I) a summary of the trustee's final report in a Chapter 7 case if the net proceeds realized exceed $1,500;

     (J) a notice under Rule 5008 regarding the presumption of abuse;

     (K) a statement under §704(b)(1) about whether the debtor's case would be presumed to be an abuse under §707(b); and

     (L) the time to request a delay in granting the discharge under §1141(d)(5)(C), 1228(f), or 1328(h).

  (2) *Notice of the Time to Accept or Reject a Plan.* Notice of the time to accept or reject a plan under Rule 3017(c) must be given in accordance with Rule 3017(d).

(g) Addressing Notices.

  (1) *In General.* A notice mailed to a creditor, indenture trustee, or equity security holder must be addressed as the entity or its authorized agent provided in its last request filed in the case. The request may be:

     (A) a proof of claim filed by a creditor or an indenture trustee designating a mailing address (unless a notice of no dividend has been given under (e) and a later notice of a possible dividend under Rule 3002(c)(5) has not been given); or

     (B) a proof of interest filed by an equity security holder designating a mailing address.

  (2) *When No Request Has Been Filed.* Except as §342(f) provides otherwise, if a creditor or indenture trustee has not filed a request under (1) or Rule 5003(e), the notice must be mailed to the address shown on the list of creditors or schedule of liabilities, whichever is filed later. If an equity security holder has not filed a request, the notice must be mailed to the address shown on the list of equity security holders.

  (3) *Notices to Representatives of an Infant or Incompetent Person.* This paragraph (3) applies if a list or schedule filed under Rule 1007 includes a name and address of an infant's or an incompetent person's representative, and a person other than that representative files a request or proof of claim designating a different name and mailing address. Unless the court orders otherwise, the notice must be mailed to the designated address of:

     (A) the representative; and

     (B) the person filing the request or proof of claim.

  (4) *Using an Address Agreed to Between an Entity and a Notice Provider.* Notwithstanding (g)(1)–(3), when the court orders that notice be given, the notice provider may do so in the manner agreed to between the provider and an entity, and at the address or addresses the entity supplies. An address supplied by the entity is conclusively presumed to be a proper address. But a failure to use a supplied address does not invalidate a notice that is otherwise effective under applicable law.

  (5) *When a Notice Is Not Brought to a Creditor's Attention.* A creditor may treat a notice as not having been brought to the creditor's attention

under §342(g)(1) only if, before the notice was issued, the creditor has filed a statement:

(A) designating the name and address of the person or organizational subdivision responsible for receiving notices; and

(B) describing the creditor's procedures for delivering notices to the designated person or organizational subdivision.

(h) **Notice to Creditors Who Filed Proofs of Claim in a Chapter 7, 12, or 13 Case.**

   (1) *Voluntary Case.* This paragraph (1) applies in a voluntary Chapter 7 case, or in a Chapter 12 or 13 case. After 70 days following the order for relief under that chapter or the date of the order converting the case to Chapter 12 or 13, the court may direct that all notices required by (a) be mailed only to:

- the debtor;
- the trustee;
- indenture trustees;
- creditors with claims for which proofs of claim have been filed; and
- creditors that are still permitted to file proofs of claim because they have received an extension of time under Rule 3002(c)(1) or (2).

   (2) *Involuntary Case.* In an involuntary chapter 2 7 case, after 90 days following the order for relief, the court may order that all notices required by (a) be mailed only to those entities listed in (1).

   (3) *When Notice of Insufficient Assets Has Been Given.* If notice of insufficient assets to pay a dividend has been given to creditors under (e), after 90 days following the mailing of a notice of the time to file proofs of claim under Rule 3002(c)(5), the court may order that notices be mailed only to those entities listed in (1).

(i) **Notice to a Committee.**

   (1) *In General.* Any notice required to be mailed under this Rule 2002 must also be mailed to a committee elected under §705 or appointed under §1102, or to its authorized agent.

   (2) *Limiting Notices.* The court may order that a notice required by (a)(2), (3), or (6) be:

(A) sent to the United States trustee; and

(B) mailed only to:

   (i) the committees elected under §705 or appointed under §1102, or to their authorized agents; and

   (ii) those creditors and equity security holders who file—and serve on the trustee or debtor in possession—a request that all notices be mailed to them.

(3) *Copy to a Committee*. A notice required under (a)(1), (a)(5), (b), (f)(1)(B)–(C), or (f)(1)(H)—and any other notice as the court orders— must be sent to a committee appointed under §1114.

(j) **Notice to the United States**. A notice required to be mailed to all creditors under this Rule 2002 must also be mailed:

  (1) in a Chapter 11 case in which the Securities and Exchange Commission has filed either a notice of appearance or a request to receive notices, to the SEC at any place it designates;

  (2) in a commodity-broker case, to the Commodity Futures Trading Commission at Washington, D.C.;

  (3) in a Chapter 11 case, to the Internal Revenue Service at the address in the register maintained under Rule 5003(e) for the district where the case is pending;

  (4) in a case in which the documents disclose that a debt (other than for taxes) is owed to the United States, to the United States attorney for the district where the case is pending and to the United States department, agency, or instrumentality through which the debtor became indebted; or

  (5) in a case in which the filed documents disclose a stock interest of the United States, to the Secretary of the Treasury at Washington, D.C.

(k) **Notice to the United States Trustee**.

  (1) *In General*. Except in a Chapter 9 case or unless the United States trustee requests otherwise, the clerk or the court's designee must send to the United States trustee notice of:

    (A) all matters described in (a)(2)–(4), (a)(8)–(9), (b), (f)(1)(A)–(C), (f)(1)(E), (f)(1)(G)–(I), and (q);

    (B) all hearings on applications for compensation or for reimbursement of expenses; and

    (C) any other matter if the United States trustee requests it or the court orders it.

  (2) *Time to Send*. The notice must be sent within the time that (a) or (b) prescribes.

  (3) *Exception Under the Securities Investor Protection Act*. In a case under the Securities Investor Protection Act, 15 U.S.C. §78aaa et seq., these rules do not require any document to be sent to the United States trustee.

(l) **Notice by Publication**. The court may order notice by publication if notice by mail is impracticable or if it is desirable to supplement the notice.

(m) **Orders Concerning Notices**. Except as these rules provide otherwise, the court may designate the matters about which, the entity to whom, and the form and manner in which a notice must be sent.

(n) **Notice of an Order for Relief in a Consumer Case**. In a voluntary case commenced under the Code by an individual debtor whose debts are primarily consumer debts, the clerk, or some other person as the court may direct, shall give the trustee and all creditors notice by mail of the order for relief not more than 20 days after the entry of such order.

(o) **Caption**. The caption of a notice given under this Rule 2002 must conform to Rule 1005. The caption of a debtor's notice to a creditor must also include the information that §342(c) requires.

(p) **Notice to a Creditor with a Foreign Address**.

    (1) *When Notice by Mail Does Not Suffice*. At the request of the United States trustee or a party in interest, or on its own, the court may find that a notice mailed to a creditor with a foreign address within the time these rules prescribe would not give the creditor reasonable notice. The court may then order that the notice be supplemented with notice by other means or that the time prescribed for the notice by mail be extended.

    (2) *Notice of the Time to File a Proof of Claim*. Unless the court, for cause, orders otherwise, a creditor with a foreign address must be given at least 30 days' notice of the time to file a proof of claim under Rule 3002(c) or Rule 3003(c).

    (3) *Determining a Foreign Address*. Unless the court, for cause, orders otherwise, the mailing address of a creditor with a foreign address must be determined under (g).

(q) **Notice of a Petition for Recognition of a Foreign Proceeding; Notice of an Intent to Communicate with a Foreign Court or Foreign Representative**.

    (1) *Timing of the Notice; Who Must Receive It*. After a petition for recognition of a foreign proceeding is filed, the court must promptly hold a hearing on it. The clerk or the court's designee must promptly give at least 21 days' notice by mail of the hearing to:

- the debtor;
- all persons or bodies authorized to administer the debtor's foreign proceedings;
- all entities against whom provisional relief is being sought under §1519;
- all parties to litigation pending in the United States in which the debtor was a party when the petition was filed; and
- any other entities as the court orders.

If the court consolidates the hearing on the petition with a hearing on a request for provisional relief, the court may set a shorter notice period.

    (2) *Content of the Notice*. The notice must:

        (A) state whether the petition seeks recognition as a foreign main proceeding or a foreign nonmain proceeding; and

        (B) include a copy of the petition and any other document the court specifies.

(3) Communicating with a Foreign Court or Foreign Representative. If the court intends to communicate with a foreign court or foreign representative, the clerk or the court's designee must give notice by mail of the court's intention to all those listed in (q)(1).

(As amended Pub. L. 98–91, §2(a), Aug. 30, 1983, 97 Stat. 607; Pub. L. 98–353, title III, §321, July 10, 1984, 98 Stat. 357; Mar. 30, 1987, eff. Aug. 1, 1987; Apr. 30, 1991, eff. Aug. 1, 1991; Apr. 22, 1993, eff. Aug. 1, 1993; Apr. 23, 1996, eff. Dec. 1, 1996; Apr. 11, 1997, eff. Dec. 1, 1997; Apr. 26, 1999, eff. Dec. 1, 1999; Apr. 17, 2000, eff. Dec. 1, 2000; Apr. 23, 2001, eff. Dec. 1, 2001; Mar. 27, 2003, eff. Dec. 1, 2003; Apr. 26, 2004, eff. Dec. 1, 2004; Apr. 25, 2005, eff. Dec. 1, 2005; Apr. 23, 2008, eff. Dec. 1, 2008; Mar. 26, 2009, eff. Dec. 1, 2009; Apr. 28, 2016, eff. Dec. 1, 2016; Apr. 27, 2017, eff. Dec. 1, 2017; Apr. 27, 2020, eff. Dec. 1, 2020; Apr. 2, 2024, eff. Dec. 1, 2024.)

Rule 2003. Meeting of Creditors or Equity Security Holders

(a) **Date and Place of the Meeting**.
  (1) *Date.* Except as provided in §341(e), the United States trustee must call a meeting of creditors to be held:
    (A) in a Chapter 7 or 11 case, no fewer than 21 days and no more than 40 days after the order for relief;
    (B) in a Chapter 12 case, no fewer than 21 days and no more than 35 days after the order for relief; or
    (C) in a Chapter 13 case, no fewer than 21 days and no more than 50 days after the order for relief.
  (2) *Effect of a Motion or an Appeal.* The United States trustee may set a later date for the meeting if there is a motion to vacate the order for relief, an appeal from such an order, or a motion to dismiss the case.
  (3) *Place; Possible Change in the Meeting Date.* The meeting may be held at a regular place for holding court. Or the United States trustee may designate any other place in the district that is convenient for the parties in interest. If the designated meeting place is not regularly staffed by the United States trustee or an assistant who may preside, the meeting may be held no more than 60 days after the order for relief.
(b) **Conducting the Meeting; Agenda; Who May Vote**.
  (1) *At a Meeting of Creditors.*
    (A) Generally. The United States trustee must preside at the meeting of creditors. The meeting must include an examination of the debtor under oath. The presiding officer has the authority to administer oaths.
    (B) Chapter 7 Cases. In a Chapter 7 case, the meeting may include the election of a creditors' committee; and if the case is not under Subchapter V, the meeting may include electing a trustee.

   (2) *At a Meeting of Equity Security Holders.* If the United States trustee convenes a meeting of equity security holders under §341(b), the United States trustee must set a date for the meeting and preside over it.

   (3) *Who Has a Right to Vote; Objecting to the Right to Vote.*

      (A) In a Chapter 7 Case. A creditor in a Chapter 7 case may vote if, at or before the meeting:

         (i) the creditor has filed a proof of claim or a writing setting forth facts evidencing a right to vote under §702(a);

         (ii) the proof of claim is not insufficient on its face; and

         (iii) no objection is made to the claim.

      (B) In a Partnership Case. A creditor in a partnership case may file a proof of claim or a writing evidencing a right to vote for a trustee for the general partner's estate even if a trustee for the partnership's estate has previously qualified.

      (C) Objecting to the Amount or Allowability of a Claim for Voting Purposes. Unless the court orders otherwise, if there is an objection to the amount or allowability of a claim for voting purposes, the United States trustee must tabulate the votes for each alternative presented by the dispute. If resolving the dispute is necessary to determine the election's result, the United States trustee must report to the court the tabulations for each alternative.

 (c) **Recording the Proceedings**. At the meeting of creditors under §341(a), the United States trustee must:

   (1) record verbatim—using electronic sound-recording equipment or other means of recording—all examinations under oath;

   (2) preserve the recording and make it available for public access for 2 years after the meeting concludes; and

   (3) upon request, certify and provide a copy or transcript of the recording to any entity at that entity's expense.

 (d) **Reporting Election Results in a Chapter 7 Case**.

   (1) *Undisputed Election.* In a Chapter 7 case, if the election of a trustee or a member of a creditors' committee is undisputed, the United States trustee must promptly file a report of the election. The report must include the name and address of the person or entity elected and a statement that the election was undisputed.

   (2) *Disputed Election.*

      (A) United States Trustee's Report. If the election is disputed, the United States trustee must:

         (i) promptly file a report informing the court of the nature of the dispute and listing the name and address of any candidate elected under any alternative presented by the dispute; and

         (ii) no later than the date on which the report is filed, mail a copy to any party in interest that has requested one.

    (B) Interim Trustee. Until the court resolves the dispute, the interim trustee continues in office. Unless a motion to resolve the dispute is filed within 14 days after the report is filed, the interim trustee serves as trustee in the case.

(e) **Adjournment**. The presiding official may adjourn the meeting from time to time by announcing at the meeting the date and time to reconvene. The presiding official must promptly file a statement showing the adjournment and the date and time to reconvene.

(f) **Special Meetings of Creditors**. The United States trustee may call a special meeting of creditors or may do so on request of a party in interest.

(g) **Final Meeting of Creditors**. If the United States trustee calls a final meeting of creditors in a case in which the net proceeds realized exceed $1,500, the clerk must give notice of the meeting to the creditors. The notice must include a summary of the trustee's final account and a statement of the amount of the claims allowed. The trustee must attend the meeting and, if requested, report on the estate's administration.

(As amended Mar. 30, 1987, eff. Aug. 1, 1987; Apr. 30, 1991, eff. Aug. 1, 1991; Apr. 22, 1993, eff. Aug. 1, 1993; Apr. 26, 1999, eff. Dec. 1, 1999; Mar. 27, 2003, eff. Dec. 1, 2003; Apr. 23, 2008, eff. Dec. 1, 2008; Mar. 26, 2009, eff. Dec. 1, 2009; Apr. 26, 2011, eff. Dec. 1, 2011; Apr. 2, 2024, eff. Dec. 1, 2024.)

Rule 2004. Examinations

(a) **In General**. On a party in interest's motion, the court may order the examination of any entity.

(b) **Scope of the Examination**.

    (1) *In General*. The examination of an entity under this Rule 2004, or of a debtor under §343, may relate only to:

        (A) the debtor's acts, conduct, or property;

        (B) the debtor's liabilities and financial condition;

        (C) any matter that may affect the administration of the debtor's estate; or

        (D) the debtor's right to a discharge.

    (2) *Other Topics in Certain Cases*. In a Chapter 12 or 13 case, or in a Chapter 11 case that is not a railroad reorganization, the examination may also relate to:

        (A) the operation of any business and the desirability of its continuing;

        (B) the source of any money or property the debtor acquired or will acquire for the purpose of consummating a plan and the consideration given or offered; and

        (C) any other matter relevant to the case or to formulating a plan.

(c) **Compelling Attendance and the Production of Documents or Electronically Stored Information**. Regardless of the district where the examination will be conducted, an entity may be compelled under Rule

9016 to attend and produce documents or electronically stored information. An attorney may issue and sign a subpoena on behalf of the court where the case is pending if the attorney is admitted to practice in that court.

(d) **Time and Place to Examine the Debtor**. The court may, for cause and on terms it may impose, order the debtor to be examined under this Rule 2004 at any designated time and place, in or outside the district.

(e) **Witness Fees and Mileage**.

    (1) *For a Nondebtor Witness*. An entity, except the debtor, may be required to attend as a witness only if the lawful mileage and witness fee for 1 day's attendance are first tendered.

    (2) *For a Debtor Witness*. A debtor who is required to appear for examination more than 100 miles from the debtor's residence must be tendered a mileage fee. The fee need cover only the distance exceeding 100 miles from the nearer of where the debtor resides:

        (A) when the first petition was filed; or

        (B) when the examination takes place.

(As amended Mar. 30, 1987, eff. Aug. 1, 1987; Apr. 30, 1991, eff. Aug. 1, 1991; Apr. 29, 2002, eff. Dec. 1, 2002; Apr. 27, 2020, eff. Dec. 1, 2020; Apr. 2, 2024, eff. Dec. 1, 2024.)

Rule 2005. Apprehending and Removing a Debtor for Examination

(a) **Compelling the Debtor's Attendance**.

    (1) *Order to Apprehend the Debtor*. On a party in interest's motion supported by an affidavit, the court may order a marshal, or other official authorized by law, to bring the debtor before the court without unnecessary delay. The affidavit must allege that:

        (A) the examination is necessary to properly administer the estate, and there is reasonable cause to believe that the debtor is about to leave or has left the debtor's residence or principal place of business to avoid the examination;

        (B) the debtor has evaded service of a subpoena or an order to attend the examination; or

        (C) the debtor has willfully disobeyed a duly served subpoena or order to attend the examination.

    (2) *Ordering an Immediate Examination*. If, after hearing, the court finds the allegations to be true, it must:

        (A) order the immediate examination of the debtor; and

        (B) if necessary, set conditions for further examination and for the debtor's obedience to any further order regarding it.

(b) **Removing a Debtor to Another District for Examination**.

    (1) *In General*. When an order is issued under (a)(1) and the debtor is found in another district, the debtor may be taken into custody and removed as provided in (2) and (3).

(2) *Within 100 Miles.* A debtor who is taken into custody less than 100 miles from where the order was issued must be brought promptly before the court that issued the order.

(3) *At 100 Miles or More.* A debtor who is taken into custody 100 miles or more from where the order was issued must be brought without unnecessary delay for a hearing before the nearest available United States magistrate judge, bankruptcy judge, or district judge. If, after hearing, the judge finds that the person in custody is the debtor and is subject to an order under (a)(1), or if the person waives a hearing, the judge must order removal, and must release the person in custody on conditions ensuring prompt appearance before the court that issued the order compelling attendance.

(4) *Conditions of Release.* The relevant provisions and policies of 18 U.S.C. §3142 govern the court's determination of what conditions will reasonably assure attendance and obedience under this Rule 2005.

(As amended Mar. 30, 1987, eff. Aug. 1, 1987; Apr. 22, 1993, eff. Aug. 1, 1993; Apr. 14, 2021, eff. Dec. 1, 2021; Apr. 2, 2024, eff. Dec. 1, 2024.)

Rule 2006. Soliciting and Voting Proxies in a Chapter 7 Case

(a) **Applicability**. This Rule 2006 applies only in a Chapter 7 case.

(b) **Definitions**.

(1) *Proxy.* A "proxy" is a written power of attorney that authorizes an entity to vote the claim or otherwise act as the holder's attorney-in-fact in connection with the administration of the estate.

(2) *Soliciting a Proxy.* "Soliciting a proxy" means any communication by which a creditor is asked, directly or indirectly, to give a proxy after or in contemplation of a Chapter 7 petition filed by or against the debtor. But such a communication is not considered soliciting a proxy if it comes from an attorney to a claim owner who is a regular client or who has requested the attorney's representation.

(c) **Who May Solicit a Proxy**. A proxy may be solicited only in writing and only by:

(1) a creditor that, on the date the petition was filed, held an allowable unsecured claim against the estate;

(2) a committee elected under §705;

(3) a committee elected by creditors that hold a majority of claims in number and in total amount and that:

(A) have claims that are not contingent or unliquidated;

(B) are not disqualified from voting under §702(a); and

(C) were present or represented at a creditors' meeting where:

(i) all creditors with claims over $500—or the 100 creditors with the largest claims—had at least 7 days' written notice; and

     (ii) written minutes are available that report the voting creditors' names and the amounts of their claims; or

  (4) a bona fide trade or credit association, which may solicit only creditors who, on the petition date:

     (A) were its members or subscribers in good standing; and

     (B) held allowable unsecured claims.

(d) **When Soliciting a Proxy Is Not Permitted**. This Rule 2006 does not permit soliciting a proxy:

  (1) for any interest except that of a general creditor;

  (2) by the interim trustee; or

  (3) by or on behalf of:

     (A) a custodian;

     (B) any entity not qualified to vote under §702(a);

     (C) an attorney-at-law; or

     (D) a transferee holding a claim for collection purposes only.

(e) **Duties of Holders of Multiple Proxies**. Before voting begins at any meeting of creditors under §341(a)—or at any other time the court orders—a holder of 2 or more proxies must file and send to the United States trustee a verified list of the proxies to be voted and a verified statement of the pertinent facts and circumstances regarding each proxy's execution and delivery. The statement must include:

  (1) a copy of the solicitation;

  (2) an identification of the solicitor, the forwarder (if the forwarder is neither the solicitor nor the claim owner), and the proxyholder—including their connections with the debtor and with each other—together with:

     (A) if the solicitor, forwarder, or proxyholder is an association, a statement that the creditors whose claims have been solicited and the creditors whose claims are to be voted were, on the petition date, members or subscribers in good standing with allowable unsecured claims; and

     (B) if the solicitor, forwarder, or proxyholder is a committee of creditors, a list stating:

        (i) the date and place the committee was organized;

        (ii) that the committee was organized under (c)(2) or (c)(3);

        (iii) the committee's members;

        (iv) the amounts of their claims;

        (v) when the claims were acquired;

        (vi) the amounts paid for the claims; and

        (vii) the extent to which the committee members' claims are secured or entitled to priority;

  (3) a statement that the proxyholder has neither paid nor promised any consideration for the proxy;

(4) a statement addressing whether there is any agreement—and, if so, giving its particulars—between the proxyholder and any other entity to:

    (A) pay any consideration related to voting the proxy; or

    (B) share with any entity (except a member or regular associate of the proxyholder's law firm) compensation that may be allowed to:

        (i) the trustee or any entity for services rendered in the case; or

        (ii) any person employed by the estate;

(5) if the proxy was solicited by an entity other than the proxyholder—or forwarded to the holder by an entity who is neither a solicitor of the proxy nor the claim owner—a statement signed and verified by the solicitor or forwarder:

    (A) confirming that no consideration has been paid or promised for the proxy;

    (B) addressing whether there is any agreement—and, if so, giving its particulars—between the solicitor or forwarder and any other entity to pay any consideration related to voting the proxy or to share with any entity (except a member or regular associate of the solicitor's or forwarder's law firm) compensation that may be allowed to:

        (i) the trustee or any entity for services rendered in the case; or

        (ii) any person employed by the estate; and

(6) if the solicitor, forwarder, or proxyholder is a committee, a statement signed and verified by each member disclosing the amount and source of any consideration paid or to be paid to the member in connection with the case, except a dividend on the member's claim.

(f) **Enforcing Restrictions on Soliciting Proxies**. On a party in interest's motion or on its own, the court may determine whether there has been a failure to comply with this Rule 2006 or any other impropriety related to soliciting or voting a proxy. After notice and a hearing, the court may:

(1) reject a proxy for cause;

(2) vacate an order entered because a proxy was voted that should have been rejected; or

(3) take other appropriate action.

(As amended Mar. 30, 1987, eff. Aug. 1, 1987; Apr. 30, 1991, eff. Aug. 1, 1991; Mar. 26, 2009, eff. Dec. 1, 2009; Apr. 2, 2024, eff. Dec. 1, 2024.)

Rule 2007. Reviewing the Appointment of a Creditors' Committee Organized Before a Chapter 9 or 11 Case Is Commenced

(a) **Motion to Review the Appointment**. If, in a Chapter 9 or 11 case, a committee appointed by the United States trustee under §1102(a) consists of the members of a committee organized by creditors before the case commenced, the court may determine whether the committee's appointment satisfies the requirements of §1102(b)(1). The court may do so on a party in interest's motion and after a hearing on notice to the United States trustee and other entities as the court orders.

(b) **Determining Whether the Committee Was Fairly Chosen**. The court may find that the committee was fairly chosen if:

(1) it was selected by a majority in number and amount of claims of unsecured creditors who are entitled to vote under §702(a) and who were present or represented at a meeting where:

(A) all creditors with unsecured claims of over $1,000—or the 100 unsecured creditors with the largest claims—had at least 7 days' written notice; and

(B) written minutes reporting the voting creditors' names and the amounts of their claims are available for inspection;

(2) all proxies voted at the meeting were solicited under Rule 2006;

(3) the lists and statements required by Rule 2006(e) have been sent to the United States trustee; and

(4) the committee's organization was in all other respects fair and proper.

(c) **Failure to Comply with Appointment Requirements**. If, after a hearing on notice under (a), the court finds that a committee appointment fails to satisfy the requirements of §1102(b)(1), it:

(1) must order the United States trustee to vacate the appointment; and

(2) may order other appropriate action.

(As amended Mar. 30, 1987, eff. Aug. 1, 1987; Apr. 30, 1991, eff. Aug. 1, 1991; Mar. 26, 2009, eff. Dec. 1, 2009; Apr. 2, 2024, eff. Dec. 1, 2024.)

Rule 2007.1. Appointing a Trustee or Examiner in a Chapter 11 Case

(a) **In General**. In a Chapter 11 case, a motion to appoint a trustee or examiner under §1104(a) or (c) must be made in accordance with Rule 9014.

(b) **Requesting the United States Trustee to Convene a Meeting of Creditors to Elect a Trustee**.

(1) *In General*. A request to the United States trustee to convene a meeting of creditors to elect a trustee must be filed and sent to the United States trustee in accordance with Rule 5005 and within the time prescribed by §1104(b). Pending court approval of the person elected, any person appointed by the United States trustee under §1104(d) and approved under (c) below must serve as trustee.

(2) *Notice and Manner of Conducting the Election*. A trustee's election under §1104(b) must be conducted as Rules 2003(b)(3) and 2006 provide, and notice of the meeting of creditors must be given as Rule 2002 provides. The United States trustee must preside at the meeting. A proxy to vote in the election may be solicited only by a creditors'

committee appointed under §1102 or by another party entitled to solicit a proxy under Rule 2006.

(3) *Reporting Election Results; Resolving Disputes.*

   (A) Undisputed Election. If the election is undisputed, the United States trustee must promptly file a report certifying the election, including the name and address of the person elected and a statement that the election is undisputed. The report must be accompanied by a verified statement of the person elected setting forth that person's connections with:

- the debtor;
- creditors;
- any other party in interest;
- their respective attorneys and accountants;
- the United States trustee; or
- any person employed in the United States trustee's office.

   (B) Disputed Election. If the election is disputed, the United States trustee must promptly file a report stating that the election is disputed, informing the court of the nature of the dispute and listing the name and address of any candidate elected under any alternative presented by the dispute. The report must be accompanied by a verified statement by each candidate, setting forth the candidate's connections with any entity listed in (A)(i)–(vi).1 No later than the date on which the report is filed, the United States trustee must mail a copy and each verified statement to:

      (i) any party in interest that has made a request to convene a meeting under §1104(b) or to receive a copy of the report; and

      (ii) any committee appointed under §1102.

(c) **Approving an Appointment**. On application of the United States trustee, the court may approve a trustee's or examiner's appointment under §1104(d). The application must:

(1) name the person appointed and state, to the best of the applicant's knowledge, all that person's connections with any entity listed in (b)(3)(A)(i)–(vi); 1

(2) state the names of the parties in interest with whom the United States trustee consulted about the appointment; and

(3) be accompanied by a verified statement of the person appointed setting forth that person's connections with any entity listed in (b)(3)(A)(i)–(vi).1

(Added Apr. 30, 1991, eff. Aug. 1, 1991; amended Apr. 11, 1997, eff. Dec. 1, 1997; Apr. 23, 2008, eff. Dec. 1, 2008; Apr. 2, 2024, eff. Dec. 1, 2024.)

Rule 2007.2. Appointing a Patient-Care Ombudsman in a Health Care Business Case

(a) **In General**. In a Chapter 7, 9, or 11 case in which the debtor is a health care business, the court must order the appointment of a patient-care ombudsman under §333—unless the court, on motion of the United States trustee or a party in interest, finds that appointing one is not necessary to protect patients. The motion must be filed within 21 days after the case was commenced or at another time set by the court.

(b) **Deferring the Appointment**. If the court has found that appointing an ombudsman is unnecessary, or has terminated the appointment, the court may, on motion of the United States trustee or a party in interest, order an appointment later if it finds that an appointment has become necessary to protect patients.

(c) **Giving Notice**. When a patient-care ombudsman is appointed under §333, the United States trustee must promptly file a notice of the appointment, including the name and address of the person appointed. Unless that person is a State Long-Term-Care Ombudsman, the notice must be accompanied by a verified statement of the person appointed setting forth that person's connections with:

(1) the debtor;

(2) creditors;

(3) patients;

(4) any other party in interest;

(5) the attorneys and accountants of those in (1)–(4);

(6) the United States trustee; or

(7) any person employed in the United States trustee's office.

(d) **Terminating an Appointment**. On motion of the United States trustee or a party in interest, the court may terminate a patient-care ombudsman's appointment that it finds to be unnecessary to protect patients.

(e) **Procedure**. Rule 9014 governs any motion under this Rule 2007.2. The motion must be sent to the United States trustee and served on:

- the debtor;
- the trustee;
- any committee elected under §705 or appointed under §1102, or its authorized agent; and
- any other entity as the court orders.

In a Chapter 9 or 11 case, if no committee of unsecured creditors has been appointed under §1102, the motion must also be served on the creditors included on the list filed under Rule 1007(d).

(Added Apr. 23, 2008, eff. Dec. 1, 2008; amended Mar. 26, 2009, eff. Dec. 1, 2009; Apr. 2, 2024, eff. Dec. 1, 2024.)

Rule 2008. Notice to the Person Selected as Trustee

(a) **Giving Notice**. The United States trustee must immediately notify the person selected as trustee how to qualify and, if applicable, the amount of the trustee's bond.

(b) **Accepting the Position of Trustee**.

    (1) *Trustee Who Has Filed a Blanket Bond*. A trustee selected in a Chapter 7, 12, or 13 case who has filed a blanket bond under Rule 2010 may reject the office by notifying the court and the United States trustee in writing within 7 days after receiving notice of selection. Otherwise, the trustee will be considered to have accepted the office.

    (2) *Other Trustees*. Any other person selected as trustee may accept the office by notifying the court and the United States trustee in writing within 7 days after receiving notice of selection. Otherwise, the person will be considered to have rejected the office.

(As amended Mar. 30, 1987, eff. Aug. 1, 1987; Apr. 30, 1991, eff. Aug. 1, 1991; Mar. 26, 2009, eff. Dec. 1, 2009; Apr. 2, 2024, eff. Dec. 1, 2024.)

Rule 2009. Trustees for Jointly Administered Estates

(a) **Creditors' Right to Elect a Single Trustee**. Except in a case under Subchapter V of Chapter 7 or Subchapter V of Chapter 11, if the court orders that 2 or more estates be jointly administered under Rule 1015(b), the creditors may elect a single trustee for those estates.

(b) **Creditors' Right to Elect a Separate Trustee**. Except in a case under Subchapter V of Chapter 7 or Subchapter V of Chapter 11, any debtor's creditors may elect a separate trustee for the debtor's estate under §702— even if the court orders joint administration under Rule 1015(b).

(c) **United States Trustee's Right to Appoint Interim Trustees in Cases with Jointly Administered Estates**.

    (1) *Chapter 7*. Except in a case under Subchapter V of Chapter 7, the United States trustee may appoint one or more interim trustees for estates being jointly administered in Chapter 7.

    (2) *Chapter 11*. If the court orders or the Code requires the appointment of a trustee, the United States trustee may appoint one or more trustees for estates being jointly administered in Chapter 11.

    (3) *Chapter 12 or 13*. The United States trustee may appoint one or more trustees for estates being jointly administered in Chapter 12 or 13.

(d) **Conflicts of Interest**. On a showing that a common trustee's conflicts of interest will prejudice creditors or equity security holders of jointly administered estates, the court must order the selection of separate trustees for the estates.

(e) **Keeping Separate Accounts**. A trustee of jointly administered estates must keep separate accounts of each estate's property and distribution.

(As amended Mar. 30, 1987, eff. Aug. 1, 1987; Apr. 30, 1991, eff. Aug. 1, 1991; Mar. 27, 2003, eff. Dec. 1, 2003; Apr. 11, 2022, eff. Dec. 1, 2022; Apr. 2, 2024, eff. Dec. 1, 2024.)

Rule 2010. Blanket Bond; Proceedings on the Bond

(a) **Authorizing a Blanket Bond**. The United States trustee may authorize a blanket bond in the United States' favor—conditioned on the faithful performance of a trustee's official duties—to cover:
  (1) a person who qualifies as trustee in multiple cases; or
  (2) multiple trustees who qualify in a different case.

(b) **Proceedings on the Bond**. A party in interest may bring a proceeding in the United States' name on a trustee's bond for the use of the entity injured by the trustee's breach of the condition.

(As amended Mar. 30, 1987, eff. Aug. 1, 1987; Apr. 30, 1991, eff. Aug. 1, 1991; Apr. 2, 2024, eff. Dec. 1, 2024.)

Rule 2011. Evidence That a Debtor Is a Debtor in Possession or That a Trustee Has Qualified

(a) **The Clerk's Certification**. Whenever evidence is required to prove that a debtor is a debtor in possession or that a trustee has qualified, the clerk may so certify. The certification constitutes conclusive evidence of that fact.

(b) **Trustee's Failure to Qualify**. If a person elected or appointed as trustee does not qualify within the time prescribed by §322(a), the clerk must so notify the court and the United States trustee.

(As amended Apr. 30, 1991, eff. Aug. 1, 1991; Apr. 2, 2024, eff. Dec. 1, 2024.)

Rule 2012. Substituting a Trustee in a Chapter 11 or 12 Case; Successor Trustee in a Pending Proceeding

(a) **Substituting a Trustee**. The trustee is automatically substituted for the debtor in possession as a party in any pending action, proceeding, or matter if:
  (1) the trustee is appointed in a Chapter 11 case (other than under Subchapter V); or
  (2) the debtor is removed as debtor in possession in a Chapter 12 case or in a case under Subchapter V of Chapter 11.

(b) **Successor Trustee**. If a trustee dies, resigns, is removed, or otherwise ceases to hold office while a bankruptcy case is pending, the successor trustee is automatically substituted as a party in any pending action, proceeding, or matter. The successor trustee must prepare, file, and send to the United States trustee an accounting of the estate's prior administration.

(As amended Mar. 30, 1987, eff. Aug. 1, 1987; Apr. 30, 1991, eff. Aug. 1, 1991; Apr. 11, 2022, eff. Dec. 1, 2022; Apr. 2, 2024, eff. Dec. 1, 2024.)

Rule 2013. Keeping a Public Record of Compensation Awarded by the Court to Examiners, Trustees, and Professionals

(a) **In General**.

 (1) *Required Items*. The clerk must keep a public record of fees the court awards to examiners and trustees, and to attorneys, accountants, appraisers, auctioneers, and other professionals that trustees employ. The record must:

  (A) include the case name and number, the name of the individual or firm receiving the fee, and the amount awarded;

  (B) be maintained chronologically; and

  (C) be kept current and open for public examination without charge.

 (2) *Meaning of "Trustee."* As used in this rule, "trustee" does not include a debtor in possession.

(b) **Annual Summary of the Record**. At the end of each year, the clerk must prepare a summary of the public record, by individual or firm name, showing the total fees awarded during the year. The summary must be open for public examination without charge. The clerk must send a copy of the summary to the United States trustee.

(As amended Mar. 30, 1987, eff. Aug. 1, 1987; Apr. 30, 1991, eff. Aug. 1, 1991; Apr. 2, 2024, eff. Dec. 1, 2024.)

Rule 2014. Employing Professionals

(a) **Order Approving Employment; Application for Employment**.

 (1) *Order Approving Employment*. The court may approve the employment of an attorney, accountant, appraiser, auctioneer, agent, or other professional under §327, §1103, or §1114 only on the trustee's or committee's application.

 (2) *Application for Employment*. The applicant must file the application and, except in a Chapter 9 case, must send a copy to the United States trustee. The application must state specific facts showing:

  (A) the need for the employment;

  (B) the name of the person to be employed;

  (C) the reasons for the selection;

  (D) the professional services to be rendered;

  (E) any proposed arrangement for compensation; and

  (F) to the best of the applicant's knowledge, all the person's connections with:

   • the debtor;

   • creditors;

   • any other party in interest;

   • their respective attorneys and accountants;

   • the United States trustee; and

- any person employed in the United States trustee's office.

(3) *Verified Statement of the Person to Be Employed.* The application must be accompanied by a verified statement of the person to be employed, setting forth that person's connections with any entity listed in (2)(F).

(b) **Services Rendered by a Member or Associate of a Law or Accounting Firm**. If a law partnership or corporation is employed as an attorney, or an accounting partnership or corporation is employed as an accountant—or if a named attorney or accountant is employed—then any partner, member, or regular associate may act as so employed, without further court order.

(As amended Mar. 30, 1987, eff. Aug. 1, 1987; Apr. 30, 1991, eff. Aug. 1, 1991; Apr. 2, 2024, eff. Dec. 1, 2024.)

Rule 2015. Duty to Keep Records, Make Reports, and Give Notices

(a) **Duties of a Trustee or Debtor in Possession**. A trustee or debtor in possession must:

(1) in a Chapter 7 case and, if the court so orders, in a Chapter 11 case (other than under Subchapter V), file and send to the United States trustee a complete inventory of the debtor's property within 30 days after qualifying as a trustee or debtor in possession, unless such an inventory has already been filed;

(2) keep a record of receipts and the disposition of money and property received;

(3) file:

(A) the reports and summaries required by §704(a)(8); and

(B) if payments are made to employees, a statement of the amounts of deductions for all taxes required to be withheld or paid on the employees' behalf and the place where these funds are deposited;

(4) give notice of the case, as soon as possible after it commences, to the following entities, except those who know or have previously been notified of it:

(A) every entity known to be holding money or property subject to the debtor's withdrawal or order, including every bank, savings- or building-and-loan association, public utility company, and landlord with whom the debtor has a deposit; and

(B) every insurance company that has issued a policy with a cash-surrender value payable to the debtor;

(5) in a Chapter 11 case (other than under Subchapter V), on or before the last day of the month after each calendar quarter during which fees must be paid under 28 U.S.C. §1930(a)(6), file and send to the United States trustee a statement of those fees and any disbursements made during that quarter; and

(6) in a Chapter 11 small business case, unless the court, for cause, sets a different schedule, file and send to the United States trustee a report

under §308, using Form 425C, for each calendar month after the order for relief—with the following adjustments:

- if the order for relief is within the first 15 days of a calendar month, the report must be filed for the rest of that month; or
- if the order for relief is after the 15th, the information for the rest of that month must be included in the report for the next calendar month.

Each report must be filed within 21 days after the last day of the month following the month that the report covers. The obligation to file reports ends on the date that the plan becomes effective or the case is converted or dismissed.

(b) **Trustee, Debtor in Possession, and Debtor in a Case Under Subchapter V of Chapter 11**. In a case under Subchapter V of Chapter 11, the debtor in possession must perform the duties prescribed in (a)(2)–(4) and, if the court orders, must file and send to the United States trustee a complete inventory of the debtor's property within the time the court sets. If the debtor is removed as debtor in possession, the trustee must perform these duties. The debtor must perform the duties prescribed in (a)(6).

(c) **Duties of a Chapter 12 Trustee or Debtor in Possession**. In a Chapter 12 case, the debtor in possession must perform the duties prescribed in (a)(2)–(4) and, if the court orders, file and send to the United States trustee a complete inventory of the debtor's property within the time the court sets. If the debtor is removed as debtor in possession, the trustee must perform these duties.

(d) **Duties of a Chapter 13 Trustee and Debtor**.
  (1) *Chapter 13 Business Case*. In a Chapter 13 case, a debtor engaged in business must:
    (A) perform the duties prescribed by (a)(2)–(4); and
    (B) if the court so orders, file and send to the United States trustee a complete inventory of the debtor's property within the time the court sets.
  (2) *Other Chapter 13 Case*. In a Chapter 13 case in which the debtor is not engaged in business, the trustee must perform the duties prescribed by (a)(2).

(e) **Duties of a Chapter 15 Foreign Representative**. In a Chapter 15 case in which the court has granted recognition of a foreign proceeding, the foreign representative must file any notice required under §1518 within 14 days after becoming aware of the later information.

(f) **Making Reports Available in a Chapter 11 Case**. In a Chapter 11 case, the court may order that copies or summaries of annual reports and other reports be mailed to creditors, equity security holders, and indenture trustees. The court may also order that summaries of these reports be published. A copy of every such report or summary, whether mailed or published, must be sent to the United States trustee.

(As amended Mar. 30, 1987, eff. Aug. 1, 1987; Apr. 30, 1991, eff. Aug. 1, 1991; Apr. 23, 1996, eff. Dec. 1, 1996; Apr. 29, 2002, eff. Dec. 1, 2002; Apr. 23, 2008, eff. Dec. 1, 2008; Mar. 26, 2009, eff. Dec. 1, 2009; Apr. 23, 2012, eff. Dec. 1, 2012; Apr. 11, 2022, eff. Dec. 1, 2022; Apr. 2, 2024, eff. Dec. 1, 2024.)

Rule 2015.1. Patient-Care Ombudsman

(a) **Notice of the Report**. Unless the court orders otherwise, a patient-care ombudsman must give at least 14 days' notice before making a report under §333(b)(2).

(1) *Recipients of the Notice*. The notice must be sent to the United States trustee, posted conspicuously at the health-care facility that is the report's subject, and served on:

- the debtor;
- the trustee;
- all patients;
- any committee elected under §705 or appointed under §1102 or its authorized agent;
- in a Chapter 9 or 11 case, the creditors on the list filed under Rule 1007(d) if no committee of unsecured creditors has been appointed under §1102; and
- any other entity as the court orders.

(2) *Content of the Notice*. The notice must state:

(A) the date and time when the report will be made;

(B) the manner in which it will be made; and

(C) if it will be in writing, the name, address, telephone number, email address, and any website of the person from whom a copy may be obtained at the debtor's expense.

(b) **Authorization to Review Confidential Patient Records**.

(1) *Motion to Review; Service*. Rule 9014 governs a patient-care ombudsman's motion under §333(c) to review confidential patient records. The motion must:

(A) be served on the patient;

(B) be served on any family member or other contact person whose name and address have been given to the trustee or the debtor in order to provide information about the patient's health care; and

(C) be sent to the United States trustee, subject to applicable nonbankruptcy law concerning patient privacy.

(2) *Time for a Hearing*. Unless the court orders otherwise, a hearing on the motion may not commence earlier than 14 days after the motion is served.

(Added Apr. 23, 2008, eff. Dec. 1, 2008; amended Mar. 26, 2009, eff. Dec. 1, 2009; Apr. 2, 2024, eff. Dec. 1, 2024.)

Rule 2015.2. Transferring a Patient in a Health Care Business Case

Unless the court orders otherwise, if the debtor is a health care business, the trustee may transfer a patient to another health care business under §704(a)(12) only if the trustee gives at least 14 days' notice of the transfer to:

- any patient-care ombudsman;
- the patient; and
- any family member or other contact person whose name and address have been given to the trustee or the debtor in order to provide information about the patient's health care.

The notice is subject to applicable nonbankruptcy law concerning patient privacy.

(Added Apr. 23, 2008, eff. Dec. 1, 2008; amended Mar. 26, 2009, eff. Dec. 1, 2009; Apr. 2, 2024, eff. Dec. 1, 2024.)

Rule 2015.3. Reporting Financial Information About Entities in Which a Chapter 11 Estate Holds a Substantial or Controlling Interest

(a) **Reporting Requirement; Content of the Report**. In a Chapter 11 case, the trustee or debtor in possession must file periodic financial reports of the value, operations, and profitability of each entity in which the estate holds a substantial or controlling interest—unless the entity is a publicly traded corporation or a debtor in a bankruptcy case. The reports must be prepared as prescribed by Form 426 and be based on the most recent information reasonably available to the filer.

(b) **Time to File; Service**. The first report must be filed at least 7 days before the first date set for the meeting of creditors under §341. Later reports must be filed at least every 6 months, until the date a plan becomes effective or the case is converted or dismissed. A copy of each report must be served on:

- the United States trustee;
- any committee appointed under §1102; and
- any other party in interest that has filed a request for it.

(c) **Presumption of a Substantial or Controlling Interest**.

    (1) *When a Presumption Applies*. Under this Rule 2015.3, the estate is presumed to have a substantial or controlling interest in an entity of which it controls or owns at least a 20% interest. Otherwise, the estate is presumed not to have a substantial or controlling interest.

    (2) *Rebutting the Presumption*. The entity, any holder of an interest in it, the United States trustee, or any other party in interest may move to rebut either presumption. After notice and a hearing, the court must

determine whether the estate's interest in the entity is substantial or controlling.

(d) **Modifying the Reporting Requirement**. After notice and a hearing, the court may vary the reporting requirements of (a) for cause, including that:

    (1) the trustee or debtor in possession is not able, after a good-faith effort, to comply with them; or

    (2) the required information is publicly available.

(e) **Notice to Entities in Which the Estate has a Substantial or Controlling Interest; Protective Order**. At least 14 days before filing the first report under (a), the trustee or debtor in possession must send notice to every entity in which the estate has a substantial or controlling interest—and all known holders of an interest in the entity—that the trustee or debtor in possession expects to file and serve financial information about the entity in accordance with this Rule 2015.3. Any such entity, or person holding an interest in it, may request that the information be protected under §107.

(f) **Effect of a Request**. Unless the court orders otherwise, a pending request under (c), (d), or (e) does not alter or stay the requirements of (a).

(Added Apr. 23, 2008, eff. Dec. 1, 2008; amended Mar. 26, 2009, eff. Dec. 1, 2009; Apr. 2, 2024, eff. Dec. 1, 2024.)

Rule 2016. Compensation for Services Rendered; Reimbursing Expenses

(a) **In General**.

    (1) *Application*. If an entity seeks from the estate interim or final compensation for services or reimbursement of necessary expenses, the entity must file an application showing:

        (A) in detail the amounts requested and the services rendered, time spent, and expenses incurred;

        (B) all payments previously made or promised for services rendered or to be rendered in connection with the case;

        (C) the source of the paid or promised compensation;

        (D) whether any previous compensation has been shared;

        (E) whether an agreement or understanding exists between the applicant and any other entity for sharing compensation for services rendered or to be rendered in connection with the case; and

        (F) the particulars of any compensation sharing or agreement or understanding to share, except with a member or regular associate of a law or accounting firm.

    (2) *Application for Services Rendered or to be Rendered by an Attorney or Accountant*. The requirements of (a) apply to an application for compensation for services rendered by an attorney or accountant, even though a creditor or other entity files the application.

(3) *Copy to the United States Trustee.* Except in a Chapter 9 case, the applicant must send a copy of the application to the United States trustee.

(b) **Disclosing Compensation Paid or Promised to the Debtor's Attorney**.

    (1) *Basic Requirements.* Within 14 days after the order for relief—or at another time as the court orders—every debtor's attorney (whether or not applying for compensation) must file and send to the United States trustee the statement required by §329. The statement must:

        (A) show whether the attorney has shared or agreed to share compensation with any other entity; and

        (B) if so, the particulars of any sharing or agreement to share, except with a member or regular associate of the attorney's law firm.

    (2) *Supplemental Statement.* Within 14 days after any payment or agreement to pay not previously disclosed, the attorney must file and send to the United States trustee a supplemental statement.

(c) **Disclosing Compensation Paid or Promised to a Bankruptcy-Petition Preparer**.

    (1) *Basic Requirements.* Before a petition is filed, every bankruptcy-petition preparer for a debtor must deliver to the debtor the declaration under penalty of perjury required by §110(h)(2). The declaration must:

        (A) disclose any fee, and its source, received from or on behalf of the debtor within 12 months before the petition's filing, together with all unpaid fees charged to the debtor;

        (B) describe the services performed and the documents prepared or caused to be prepared by the bankruptcy-petition preparer; and

        (C) be filed with the petition.

    (2) *Supplemental Statement.* Within 14 days after any later payment or agreement to pay not previously disclosed, the bankruptcy-petition preparer must file a supplemental statement.

(As amended Mar. 30, 1987, eff. Aug. 1, 1987; Apr. 30, 1991, eff. Aug. 1, 1991; Mar. 27, 2003, eff. Dec. 1, 2003; Mar. 26, 2009, eff. Dec. 1, 2009; Apr. 2, 2024, eff. Dec. 1, 2024.)

Rule 2017. Examining Transactions Between a Debtor and the Debtor's Attorney

(a) **Payments or Transfers to an Attorney Made in Contemplation of Filing a Petition or Before the Order for Relief**. On a party in interest's motion, or on its own, the court may, after notice and a hearing, determine whether a debtor's direct or indirect payment of money or transfer of property to an attorney for services rendered or to be rendered was excessive if it was made:

    (1) in contemplation of the filing of a bankruptcy petition by or against the debtor; or

    (2) before the order for relief is entered in an involuntary case.

(b) **Payments or Transfers to an Attorney Made After the Order for Relief Is Entered**. On motion of the debtor or the United States trustee, or on its own, the court may, after notice and a hearing, determine whether a debtor's payment of money or transfer of property—or agreement to pay money or transfer property—to an attorney after an order for relief is entered is excessive. It does not matter whether the payment or transfer is made, or to be made, directly or indirectly, if the payment, transfer, or agreement is for services related to the case.

(As amended Mar. 30, 1987, eff. Aug. 1, 1987; Apr. 30, 1991, eff. Aug. 1, 1991; Apr. 2, 2024, eff. Dec. 1, 2024.)

Rule 2018. Intervention by an Interested Entity; Right to Be Heard

(a) **In General**. After hearing on such notice as the court orders and for cause, the court may permit an interested entity to intervene generally or in any specified matter.

(b) **Intervention by a State Attorney General**. In a Chapter 7, 11, 12, or 13 case, a state attorney general may appear and be heard on behalf of consumer creditors if the court determines that the appearance is in the public interest. But the state attorney general may not appeal from any judgment, order, or decree entered in the case.

(c) **Intervention by the United States Secretary of the Treasury or a State Representative**. In a Chapter 9 case:
   (1) the United States Secretary of the Treasury may—and if requested by the court must—intervene; and
   (2) a representative of the state where the debtor is located may intervene in any matter the court specifies.

(d) **Intervention by a Labor Union or an Association Representing the Debtor's Employees**. In a Chapter 9, 11, or 12 case, a labor union or an association representing the debtor's employees has the right to be heard on the economic soundness of a plan affecting the employees' interests. Unless otherwise permitted by law, the labor union or employees' association exercising that right may not appeal any judgment, order, or decree related to the plan.

(e) **Serving Entities Covered by This Rule**. The court may issue orders governing the service of notice and documents on entities permitted to intervene or be heard under this Rule 2018.

(As amended Mar. 30, 1987, eff. Aug. 1, 1987; Apr. 30, 1991, eff. Aug. 1, 1991; Apr. 2, 2024, eff. Dec. 1, 2024.)

Rule 2019. Disclosures by Groups, Committees, and Other Entities in a Chapter 9 or 11 Case

(a) **Definitions**. In this Rule 2019:

    (1) "disclosable economic interest" means any claim, interest, pledge, lien, option, participation, derivative instrument, or other right or derivative right granting the holder an economic interest that is affected by the value, acquisition, or disposition of a claim or interest; and

    (2) "represent" or "represents" means to take a position before the court or to solicit votes regarding a plan's confirmation on another's behalf.

(b) **Who Must Disclose**.

    (1) *In General.* In a Chapter 9 or 11 case, a verified statement containing the information listed in (c) must be filed by every group or committee consisting of or representing—and every entity representing—multiple creditors or equity security holders that are:

        (A) acting in concert to advance their common interests; and

        (B) not composed entirely of affiliates or insiders of one another.

    (2) *When a Disclosure Statement Is Not Required.* Unless the court orders otherwise, an entity need not file the statement described in (1) solely because it is:

        (A) an indenture trustee;

        (B) an agent for one or more other entities under an agreement to extend credit;

        (C) a class-action representative; or

        (D) a governmental unit that is not a person.

(c) **Required Information**. The verified statement must include:

    (1) the pertinent facts and circumstances concerning:

        (A) for a group or committee (except a committee appointed under §1102 or §1114), its formation, including the name of each entity at whose instance it was formed or for whom it has agreed to act; or

        (B) for an entity, the entity's employment, including the name of each creditor or equity security holder at whose instance the employment was arranged;

    (2) if not disclosed under (1), for each member of a group or committee and for an entity:

        (A) name and address;

        (B) the nature and amount of each disclosable economic interest held in relation to the debtor when the group or committee was formed or the entity was employed; and

        (C) for each member of a group or committee claiming to represent any entity in addition to its own members (except a committee appointed under §1102 or §1114), the quarter and year in which each disclosable economic interest was acquired—unless it was acquired more than 1 year before the petition was filed;

(3) if not disclosed under (1) or (2), for each creditor or equity security holder represented by an entity, group, or committee (except a committee appointed under §1102 or §1114):

    (A) name and address; and

    (B) the nature and amount of each disclosable economic interest held in relation to the debtor on the statement's date; and

(4) a copy of any instrument authorizing the group, committee, or entity to act on behalf of creditors or equity security holders.

(d) **Supplemental Statement**. If a fact disclosed in its most recent statement has changed materially, a group, committee, or entity must file a verified supplemental statement whenever it takes a position before the court or solicits votes on a plan's confirmation. The supplemental statement must set forth any material changes in the information specified in (c).

(e) **Failure to Comply; Sanctions**.

(1) *Failure to Comply*. On a party in interest's motion, or on its own, the court may determine whether there has been a failure to comply with this Rule 2019.

(2) *Sanctions*. If the court finds a failure to comply, it may:

    (A) refuse to permit the group, committee, or entity to be heard or to intervene in the case;

    (B) hold invalid any authority, acceptance, rejection, or objection that the group, committee, or entity has given, procured, or received; or

    (C) grant other appropriate relief.

(As amended Mar. 30, 1987, eff. Aug. 1, 1987; Apr. 30, 1991, eff. Aug. 1, 1991; Apr. 26, 2011, eff. Dec. 1, 2011; Apr. 2, 2024, eff. Dec. 1, 2024.)

Rule 2020. Reviewing an Act by a United States Trustee

A proceeding to contest any act or failure to act by a United States trustee is governed by Rule 9014.

(Added Apr. 30, 1991, eff. Aug. 1, 1991; amended Apr. 2, 2024, eff. Dec. 1, 2024.)

Part III—Claims; Plans; Distributions to Creditors and Equity Security Holders

Rule 3001. Proof of Claim

(a) **Definition and Form**. A proof of claim is a written statement of a creditor's claim. It must substantially conform to Form 410.

(b) **Who May Sign a Proof of Claim**. Only a creditor or the creditor's agent may sign a proof of claim—except as provided in Rules 3004 and 3005.

(c) **Required Supporting Information**.

(1) *Claim or Interest Based on a Writing.* If a claim or an interest in the debtor's property securing the claim is based on a writing, the creditor must file a copy with the proof of claim—except for a claim based on a consumer-credit agreement under (4). If the writing has been lost or destroyed, a statement explaining the loss or destruction must be filed with the claim.

(2) *Additional Information in an Individual Debtor's Case.* If the debtor is an individual, the creditor must file with the proof of claim:

   (A) an itemized statement of the principal amount and any interest, fees, expenses, or other charges incurred before the petition was filed;

   (B) for any claimed security interest in the debtor's property, the amount needed to cure any default as of the date the petition was filed; and

   (C) for any claimed security interest in the debtor's principal residence:
      (i) Form 410A; and
      (ii) if there is an escrow account connected with the claim, an escrow-account statement, prepared as of the date the petition was filed, that is consistent in form with applicable nonbankruptcy law.

(3) *Sanctions in an Individual-Debtor Case.* If the debtor is an individual and a claim holder fails to provide any information required by (1) or (2), the court may, after notice and a hearing, take one or both of these actions:

   (A) preclude the holder from presenting the information in any form as evidence in any contested matter or adversary proceeding in the case—unless the court determines that the failure is substantially justified or is harmless; and

   (B) award other appropriate relief, including reasonable expenses and attorney's fees caused by the failure.

(4) *Claim Based on an Open-End or Revolving Consumer-Credit Agreement.*

   (A) Required Statement. Except when the claim is secured by an interest in the debtor's real property, a proof of claim for a claim based on an open-end or revolving consumer-credit agreement must be accompanied by a statement that shows the following information about the credit account:
      (i) the name of the entity from whom the creditor purchased the account;
      (ii) the name of the entity to whom the debt was owed at the time of an account holder's last transaction on the account;
      (iii) the date of that last transaction;
      (iv) the date of the last payment on the account; and
      (v) the date that the account was charged to profit and loss.

(B) Copy to a Party in Interest. On a party in interest's written request, the creditor must send a copy of the writing described in (1) to that party within 30 days after the request is sent.

(d) **Claim Based on a Security Interest in the Debtor's Property**. If a creditor claims a security interest in the debtor's property, the proof of claim must be accompanied by evidence that the security interest has been perfected.

(e) **Transferred Claim**.

    (1) *Claim Transferred Before a Proof of Claim Is Filed*. Unless the transfer was made for security, if a claim was transferred before a proof of claim is filed, only the transferee or an indenture trustee may file a proof of claim.

    (2) *Claim Transferred After a Proof of Claim Was Filed*.

        (A) Filing Evidence of the Transfer. Unless the transfer was made for security, the transferee of a claim that was transferred after a proof of claim is filed must file evidence of the transfer—except for a claim based on a publicly traded note, bond, or debenture.

        (B) Notice of the Filing and the Time for Objecting. The clerk must immediately notify the alleged transferor, by mail, that evidence of the transfer has been filed and that the alleged transferor has 21 days after the notice is mailed to file an objection. The court may extend the time to file it.

        (C) Hearing on an Objection; Substituting the Transferee. If, on timely objection by the alleged transferor and after notice and a hearing, the court finds that the claim was transferred other than for security, the court must substitute the transferee for the transferor. If the alleged transferor does not file a timely objection, the transferee must be substituted for the transferor.

    (3) *Claim Transferred for Security Before a Proof of Claim Is Filed*.

        (A) Right to File a Proof of Claim. If a claim (except one based on a publicly traded note, bond, or debenture) was transferred for security before the proof of claim is filed, either the transferor or transferee (or both) may file a proof of claim for the full amount. The proof of claim must include a statement setting forth the terms of the transfer.

        (B) Notice of a Right to Join in a Proof of Claim; Consolidating Proofs. If either the transferor or transferee files a proof of claim, the clerk must, by mail, immediately notify the other of the right to join in the claim. If both file proofs of the same claim, the claims must be consolidated.

        (C) Failure to File an Agreement About the Rights of the Transferor and Transferee. On a party in interest's motion and after notice and a hearing, the court must issue appropriate orders regarding the rights of the transferor and transferee if either one fails to file an agreement on voting the claim, receiving dividends on it, or participating in the estate's administration.

(4) *Claim Transferred for Security After a Proof of Claim Was Filed.*

    (A) Filing Evidence of the Transfer. If a claim (except one based on a publicly traded note, bond, or debenture) was transferred for security after a proof of claim was filed, the transferee must file a statement setting forth the terms of the transfer.

    (B) Notice of the Filing and the Time for Objecting. The clerk must immediately notify the alleged transferor, by mail, that evidence of the transfer has been filed and that the alleged transferor has 21 days after the notice is mailed to file an objection. The court may extend the time to file it.

    (C) Hearing on an Objection. If the alleged transferor files a timely objection, the court must, after notice and a hearing, determine whether the transfer was for security.

    (D) Failure to File an Agreement About the Rights of the Transferor and Transferee. On a party in interest's motion and after notice and a hearing, the court must issue appropriate orders regarding the rights of the transferor and transferee if either one fails to file an agreement on voting the claim, receiving dividends on it, or participating in the estate's administration.

(5) *Serving an Objection or Motion; Notice of a Hearing.* At least 30 days before a hearing, a copy of any objection filed under (2) or (4) or any motion filed under (3) or (4) must be mailed or delivered to either the transferor or transferee as appropriate, together with notice of the hearing.

(f) **Proof of Claim as Prima Facie Evidence of a Claim and Its Amount**. A proof of claim signed and filed in accordance with these rules is prima facie evidence of the claim's validity and amount.

(g) **Proving the Ownership and Quantity of Grain**. To the extent not inconsistent with the United States Warehouse Act or applicable State law, a warehouse receipt, scale ticket, or similar document of the type routinely issued as evidence of title by a grain storage facility, as defined in section 557 of title 11, shall constitute prima facie evidence of the validity and amount of a claim of ownership of a quantity of grain.

(As amended Pub. L. 98–353, title III, §354, July 10, 1984, 98 Stat. 361; Apr. 30, 1991, eff. Aug. 1, 1991; Mar. 26, 2009, eff. Dec. 1, 2009; Apr. 26, 2011, eff. Dec. 1, 2011; Apr. 23, 2012, eff. Dec. 1, 2012; Apr. 2, 2024, eff. Dec. 1, 2024.)

Rule 3002. Filing a Proof of Claim or Interest

(a) **Need to File**. Unless Rule 1019(c), 3003, 3004, or 3005 provides otherwise, every creditor must file a proof of claim—and an equity security holder must file a proof of interest—for the claim or interest to be allowed. A lien that secures a claim is not void solely because an entity failed to file a proof of claim.

(b) **Where to File**. The proof of claim or interest must be filed in the district where the case is pending and in accordance with Rule 5005.

(c) **Time to File**. In a voluntary Chapter 7 case or in a Chapter 12 or 13 case, the proof of claim is timely if filed within 70 days after the order for relief or entry of an order converting the case to Chapter 12 or 13. In an involuntary Chapter 7 case, a proof of claim is timely if filed within 90 days after the order for relief is entered. These exceptions apply in all cases:

   (1) *Governmental Unit*. A governmental unit's proof of claim is timely if filed within 180 days after the order for relief. But a proof of claim resulting from a tax return filed under §1308 is timely if filed within 180 days after the order for relief or within 60 days after the tax return is filed. On motion filed by a governmental unit before the time expires and for cause, the court may extend the time to file a proof of claim.

   (2) *Infant or Incompetent Person*. In the interests of justice, the court may extend the time for an infant or incompetent person—or a representative of either—to file a proof of claim, but only if the extension will not unduly delay case administration.

   (3) *Unsecured Claim That Arises from a Judgment*. This paragraph (3) applies if an unsecured claim arises in favor of an entity or becomes allowable because of a judgment to recover money or property from that entity or a judgment that denies or avoids the entity's interest in property. The claim may be filed within 30 days after the judgment becomes final. But the claim must not be allowed if the judgment imposes a liability that is not satisfied—or a duty that is not performed—within the 30 days or any additional time set by the court.

   (4) *Claim Arising from a Rejected Executory Contract or Unexpired Lease*. A proof of claim for a claim that arises from a rejected executory contract or an unexpired lease may be filed within the time set by the court.

   (5) *Notice That Assets May Be Available to Pay a Dividend*. The clerk must, by mail, give at least 90 days' notice to creditors that a dividend payment appears possible and that proofs of claim must be filed by the date set forth in the notice if:

      (A) a notice of insufficient assets to pay a dividend had been given under Rule 2002(e); and

      (B) the trustee later notifies the court that a dividend appears possible.

   (6) *Claim Secured by a Security Interest in the Debtor's Principal Residence*. A proof of a claim secured by a security interest in the debtor's principal residence is timely filed if:

      (A) the proof of claim and attachments required by Rule 3001(c)(2)(C) are filed within 70 days after the order for relief; and

(B) the attachments required by Rule 3001(c)(1) and (d) are filed as a supplement to the holder's claim within 120 days after the order for relief.

(7) *Extending the Time to File.* On a creditor's motion filed before or after the time to file a proof of claim has expired, the court may extend the time to file by no more than 60 days from the date of its order. The motion may be granted if the court finds that the notice was insufficient to give the creditor a reasonable time to file.

(As amended Mar. 30, 1987, eff. Aug. 1, 1987; Apr. 30, 1991, eff. Aug. 1, 1991; Apr. 23, 1996, eff. Dec. 1, 1996; Apr. 23, 2008, eff. Dec. 1, 2008; Apr. 27, 2017, eff. Dec. 1, 2017; Apr. 11, 2022, eff. Dec. 1, 2022; Apr. 2, 2024, eff. Dec. 1, 2024.)

Rule 3002.1. Notice Relating to Claims Secured by a Security Interest in the Debtor's Principal Residence in a Chapter 13 Case

(a) **In General**. This rule applies in a Chapter 13 case to a claim that is secured by a security interest in the debtor's principal residence and for which the plan provides for the trustee or debtor to make contractual installment payments. Unless the court orders otherwise, the notice requirements of this rule cease when an order terminating or annulling the automatic stay related to that residence becomes effective.

(b) **Notice of a Payment Change**.

(1) *Notice by the Claim Holder.* The claim holder must file a notice of any change in the amount of an installment payment—including any change resulting from an interest-rate or escrow-account adjustment. At least 21 days before the new payment is due, the notice must be filed and served on:

- the debtor;
- the debtor's attorney; and
- the trustee.

If the claim arises from a home-equity line of credit, the court may modify this requirement.

(2) *Party in Interest's Objection.* A party in interest who objects to the payment change may file a motion to determine whether the change is required to maintain payments under §1322(b)(5). Unless the court orders otherwise, if no motion is filed by the day before the new payment is due, the change goes into effect.

(c) **Fees, Expenses, and Charges Incurred After the Case Was Filed; Notice by the Claim Holder**. The claim holder must file a notice itemizing all fees, expenses, and charges incurred after the case was filed that the holder asserts are recoverable against the debtor or the debtor's principal residence. Within 180 days after the fees, expenses, or charges were incurred, the notice must be served on:

- the debtor;
- the debtor's attorney; and
- the trustee.

(d) **Filing Notice as a Supplement to a Proof of Claim**. A notice under (b) or (c) must be filed as a supplement to the proof of claim using Form 410S-1 or 410S-2, respectively. The notice is not subject to Rule 3001(f).

(e) **Determining Fees, Expenses, or Charges**. On a party in interest's motion filed within one year after the notice in (c) was served, the court must, after notice and a hearing, determine whether paying any claimed fee, expense, or charge is required by the underlying agreement and applicable nonbankruptcy law to cure a default or maintain payments under §1322(b)(5).

(f) **Notice of the Final Cure Payment**.

(1) *Content of a Notice*. Within 30 days after the debtor completes all payments under a Chapter 13 plan, the trustee must file a notice:

(A) stating that the debtor has paid in full the amount required to cure any default on the claim; and

(B) informing the claim holder of its obligation to file and serve a response under (g).

(2) *Serving the Notice*. The notice must be served on:

- the claim holder;
- the debtor; and
- the debtor's attorney.

(3) *The Debtor's Right to File*. The debtor may file and serve the notice if:

(A) the trustee fails to do so; and

(B) the debtor contends that the final cure payment has been made and all plan payments have been completed.

(g) **Response to a Notice of the Final Cure Payment**.

(1) *Required Statement*. Within 21 days after the notice under (f) is served, the claim holder must file and serve a statement that:

(A) indicates whether:

(i) the claim holder agrees that the debtor has paid in full the amount required to cure any default on the claim; and

(ii) the debtor is otherwise current on all payments under §1322(b)(5); and

(B) itemizes the required cure or postpetition amounts, if any, that the claim holder contends remain unpaid as of the statement's date.

(2) *Persons to be Served*. The holder must serve the statement on:

- the debtor;
- the debtor's attorney; and
- the trustee.

(3) *Statement to be a Supplement*. The statement must be filed as a supplement to the proof of claim and is not subject to Rule 3001(f).

(h) **Determining the Final Cure Payment**. On the debtor's or trustee's motion filed within 21 days after the statement under (g) is served, the court must, after notice and a hearing, determine whether the debtor has cured the default and made all required postpetition payments.

(i) **Failure to Give Notice**. If the claim holder fails to provide any information as required by (b), (c), or (g), the court may, after notice and a hearing, take one or both of these actions:

    (1) preclude the holder from presenting the omitted information in any form as evidence in a contested matter or adversary proceeding in the case—unless the failure was substantially justified or is harmless; and

    (2) award other appropriate relief, including reasonable expenses and attorney's fees caused by the failure.

(Added Apr. 26, 2011, eff. Dec. 1, 2011; amended Apr. 28, 2016, eff. Dec. 1, 2016; Apr. 26, 2018, eff. Dec. 1, 2018; Apr. 2, 2024, eff. Dec. 1, 2024.)

Rule 3003. Chapter 9 or 11—Filing a Proof of Claim or Equity Interest

(a) **Scope**. This rule applies only in a Chapter 9 or 11 case.

(b) **Scheduled Liabilities and Listed Equity Security Holders as Prima Facie Evidence of Validity and Amount**.

    (1) *Creditor's Claim*. An entry on the schedule of liabilities filed under §521(a)(1)(B)(i) is prima facie evidence of the validity and the amount of a creditor's claim—except for a claim scheduled as disputed, contingent, or unliquidated. Filing a proof of claim is unnecessary except as provided in (c)(2).

    (2) *Interest of an Equity Security Holder*. An entry on the list of equity security holders filed under Rule 1007(a)(3) is prima facie evidence of the validity and the amount of the equity interest. Filing a proof of the interest is unnecessary except as provided in (c)(2).

(c) **Filing a Proof of Claim**.

    (1) *Who May File a Proof of Claim*. A creditor or indenture trustee may file a proof of claim.

    (2) *Who Must File a Proof of Claim or Interest*. A creditor or equity security holder whose claim or interest is not scheduled—or is scheduled as disputed, contingent, or unliquidated—must file a proof of claim or interest. A creditor who fails to do so will not be treated as a creditor for that claim for voting and distribution.

    (3) *Time to File*. The court must set the time to file a proof of claim or interest and may, for cause, extend the time. If the time has expired, the proof of claim or interest may be filed to the extent and under the conditions stated in Rule 3002(c)(2), (3), (4), and (7).

(4) *Proof of Claim by an Indenture Trustee.* An indenture trustee may file a proof of claim on behalf of all known or unknown holders of securities issued under the trust instrument under which it is trustee.

(5) *Effect of Filing a Proof of Claim or Interest.* A proof of claim or interest signed and filed under (c) supersedes any scheduling of the claim or interest under §521(a)(1).

(d) **Treating a Nonrecord Holder of a Security as the Record Holder**. For the purpose of Rules 3017, 3018, and 3021 and receiving notices, an entity that is not a record holder of a security may file a statement setting forth facts that entitle the entity to be treated as the record holder. A party in interest may file an objection to the statement.

(As amended Mar. 30, 1987, eff. Aug. 1, 1987; Apr. 30, 1991, eff. Aug. 1, 1991; Apr. 23, 2008, eff. Dec. 1, 2008; Apr. 2, 2024, eff. Dec. 1, 2024.)

Rule 3004. Proof of Claim Filed by the Debtor or Trustee for a Creditor

(a) **Filing by the Debtor or Trustee**. If a creditor does not file a proof of claim within the time prescribed by Rule 3002(c) or Rule 3003(c), the debtor or trustee may do so within 30 days after the creditor's time to file expires.

(b) **Notice by the Clerk**. The clerk must promptly give notice of the filing to:
- the creditor;
- the debtor; and
- the trustee.

(As amended Mar. 30, 1987, eff. Aug. 1, 1987; Apr. 25, 2005, eff. Dec. 1, 2005; Apr. 2, 2024, eff. Dec. 1, 2024.)

Rule 3005. Filing a Proof of Claim or Accepting or Rejecting a Plan by a Surety, Endorser, Guarantor, or Other Codebtor

(a) **In General**. If a creditor fails to file a proof of claim within the time prescribed by Rule 3002(c) or Rule 3003(c), it may be filed by an entity that, along with the debtor, is or may be liable to the creditor or has given security for the creditor's debt. The entity must do so within 30 days after the creditor's time to file expires. A distribution on such a claim may be made only on satisfactory proof that the distribution will diminish the original debt.

(b) **Accepting or Rejecting a Plan in a Creditor's Name**. An entity that has filed a proof of claim on a creditor's behalf under (a) may accept or reject a plan in the creditor's name. If the creditor's name is unknown, the entity may do so in its own name. But the creditor must be substituted for the entity on that claim if the creditor:

(1) files a proof of claim within the time permitted by Rule 3003(c); or

(2) files notice, before the plan is confirmed, of an intent to act on the creditor's own behalf.

(As amended Mar. 30, 1987, eff. Aug. 1, 1987; Apr. 30, 1991, eff. Aug. 1, 1991; Apr. 25, 2005, eff. Dec. 1, 2005; Apr. 2, 2024, eff. Dec. 1, 2024.)

Rule 3006. Withdrawing a Proof of Claim; Effect on a Plan

(a) **Notice of Withdrawal; Limitations**. A creditor may withdraw a proof of claim by filing a notice of withdrawal. But unless the court orders otherwise after notice and a hearing, a creditor may not withdraw a proof of claim if:

(1) an objection to it has been filed;

(2) a complaint has been filed against the creditor in an adversary proceeding; or

(3) the creditor has accepted or rejected the plan or has participated significantly in the case.

(b) **Notice of the Hearing; Order Permitting Withdrawal**. Notice of the hearing must be served on:

- the trustee or debtor in possession; and
- any creditors' committee elected under §705(a) or appointed under §1102.

The court's order permitting a creditor to withdraw a proof of claim may contain any terms and conditions the court considers proper.

(c) **Effect of Withdrawing a Proof of Claim**. Unless the court orders otherwise, an authorized withdrawal constitutes withdrawal of any related acceptance or rejection of a plan.

(As amended Apr. 30, 1991, eff. Aug. 1, 1991; Apr. 2, 2024, eff. Dec. 1, 2024.)

Rule 3007. Objecting to a Claim

(a) **Time and Manner of Serving the Objection**.

(1) *Time to Serve*. An objection to a claim and a notice of the objection must be filed and served at least 30 days before a scheduled hearing on the objection or any deadline for the claim holder to request a hearing.

(2) *Whom to Serve; Manner of Service*.

(A) Serving the Claim Holder. The notice—substantially conforming to Form 420B—and objection must be served by mail on the person the claim holder most recently designated to receive notices on the claim holder's original or latest amended proof of claim, at the address so indicated. If the objection is to a claim of:

(i) the United States or one of its officers or agencies, service must also be made as if it were a summons and complaint under Rule 7004(b)(4) or (5); or

(ii) an insured depository institution as defined in section 3 of the Federal Deposit Insurance Act, service must also be made under Rule 7004(h).

(B) **Serving Others.** The notice and objection must also be served, by mail (or other permitted means), on:

- the debtor or debtor in possession;
- the trustee; and
- if applicable, the entity that filed the proof of claim under Rule 3005.

(b) **Demanding Relief That Requires an Adversary Proceeding Not Permitted.** In objecting to a claim, a party in interest must not include a demand for a type of relief specified in Rule 7001 but may include the objection in an adversary proceeding.

(c) **Limit on Omnibus Objections.** Unless the court orders otherwise or (d) permits, objections to more than one claim may not be joined in a single objection.

(d) **Omnibus Objection.** Subject to (e), objections to more than one claim may be joined in a single objection if:

(1) all the claims were filed by the same entity; or

(2) the objections are based solely on grounds that the claims should be disallowed, in whole or in part, because they:

(A) duplicate other claims;

(B) were filed in the wrong case;

(C) have been amended by later proofs of claim;

(D) were not timely filed;

(E) have been satisfied or released during the case in accordance with the Code, applicable rules, or a court order;

(F) were presented in a form that does not comply with applicable rules and the objection states that the objector is therefore unable to determine a claim's validity;

(G) are interests, not claims; or

(H) assert a priority in an amount that exceeds the maximum amount allowable under §507.

(e) **Required Content of an Omnibus Objection.** An omnibus objection must:

(1) state in a conspicuous place that claim holders can find their names and claims in the objection;

(2) list the claim holders alphabetically, provide a cross-reference to claim numbers, and, if appropriate, list claim holders by category of claims;

(3) state for each claim the grounds for the objection and provide a cross-reference to the pages where pertinent information about the grounds appears;

(4) state in the title the objector's identity and the grounds for the objections;

(5) be numbered consecutively with other omnibus objections filed by the same objector; and

(6) contain objections to no more than 100 claims.

(f) **Finality of an Order When Objections Are Joined**. When objections are joined, the finality of an order regarding any claim must be determined as though the claim had been subject to an individual objection.

(As amended Apr. 30, 1991, eff. Aug. 1, 1991; Apr. 30, 2007, eff. Dec. 1, 2007; Apr. 27, 2017, eff. Dec. 1, 2017; Apr. 14, 2021, eff. Dec. 1, 2021; Apr. 2, 2024, eff. Dec. 1, 2024.)

Rule 3008. Reconsidering an Order Allowing or Disallowing a Claim

A party in interest may move to reconsider an order allowing or disallowing a claim. After notice and a hearing, the court must issue an appropriate order.

(As amended Apr. 2, 2024, eff. Dec. 1, 2024.)

Rule 3009. Chapter 7—Paying Dividends

In a Chapter 7 case, dividends to creditors on claims that have been allowed must be paid as soon as practicable. A dividend check must be made payable to and mailed to the creditor. But if a power of attorney authorizing another entity to receive payment has been filed under Rule 9010, the check must be:

(a) made payable to both the creditor and the other entity; and

(b) mailed to the other entity.

(As amended Mar. 30, 1987, eff. Aug. 1, 1987; Apr. 22, 1993, eff. Aug. 1, 1993; Apr. 2, 2024, eff. Dec. 1, 2024.)

Rule 3010. Chapter 7, Subchapter V of Chapter 11, Chapter 12, and Chapter 13— Limits on Small Dividends and Payments

(a) **Chapter 7**. In a Chapter 7 case, the trustee must not distribute to a creditor any dividend less than $5 unless authorized to do so by local rule or court order. A dividend not distributed must be treated in the same manner as unclaimed funds under §347.

(b) **Subchapter V of Chapter 11, Chapter 12, and Chapter 13**. In a case under Subchapter V of Chapter 11, or under Chapter 12 or 13, the trustee must not distribute to a creditor any payment less than $15 unless authorized to do so by local rule or court order. Distribution must be made when accumulated funds total $15 or more. Any remaining funds must be distributed with the final payment.

(As amended Mar. 30, 1987, eff. Aug. 1, 1987; Apr. 30, 1991, eff. Aug. 1, 1991; Apr. 11, 2022, eff. Dec. 1, 2022; Apr. 2, 2024, eff. Dec. 1, 2024.)

Rule 3011. Chapter 7, Subchapter V of Chapter 11, Chapter 12, and Chapter 13—Listing Unclaimed Funds

(a) **Filing the List**. The trustee must:
   (1) file a list of the known names and addresses of entities entitled to payment from any remaining property of the estate that is paid into court under §347(a); and
   (2) include the amount due each entity.
(b) **Making the Information Searchable**. On the court's website, the clerk must provide searchable access to information about funds deposited under §347(a). The court may, for cause, limit access to that information in a specific case.

(As amended Mar. 30, 1987, eff. Aug. 1, 1987; Apr. 30, 1991, eff. Aug. 1, 1991; Apr. 11, 2022, eff. Dec. 1, 2022; Apr. 24, 2023, eff. Dec. 1, 2023; Apr. 2, 2024, eff. Dec. 1, 2024.)

Rule 3012. Determining the Amount of a Secured or Priority Claim

(a) **In General**. On a party in interest's request, after notice and a hearing, the court may determine the amount of a secured claim under §506(a) or the amount of a priority claim under §507. The notice must be served on:
   • the claim holder; and
   • any other entity the court designates.
(b) **Determining the Amount of a Claim.**
   (1) *Secured Claim*. Except as provided in (c), a request to determine the amount of a secured claim may be made by motion, in an objection to a claim, or in a plan filed in a Chapter 12 or 13 case. If the request is included in a plan, a copy of the plan must be served on the claim holder and any other entity the court designates as if it were a summons and complaint under Rule 7004.
   (2) *Priority Claim*. A request to determine the amount of a priority claim may be made only by motion after the claim is filed or in an objection to the claim.
(c) **Governmental Unit's Secured Claim**. A request to determine the amount of a governmental unit's secured claim may be made only by motion—or in an objection to a claim—filed after:
   (1) the governmental unit has filed the proof of claim; or
   (2) the time to file it under Rule 3002(c)(1) has expired.

(As amended Mar. 30, 1987, eff. Aug. 1, 1987; Apr. 27, 2017, eff. Dec. 1, 2017; Apr. 2, 2024, eff. Dec. 1, 2024.)

Rule 3013. Determining Classes of Creditors and Equity Security Holders

For purposes of a plan and its acceptance, the court may—on motion after hearing on notice as the court orders—determine classes of creditors and equity security holders under §§1122, 1222(b)(1), and 1322(b)(1).

(As amended Apr. 30, 1991, eff. Aug. 1, 1991; Apr. 2, 2024, eff. Dec. 1, 2024.)

Rule 3014. Chapter 9 or 11—Secured Creditors' Election to Apply §1111(b)

(a) **Time for an Election**.
  (1) *Chapter 9 or 11*. In a Chapter 9 or 11 case, before a hearing on the disclosure statement concludes, a class of secured creditors may elect to apply §1111(b)(2). If the disclosure statement is conditionally approved under Rule 3017.1 and a final hearing on it is not held, the election must be made within the time provided in Rule 3017.1(a)(2). In either situation, the court may set another time for the election.
  (2) *Subchapter V of Chapter 11*. In a case under Subchapter V of Chapter 11 in which §1125 does not apply, the election may be made no later than a date the court sets.
(b) **Signed Writing; Binding Effect**. The election must be made in writing and signed, unless made at the hearing on the disclosure statement. An election made by the majorities required by §1111(b)(1)(A)(i) is binding on all members of the class.

(As amended Apr. 11, 1997, eff. Dec. 1, 1997; Apr. 11, 2022, eff. Dec. 1, 2022; Apr. 2, 2024, eff. Dec. 1, 2024.)

Rule 3015. Chapter 12 or 13—Time to File a Plan; Nonstandard Provisions; Objection to Confirmation; Effect of Confirmation; Modifying a Plan

(a) **Time to File a Chapter 12 Plan**. The debtor must file a Chapter 12 plan:
  (1) with the petition; or
  (2) within the time prescribed by §1221.
(b) **Time to File a Chapter 13 Plan**.
  (1) In General. The debtor must file a Chapter 13 plan with the petition or within 14 days after the petition is filed. The time to file must not be extended except for cause and on notice as the court orders.
  (2) Case Converted to Chapter 13. If a case is converted to Chapter 13, the plan must be filed within 14 days after conversion. The time must not be extended except for cause and on notice as the court orders.
(c) **Form of a Chapter 13 Plan**.

(1) *In General.* In filing a Chapter 13 plan, the debtor must use Form 113, unless the court has adopted a local form under Rule 3015.1.

(2) *Nonstandard Provision.* With either form, a nonstandard provision is effective only if it is included in the section of the form that is designated for nonstandard provisions and is identified in accordance with any other requirements of the form. A nonstandard provision is one that is not included in the form or deviates from it.

(d) **Serving a Copy of the Plan.** If the plan was not included with the notice of a confirmation hearing mailed under Rule 2002, the debtor must serve the plan on the trustee and creditors when it is filed.

(e) **Copy to the United States Trustee.** The clerk must promptly send to the United States trustee a copy of any plan filed under (a) or (b) or any modification of it.

(f) **Objection to Confirmation; Determining Good Faith When No Objection is Filed.**

(1) *Serving an Objection.* An entity that objects to a plan's confirmation must file and serve the objection on the debtor, trustee, and any other entity the court designates, and must send a copy to the United States trustee. Unless the court orders otherwise, the objection must be filed, served, and sent at least 7 days before the date set for the confirmation hearing. The objection is governed by Rule 9014.

(2) *When No Objection Is Filed.* If no objection is timely filed, the court may, without receiving evidence, determine that the plan has been proposed in good faith and not by any means forbidden by law.

(g) **Effect of Confirmation of a Chapter 12 or 13 Plan on the Amount of a Secured Claim; Terminating the Stay.**

(1) *Secured Claim.* When a plan is confirmed, the amount of a secured claim—determined in the plan under Rule 3012—becomes binding on the claim holder. That is the effect even if the holder files a contrary proof of claim, the debtor schedules that claim, or an objection to the claim is filed.

(2) *Terminating the Stay.* When a plan is confirmed, a request in the plan to terminate the stay imposed under §362(a), §1201(a), or §1301(a) is granted.

(h) **Modifying a Plan After It Is Confirmed.**

(1) *Request to Modify a Plan After It Is Confirmed.* A request to modify a confirmed plan under §1229 or §1329 must identify the proponent and include the proposed modification. Unless the court orders otherwise for creditors not affected by the modification, the clerk or the court's designee must:

(A) give the debtor, trustee, and creditors at least 21 days' notice, by mail, of the time to file objections and the date of any hearing;

(B) send a copy of the notice to the United States trustee; and

(C) include a copy or summary of the modification.

(2) *Objecting to a Modification.* Rule 9014 governs an objection to a proposed modification. An objection must be filed and served on:

- the debtor;
- the trustee; and
- any other entity the court designates.

A copy must also be sent to the United States trustee.

(As amended Apr. 30, 1991, eff. Aug. 1, 1991; Apr. 22, 1993, eff. Aug. 1, 1993; Mar. 26, 2009, eff. Dec. 1, 2009; Apr. 27, 2017, eff. Dec. 1, 2017; Apr. 2, 2024, eff. Dec. 1, 2024.)

Rule 3015.1. Requirements for a Local Form for a Chapter 13 Plan

As an exception to Rule 9029(a)(1), a district may require that a single local form be used for a Chapter 13 plan instead of Form 113 if it:

(a) is adopted for the district after public notice and an opportunity for comment;
(b) numbers and labels each paragraph in boldface type with a heading that states its general subject matter;
(c) includes an opening paragraph for the debtor to indicate that the plan does or does not:
    (1) contain a nonstandard provision;
    (2) limit the amount of a secured claim based on a valuation of the collateral; or
    (3) avoid a security interest or lien;
(d) contains separate paragraphs relating to:
    (1) curing any default and maintaining payments on a claim secured by the debtor's principal residence;
    (2) paying a domestic support obligation;
    (3) paying a claim described in the final paragraph of §1325(a); and
    (4) surrendering property that secures a claim and requesting that the stay under §362(a) or 1301(a) related to the property be terminated; and
(e) contains a final paragraph providing a place for:
    (1) nonstandard provisions as defined in Rule 3015(c), with a warning that any nonstandard provision placed elsewhere is void; and
    (2) a certification by the debtor's attorney, or by an unrepresented debtor, that the plan does not contain any nonstandard provision except as set out in the final paragraph.

(Added Apr. 27, 2017, eff. Dec. 1, 2017; amended Apr. 2, 2024, eff. Dec. 1, 2024.)

Rule 3016. Chapter 9 or 11—Plan and Disclosure Statement

(a) **In General.** In a Chapter 9 or 11 case, every proposed plan or modification must be dated. In a Chapter 11 case, the plan or modification must also name the entity or entities proposing or filing it.

(b) **Filing a Disclosure Statement**.

    (1) *In General*. In a Chapter 9 or 11 case, unless (2) applies, the disclosure statement, if required by §1125—or evidence showing compliance with §1126(b)—must be filed with the plan or at another time set by the court.

    (2) *Providing Information Under §1125(f)(1)*. A plan intended to provide adequate information under §1125(f)(1) must be so designated. Rule 3017.1 then applies as if the plan were a disclosure statement.

(c) **Injunction in a Plan**. If the plan provides for an injunction against conduct not otherwise enjoined by the Code, the plan and disclosure statement must:

    (1) describe in specific and conspicuous language (bold, italic, or underlined text) all acts to be enjoined; and

    (2) identify the entities that would be subject to the injunction.

(d) **Form of a Disclosure Statement and Plan in a Small Business Case or a Case Under Subchapter V of Chapter 11**. In a small business case or a case under Subchapter V of Chapter 11, the court may approve a disclosure statement that substantially conforms to Form 425B and confirm a plan that substantially conforms to Form 425A—or, in either instance, to a standard form approved by the court.

(As amended Mar. 30, 1987, eff. Aug. 1, 1987; Apr. 30, 1991, eff. Aug. 1, 1991; Apr. 23, 1996, eff. Dec. 1, 1996; Apr. 23, 2001, eff. Dec. 1, 2001; Apr. 23, 2008, eff. Dec. 1, 2008; Apr. 11, 2022, eff. Dec. 1, 2022; Apr. 2, 2024, eff. Dec. 1, 2024.)

Rule 3017. Chapter 9 or 11—Hearing on a Disclosure Statement and Plan

(a) **Hearing on a Disclosure Statement; Objections**.

    (1) *Notice and Hearing*.

        (A) Notice. Except as provided in Rule 3017.1 for a small business case, the court must hold a hearing on a disclosure statement filed under Rule 3016(b) and any objection or modification to it. The hearing must be held on at least 28 days' notice under Rule 2002(b) to:

            • the debtor;

            • creditors;

            • equity security holders; and

            • other parties in interest.

        (B) Limit on Sending the Plan and Disclosure Statement. A copy of the plan and disclosure statement must be mailed with the notice of a hearing to:

            • the debtor;

            • any trustee or appointed committee;

            • the Securities and Exchange Commission; and

- any party in interest that, in writing, requests a copy of the disclosure statement or plan.

(2) *Objecting to a Disclosure Statement.* An objection to a disclosure statement must be filed and served before the disclosure statement is approved or by an earlier date the court sets. The objection must be served on:

- the debtor;
- the trustee;
- any appointed committee; and
- any other entity the court designates.

(3) *Chapter 11—Copies to the United States Trustee.* In a Chapter 11 case, a copy of every item required to be served or mailed under this Rule 3017(a) must also be sent to the United States trustee within the prescribed time.

(b) **Court Ruling on the Disclosure Statement**. After the hearing, the court must determine whether the disclosure statement should be approved.

(c) **Time to Accept or Reject a Plan and for the Confirmation Hearing**. At the time or before the disclosure statement is approved, the court:

(1) must set a deadline for the holders of claims and interests to accept or reject the plan; and

(2) may set a date for a confirmation hearing.

(d) **Hearing on Confirmation**.

(1) *Sending the Plan and Related Documents.*

(A) In General. After the disclosure statement has been approved, the court must order the debtor in possession, the trustee, the plan proponent, or the clerk to mail the following items to creditors and equity security holders and, in a Chapter 11 case, to send a copy of each to the United States trustee:

(i) the court-approved disclosure statement;

(ii) the plan or a court-approved summary of it;

(iii) a notice of the time to file acceptances and rejections of the plan; and

(iv) any other information as the court orders—including any opinion approving the disclosure statement or a court-approved summary of the opinion.

(B) Exception. The court may vary the requirements for an unimpaired class of creditors or equity security holders.

(2) *Time to Object to a Plan; Notice of the Confirmation Hearing.* Notice of the time to file an objection to a plan's confirmation and the date of the hearing on confirmation must be mailed to creditors and equity security holders in accordance with Rule 2002(b). A ballot that conforms to Form 314 must also be mailed to creditors and equity security holders who are entitled to vote on the plan. If the court's

opinion is not sent (or only a summary of the plan was sent), a party in interest may request a copy of the opinion or plan, which must be provided at the plan proponent's expense.

(3) *Notice to Unimpaired Classes.* If the court orders that the disclosure statement and plan (or the plan summary) not be mailed to an unimpaired class, a notice that the class has been designated as unimpaired must be mailed to the class members. The notice must show:

    (A) the name and address of the person from whom the plan (or summary) and the disclosure statement may be obtained at the plan proponent's expense;

    (B) the time to file an objection to the plan's confirmation; and

    (C) the date of the confirmation hearing.

(4) *Definition of "Creditors" and "Equity Security Holders."* In this Rule 3017(d), "creditors" and "equity security holders" include record holders of stock, bonds, debentures, notes, and other securities on the date the order approving the disclosure statement is entered—or another date the court sets for cause and after notice and a hearing.

(e) **Procedure for Sending Information to Beneficial Holders of Securities**. At the hearing under (a), the court must:

(1) determine the adequacy of the procedures for sending the documents and information listed in (d)(1) to beneficial holders of stock, bonds, debentures, notes, and other securities; and

(2) issue any appropriate orders.

(f) **Sending Information to Entities Subject to an Injunction**.

(1) *Timing of the Notice.* This Rule 3017(f) applies if, under a plan, an entity that is not a creditor or equity security holder is subject to an injunction against conduct not otherwise enjoined by the Code. At the hearing under (a), the court must consider procedures to provide the entity with at least 28 days' notice of:

    (A) the time to file an objection; and

    (B) the date of the confirmation hearing.

(2) *Content of the Notice.* The notice must:

    (A) provide the information required by Rule 2002(c)(3); and

    (B) if feasible, include a copy of the plan and disclosure statement.

(As amended Mar. 30, 1987, eff. Aug. 1, 1987; Apr. 30, 1991, eff. Aug. 1, 1991; Apr. 11, 1997, eff. Dec. 1, 1997; Apr. 23, 2001, eff. Dec. 1, 2001; Mar. 26, 2009, eff. Dec. 1, 2009; Apr. 2, 2024, eff. Dec. 1, 2024.)

Rule 3017.1. Disclosure Statement in a Small Business Case or a Case Under Subchapter V of Chapter 11

(a) **Conditionally Approving a Disclosure Statement**. This section (a) applies in a small business case or in a case under Subchapter V of Chapter 11 in which the court has ordered that §1125 applies. The court may, on motion of the plan proponent or on its own, conditionally approve a disclosure statement filed under Rule 3016. On or before doing so, the court must:

(1) set the time within which the claim holders and interest holders may accept or reject the plan;

(2) set the time to file an objection to the disclosure statement;

(3) if a timely objection is filed, set the date to hold the hearing on final approval of the disclosure statement; and

(4) set a date for the confirmation hearing.

(b) **Effect of a Conditional Approval**. Rule 3017(a)–(c) and (e) do not apply to a conditionally approved disclosure statement. But conditional approval is considered approval in applying Rule 3017(d).

(c) **Time to File an Objection; Date of a Hearing**.

(1) *Notice*. Notice must be given under Rule 2002(b) of the time to file an objection and the date of a hearing to consider final approval of the disclosure statement. The notice may be combined with notice of the confirmation hearing.

(2) *Time to File an Objection to the Disclosure Statement*. An objection to the disclosure statement must be filed before it is finally approved or by an earlier date set by the court. The objection must be served on:

- the debtor;
- the trustee;
- any appointed committee; and
- any other entity the court designates.

A copy must also be sent to the United States trustee.

(3) *Hearing on an Objection to the Disclosure Statement*. If a timely objection to the disclosure statement is filed, the court must hold a hearing on final approval either before or combined with the confirmation hearing.

(Added Apr. 11, 1997, eff. Dec. 1, 1997; amended Apr. 23, 2008, eff. Dec. 1, 2008; Apr. 11, 2022, eff. Dec. 1, 2022; Apr. 2, 2024, eff. Dec. 1, 2024.)

Rule 3017.2. Setting Dates in a Case Under Subchapter V of Chapter 11 in Which There Is No Disclosure Statement

In a case under Subchapter V of Chapter 11 in which §1125 does not apply, the court must set:

(a) a time within which the holders of claims and interests may accept or reject the plan;

(b) a date on which an equity security holder or a creditor whose claim is based on a security must be the record holder of the security in order to be eligible to accept or reject the plan;

(c) a date for the hearing on confirmation; and

(d) a date for sending the plan, notice of the time within which the holders of claims and interests may accept or reject it, and notice of the date for the hearing on confirmation.

(Added Apr. 11, 2022, eff. Dec. 1, 2022; amended Apr. 2, 2024, eff. Dec. 1, 2024.)

Rule 3018. Chapter 9 or 11—Accepting or Rejecting a Plan

(a) In General.

(1) *Who May Accept or Reject a Plan.* Within the time set by the court under Rule 3017, 3017.1, or 3017.2, a claim holder or equity security holder may accept or reject a Chapter 9 or Chapter 11 plan under §1126.

(2) *Claim Based on a Security of Record.* Subject to (b), an equity security holder or creditor whose claim is based on a security of record may accept or reject a plan only if the equity security holder or creditor is the holder of record:

  (A) on the date the order approving the disclosure statement is entered; or

  (B) on another date the court sets:

   (i) under Rule 3017.2; or

   (ii) after notice and a hearing and for cause.

(3) *Changing or Withdrawing an Acceptance or Rejection.* After notice and a hearing and for cause, the court may permit a creditor or equity security holder to change or withdraw an acceptance or rejection.

(4) *Temporarily Allowing a Claim or Interest.* Even if an objection to a claim or interest has been filed, the court may, after notice and a hearing, temporarily allow a claim or interest in an amount that the court considers proper for voting to accept or reject a plan.

(b) Treatment of Acceptances or Rejections Obtained Before the Petition Was Filed.

(1) *Acceptance or Rejection by a Nonholder of Record.* An equity security holder or creditor who accepted or rejected a plan before the petition was filed will not be considered to have accepted or rejected the plan under §1126(b) if the equity security holder or creditor:

  (A) has a claim or interest based on a security of record; and

  (B) was not the security's holder of record on the date specified in the solicitation of the acceptance or rejection.

(2) *Defective Solicitations.* A holder of a claim or interest who accepted or rejected a plan before the petition was filed will not be considered to have accepted or rejected the plan if the court finds, after notice and a hearing, that:

  (A) the plan was not sent to substantially all creditors and equity security holders of the same class;

    (B) an unreasonably short time was prescribed for those creditors and equity security holders to accept or reject the plan; or

    (C) the solicitation did not comply with §1126(b).

(c) **Form for Accepting or Rejecting a Plan; Procedure When More Than One Plan Is Filed**.

  (1) *Form*. An acceptance or rejection of a plan must:

    (A) be in writing;

    (B) identify the plan or plans;

    (C) be signed by the creditor or equity security holder—or an authorized agent; and

    (D) conform to Form 314.

  (2) *When More Than One Plan Is Distributed*. If more than one plan is sent under Rule 3017, a creditor or equity security holder may accept or reject one or more plans and may indicate preferences among those accepted.

(d) **Partially Secured Creditor**. If a creditor's claim has been allowed in part as a secured claim and in part as an unsecured claim, the creditor may accept or reject a plan in both capacities.

(As amended Mar. 30, 1987, eff. Aug. 1, 1987; Apr. 30, 1991, eff. Aug. 1, 1991; Apr. 22, 1993, eff. Aug. 1, 1993; Apr. 11, 1997, eff. Dec. 1, 1997; Apr. 11, 2022, eff. Dec. 1, 2022; Apr. 2, 2024, eff. Dec. 1, 2024.)

Rule 3019. Chapter 9 or 11—Modifying a Plan

(a) **Modifying a Plan Before Confirmation**. In a Chapter 9 or 11 case, after a plan has been accepted and before confirmation, the plan proponent may file a modification. The modification is considered accepted by any creditor or equity security holder who has accepted it in writing. For others who have not accepted it in writing but have accepted the plan, the modification is considered accepted if, after notice and a hearing, the court finds that it does not adversely change the treatment of their claims or interests. The notice must be served on:

- the trustee;
- any appointed committee; and
- any other entity the court designates.

(b) **Modifying a Plan After Confirmation in an Individual Debtor's Chapter 11 Case**.

  (1) *In General*. When a plan in an individual debtor's Chapter 11 case has been confirmed, a request to modify it under §1127(e) is governed by Rule 9014. The request must identify the proponent, and the proposed modification must be filed with it.

  (2) *Time to File an Objection; Service*.

    (A) Time. Unless the court orders otherwise for creditors who are not affected by the proposed modification, the clerk—or the court's designee—must give the debtor, trustee, and creditors at least 21 days' notice, by mail, of:

(i) the time to file an objection; and

(ii) if an objection is filed, the date of a hearing to consider the proposed modification.

(B) Service. Any objection must be served on:

- the debtor;
- the entity proposing the modification;
- the trustee; and
- any other entity the court designates.

A copy of the notice, modification, and objection must also be sent to the United States trustee.

(c) **Modifying a Plan After Confirmation in a Case Under Subchapter V of Chapter 11**. In a case under Subchapter V of Chapter 11, Rule 9014 governs a request to modify the plan under §1193(b) or (c), and (b) of this rule applies.

(As amended Mar. 30, 1987, eff. Aug. 1, 1987; Apr. 22, 1993, eff. Aug. 1, 1993; Apr. 23, 2008, eff. Dec. 1, 2008; Mar. 26, 2009, eff. Dec. 1, 2009; Apr. 11, 2022, eff. Dec. 1, 2022; Apr. 2, 2024, eff. Dec. 1, 2024.)

Rule 3020. In a Chapter 11 Case, Depositing Funds Before the Plan is Confirmed; Confirmation in a Chapter 9 or 11 Case

(a) **Chapter 11—Depositing Funds Before the Plan is Confirmed**. Before a plan is confirmed in a Chapter 11 case, the court may order that the consideration required to be distributed upon confirmation be deposited with the trustee or debtor in possession. Any funds deposited must be kept in a special account established for the sole purpose of making the distribution.

(b) **Chapter 9 or 11—Objecting to Confirmation; Confirmation Hearing**.

(1) *Objecting to Confirmation*. In a Chapter 9 or 11 case, an objection to confirmation is governed by Rule 9014. The objection must be filed and served within the time set by the court and be served on:

- the debtor;
- the trustee;
- the plan proponent;
- any appointed committee; and
- any other entity the court designates.

(2) *Copy to the United States Trustee*. In a Chapter 11 case, the objecting party must send a copy of the objection to the United States trustee within the time set to file an objection.

(3) *Hearing on the Objection; Procedure If No Objection Is Filed*. After notice and a hearing as provided in Rule 2002, the court must rule on

confirmation. If no objection is timely filed, the court may, without receiving evidence, determine that the plan was proposed in good faith and not by any means forbidden by law.

(c) **Confirmation Order**.

    (1) *Form of the Order; Injunctive Relief.* A confirmation order must conform to Form 315. If the plan provides for an injunction against conduct not otherwise enjoined under the Code, the order must:

        (A) describe the acts enjoined in reasonable detail;

        (B) be specific in its terms regarding the injunction; and

        (C) identify the entities subject to the injunction.

    (2) *Notice of Confirmation.* Notice of entry of a confirmation order must be promptly mailed to:

- the debtor;
- the trustee;
- creditors;
- equity security holders;
- other parties in interest; and
- if known, identified entities subject to an injunction described in (1).

    (3) *Copy to the United States Trustee.* In a Chapter 11 case, a copy of the order must be sent to the United States trustee under Rule 2002(k).

(d) **Retained Power to Issue Future Orders Relating to Administration**. After a plan is confirmed, the court may continue to issue orders needed to administer the estate.

(e) **Staying a Confirmation Order**. Unless the court orders otherwise, a confirmation order is stayed for 14 days after its entry.

(As amended Mar. 30, 1987, eff. Aug. 1, 1987; Apr. 30, 1991, eff. Aug. 1, 1991; Apr. 22, 1993, eff. Aug. 1, 1993; Apr. 26, 1999, eff. Dec. 1, 1999; Apr. 23, 2001, eff. Dec. 1, 2001; Mar. 26, 2009, eff. Dec. 1, 2009; Apr. 2, 2024, eff. Dec. 1, 2024.)

Rule 3021. Distributing Funds Under a Plan

(a) In General. After confirmation and when any stay under Rule 3020(e) expires, payments under the plan must be distributed to:

- creditors whose claims have been allowed;
- interest holders whose interests have not been disallowed; and
- indenture trustees whose claims under Rule 3003(c)(5) have been allowed.

(b) **Definition of "Creditors" and "Interest Holders."** In this Rule 3021:

    (1) "creditors" include record holders of bonds, debentures, notes, and other debt securities as of the initial distribution date, unless the plan or confirmation order states a different date; and

(2) "interest holders" include record holders of stock and other equity securities as of the initial distribution date, unless the plan or confirmation order states a different date.

(As amended Apr. 11, 1997, eff. Dec. 1, 1997; Apr. 26, 1999, eff. Dec. 1, 1999; Apr. 2, 2024, eff. Dec. 1, 2024.)

Rule 3022. Chapter 11—Final Decree

After the estate is fully administered in a Chapter 11 case, the court must, on its own or on a party in interest's motion, enter a final decree closing the case.

(As amended Mar. 30, 1987, eff. Aug. 1, 1987; Apr. 30, 1991, eff. Aug. 1, 1991; Apr. 2, 2024, eff. Dec. 1, 2024.)

Part IV—The Debtor's Duties and Benefits

Rule 4001. Relief from the Automatic Stay; Prohibiting or Conditioning the Use, Sale, or Lease of Property; Using Cash Collateral; Obtaining Credit; Various Agreements

(a) **Relief from the Automatic Stay; Prohibiting or Conditioning the Use, Sale, or Lease of Property**.
  (1) *Motion.* A motion under §362(d) for relief from the automatic stay—or a motion under §363(e) to prohibit or condition the use, sale, or lease of property—must comply with Rule 9014. The motion must be served on:
  (A) the following, as applicable:
  - a committee elected under §705 or appointed under §1102;
  - the committee's authorized agent; or
  - the creditors included on the list filed under Rule 1007(d) if the case is a Chapter 9 or Chapter 11 case and no committee of unsecured creditors has been appointed under §1102; and
  (B) any other entity the court designates.
  (2) *Relief Without Notice.* Relief from a stay under §362(a)—or a request under §363(e) to prohibit or condition the use, sale, or lease of property—may be granted without prior notice only if:
  (A) specific facts—shown by either an affidavit or a verified motion—clearly demonstrate that the movant will suffer immediate and irreparable injury, loss, or damage before the adverse party or its attorney can be heard in opposition; and
  (B) the movant's attorney certifies to the court in writing what efforts, if any, have been made to give notice and why it should not be required.
  (3) *Notice of Relief; Motion for Reinstatement or Reconsideration.*

     (A) Notice of Relief. A party who obtains relief under (2) and under §362(f) or §363(e) must:

        (i) immediately give oral notice both to the debtor and to the trustee or the debtor in possession; and

        (ii) promptly send them a copy of the order granting relief.

     (B) Motion for Reinstatement or Reconsideration. On 2 days' notice to the party who obtained relief under (2)—or on shorter notice as the court may order—the adverse party may move to reinstate the stay or reconsider the order prohibiting or conditioning the use, sale, or lease of property. The court must proceed expeditiously to hear and decide the motion.

   (4) *Stay of an Order Granting Relief from the Automatic Stay.* Unless the court orders otherwise, an order granting a motion for relief from the automatic stay under (1) is stayed for 14 days after it is entered.

(b) Using Cash Collateral.

   (1) *Motion; Content; Service.*

     (A) Motion. A motion for authorization to use cash collateral must comply with Rule 9014 and must be accompanied by a proposed form of order.

     (B) Content. The motion must consist of—or if the motion exceeds five pages, begin with—a concise statement of the relief requested, no longer than five pages. The statement must list or summarize all material provisions (citing their locations in the relevant documents), including:

- the name of each entity with an interest in the cash collateral;
- how it will be used;
- the material terms of its use, including duration; and
- all liens, cash payments, or other adequate protection that will be provided to each entity with an interest in the cash collateral—or if no such protection is proposed, an explanation of how each entity's interest is adequately protected.

     (C) Service. The motion must be served on:

- each entity with an interest in the cash collateral;
- all those who must be served under (a)(1)(A); and
- any other entity the court designates.

   (2) *Hearings; Notice.*

     (A) Preliminary and Final Hearings. The court may begin a final hearing on the motion no earlier than 14 days after it has been served. If the motion so requests, the court may conduct a preliminary hearing before that 14-day period ends. After a preliminary hearing, the court may authorize using only the cash collateral necessary to avoid immediate and irreparable harm to the estate pending a final hearing.

(B) Notice. Notice of a hearing must be given to the parties who must be served with the motion under (1)(C) and to any other entity the court designates.

(c) **Obtaining Credit.**

    (1) *Motion; Content; Service.*

        (A) Motion. A motion for authorization to obtain credit must comply with Rule 9014 and must be accompanied by a copy of the credit agreement and a proposed form of order.

        (B) Content. The motion must consist of—or if the motion exceeds five pages, begin with—a concise statement of the relief requested, no longer than five pages. The statement must list or summarize all material provisions of the credit agreement and form of order (citing their locations in the relevant documents), including interest rates, maturity dates, default provisions, liens, and borrowing limits and conditions. If the credit agreement or form of order includes any of the provisions listed below in (i)–(xi), the concise statement must also list or summarize each one, describe its nature and extent, cite its location in the proposed agreement and form of order, and identify any that would remain effective if interim approval were to be granted but final relief denied under (2). The provisions are:

            (i) a grant of priority or a lien on property of the estate under §364(c) or (d);

            (ii) the providing of adequate protection or priority for a claim that arose before the case commenced—including a lien on property of the estate, or its use, or of credit obtained under §364 to make cash payments on the claim;

            (iii) a determination of the validity, enforceability, priority, or amount of a claim that arose before the case commenced, or of any lien securing the claim;

            (iv) a waiver or modification of Code provisions or applicable rules regarding the automatic stay;

            (v) a waiver or modification of an entity's right to file a plan, seek to extend the time in which the debtor has the exclusive right to file a plan, request the use of cash collateral under §363(c), or request authorization to obtain credit under §364;

            (vi) the establishment of deadlines for filing a plan of reorganization, approving a disclosure statement, holding a hearing on confirmation, or entering a confirmation order;

            (vii) a waiver or modification of applicable nonbankruptcy law regarding perfecting or enforcing a lien on property of the estate;

(viii) a release, waiver, or limitation on a claim or other cause of action belonging to the estate or the trustee, including any modification of the statute of limitations or other deadline to commence an action;

(ix) the indemnification of any entity;

(x) a release, waiver, or limitation of any right under §506(c); or

(xi) the granting of a lien on a claim or cause of action arising under §544, 545, 547, 548, 549, 553(b), 723(a), or 724(a).

(C) Service. The motion must be served on all those who must be served under (a)(1)(A) and any other entity the court designates.

(2) *Hearings; Notice.*

(A) Preliminary and Final Hearings. The court may begin a final hearing on the motion no earlier than 14 days after it has been served. If the motion so requests, the court may conduct a preliminary hearing before that 14-day period ends. After a preliminary hearing, the court may authorize obtaining credit only to the extent necessary to avoid immediate and irreparable harm to the estate pending a final hearing.

(B) Notice. Notice of a hearing must be given to the parties who must be served with the motion under (1)(C) and to any other entity the court designates.

(3) *Inapplicability in a Chapter 13 Case.* This subdivision (c) does not apply in a Chapter 13 case.

(d) **Various Agreements: Relief from the Automatic Stay; Prohibiting or Conditioning the Use, Sale, or Lease of Property; Providing Adequate Protection; Using Cash Collateral; or Obtaining Credit.**

(1) *Motion; Content; Service.*

(A) Motion. A motion to approve any of the following must be accompanied by a copy of the agreement and a proposed form of order:

(i) an agreement to provide adequate protection;

(ii) an agreement to prohibit or condition the use, sale, or lease of property;

(iii) an agreement to modify or terminate the stay provided for in §362;

(iv) an agreement to use cash collateral; or

(v) an agreement between the debtor and an entity that has a lien or interest in property of the estate under which the entity consents to creating a lien that is senior or equal to the entity's lien or interest.

(B) Content. The motion must consist of—or if the motion exceeds five pages, begin with—a concise statement of the relief requested, no longer than five pages. The statement must:

(i) list or summarize all the agreement's material provisions (citing their locations in the relevant documents); and

(ii) briefly list or summarize, cite the location of, and describe the nature and extent of each provision in the proposed form of order, agreement, or other document of the type listed in (c)(1)(B).

(C) *Service.* The motion must be served on all those who must be served under (a)(1)(A) and any other entity the court designates.

(2) *Objection.* Notice of the motion must be mailed to the parties on whom service of the motion is required and any other entity the court designates. The notice must include the time within which objections may be filed and served on the debtor in possession or trustee. Unless the court sets a different time, any objections must be filed within 14 days after the notice is mailed.

(3) *Disposition Without a Hearing.* If no objection is filed, the court may enter an order approving or disapproving the agreement without holding a hearing.

(4) *Hearing.* If an objection is filed or if the court decides that a hearing is appropriate, the court must hold one after giving at least 7 days' notice to:

- the objector;
- the movant;
- the parties who must be served with the motion under (1)(C); and
- any other entity the court designates.

(5) *Agreement to Settle a Motion.* The court may decide that a motion made under (a), (b), or (c) was sufficient to give reasonable notice of the agreement's material provisions and an opportunity for a hearing. If so, the court may order that the procedures prescribed in (1)–(4) do not apply and may approve the agreement without further notice.

(As amended Mar. 30, 1987, eff. Aug. 1, 1987; Apr. 30, 1991, eff. Aug. 1, 1991; Apr. 26, 1999, eff. Dec. 1, 1999; Apr. 30, 2007, eff. Dec. 1, 2007; Mar. 26, 2009, eff. Dec. 1, 2009; Apr. 28, 2010, eff. Dec. 1, 2010; Apr. 25, 2019, eff. Dec. 1, 2019; Apr. 2, 2024, eff. Dec. 1, 2024.)

Rule 4002. Debtor's Duties

(a) **In General**. In addition to performing other duties that are required by the Code or these rules, the debtor must:

(1) attend and submit to an examination when the court orders;

(2) attend the hearing on a complaint objecting to discharge and, if called, testify as a witness;

(3) if a schedule of property has not yet been filed under Rule 1007, report to the trustee immediately in writing:

(A) the location of any real property in which the debtor has an interest; and

(B) the name and address of every person holding money or property subject to the debtor's withdrawal or order;

(4) cooperate with the trustee in preparing an inventory, examining proofs of claim, and administering the estate; and

(5) file a statement of any change in the debtor's address.

(b) **Individual Debtor's Duty to Provide Documents**.

(1) *Personal Identifying Information.* An individual debtor must bring to the §341 meeting of creditors:

(A) a government-issued identification with the debtor's picture, or other personal information that establishes the debtor's identity; and

(B) evidence of any social-security number, or a written statement that no such evidence exists.

(2) *Financial Documents.* An individual debtor must bring the following documents (or copies) to the §341 meeting of creditors and make them available to the trustee—or provide a written statement that they do not exist or are not in the debtor's possession:

(A) evidence of current income, such as the most recent payment advice;

(B) unless the trustee or the United States trustee instructs otherwise, a statement for each depository or investment account—including a checking, savings, or money-market account, mutual fund or brokerage account—for the period that includes the petition's filing date; and

(C) if required by §707(b)(2)(A) or (B), documents showing claimed monthly expenses.

(3) *Tax Return to Be Provided to the Trustee.* At least 7 days before the first date set for the §341 meeting of creditors, the debtor must provide the trustee with:

(A) a copy of the debtor's federal income-tax return, including any attachments to it, for the most recent tax year ending before the case was commenced and for which the debtor filed a return;

(B) a transcript of the return; or

(C) a written statement that the documents do not exist.

(4) *Tax Return to Be Provided to a Creditor.* Upon a creditor's request at least 14 days before the first date set for the §341 meeting of creditors, the debtor must provide the creditor with the documents to be provided to the trustee under (3). The debtor must do so at least 7 days before the meeting.

(5) *Safeguarding Confidential Tax Information.* The debtor's obligation to provide tax returns under (3) and (4) is subject to procedures

established by the Director of the Administrative Office of the United States Courts for safeguarding confidential tax information.

(As amended Mar. 30, 1987, eff. Aug. 1, 1987; Apr. 23, 2008, eff. Dec. 1, 2008; Mar. 26, 2009, eff. Dec. 1, 2009; Apr. 2, 2024, eff. Dec. 1, 2024.)

Rule 4003. Exemptions

(a) **Claiming an Exemption**. A debtor must list the property claimed as exempt under §522 on Form 106C filed under Rule 1007. If the debtor fails to do so within the time specified in Rule 1007(c), a debtor's dependent may file the list within 30 days after the debtor's time to file expires.

(b) **Objecting to a Claimed Exemption**.

   (1) *By a Party in Interest*. Except as (2) and (3) provide, a party in interest may file an objection to a claimed exemption within 30 days after the later of:

- the conclusion of the §341 meeting of creditors;
- the filing of an amendment to the list; or
- the filing of a supplemental schedule.

On a party in interest's motion filed before the time to object expires, the court may, for cause, extend the time to file an objection.

   (2) *By the Trustee for a Fraudulently Claimed Exemption*. If the debtor has fraudulently claimed an exemption, the trustee may file an objection to it within one year after the case is closed. The trustee must deliver or mail the objection to:

- the debtor;
- the debtor's attorney;
- the person who filed the list of exempt property; and
- that person's attorney.

   (3) *Objection Based on §522(q)*. An objection based on §522(q) must be filed:

(A) before the case is closed; or

(B) if an exemption is first claimed after a case has been reopened, before the reopened case is closed.

   (4) *Distributing Copies of the Objection*. A copy of any objection, other than one filed by the trustee under (b)(2), must be delivered or mailed to:

- the trustee;
- the debtor;
- the debtor's attorney;
- the person who filed the list of exempt property; and
- that person's attorney.

(c) **Burden of Proof**. In a hearing under this Rule 4003, the objecting party has the burden of proving that an exemption was not properly claimed. After notice and a hearing, the court must determine the issues presented.

(d) **Avoiding a Lien or Other Transfer of Exempt Property**.

    (1) *Bringing a Proceeding*. A proceeding under §522(f) to avoid a lien or other transfer of exempt property must be commenced by:

        (A) filing a motion under Rule 9014; or

        (B) serving a Chapter 12 or 13 plan on the affected creditors as Rule 7004 provides for serving a summons and complaint.

    (2) *Objecting to a Request Under §522(f)*. As an exception to (b), a creditor may object to a request under §522(f) by challenging the validity of the exemption asserted to be impaired by the lien.

(As amended Mar. 30, 1987, eff. Aug. 1, 1987; Apr. 30, 1991, eff. Aug. 1, 1991; Apr. 17, 2000, eff. Dec. 1, 2000; Apr. 23, 2008, eff. Dec. 1, 2008; Apr. 27, 2017, eff. Dec. 1, 2017; Apr. 2, 2024, eff. Dec. 1, 2024.)

Rule 4004. Granting or Denying a Discharge

(a) **Time to Object to a Discharge; Notice**.

    (1) *Chapter 7*. In a Chapter 7 case, a complaint—or a motion under §727(a)(8) or (9)—objecting to a discharge must be filed within 60 days after the first date set for the §341(a) meeting of creditors.

    (2) *Chapter 11*. In a Chapter 11 case, a complaint objecting to a discharge must be filed on or before the first date set for the hearing on confirmation.

    (3) *Chapter 13*. In a Chapter 13 case, a motion objecting to a discharge under §1328(f) must be filed within 60 days after the first date set for the §341(a) meeting of creditors.

    (4) *Notice to the United States Trustee, the Creditors, and the Trustee*. At least 28 days' notice of the time for filing must be given to:

      • the United States trustee under Rule 2002(k);

      • all creditors under Rule 2002(f);

      • the trustee; and

      • the trustee's attorney.

(b) **Extending the Time to File an Objection**.

    (1) *Motion Before the Time Expires*. On a party in interest's motion and after notice and a hearing, the court may, for cause, extend the time to object to a discharge. The motion must be filed before the time has expired.

    (2) *Motion After the Time Has Expired*. After the time to object has expired and before a discharge is granted, a party in interest may file a motion to extend the time if:

        (A) the objection is based on facts that, if learned after the discharge is granted, would provide a basis for revocation under §727(d);

(B) the movant did not know those facts in time to object; and

(C) the movant files the motion promptly after learning about them.

(c) **Granting a Discharge**.

(1) *Chapter 7*. In a Chapter 7 case, when the times to object to discharge and to file a motion to dismiss the case under Rule 1017(e) expire, the court must promptly grant the discharge—except under these circumstances:

(A) the debtor is not an individual;

(B) a complaint—or a motion under §727(a)(8) or (9)—objecting to the discharge is pending;

(C) the debtor has filed a waiver under §727(a)(10);

(D) a motion is pending to dismiss the case under §707;

(E) a motion is pending to extend the time to file a complaint objecting to the discharge;

(F) a motion is pending to extend the time to file a motion to dismiss the case under Rule 1017(e)(1);

(G) the debtor has not fully paid the filing fee required by 28 U.S.C. §1930(a)—together with any other fee prescribed by the Judicial Conference of the United States under 28 U.S.C. §1930(b) that is payable to the clerk upon commencing a case—unless the court has waived the fees under 28 U.S.C. §1930(f);

(H) the debtor has not filed a certificate showing that a course on personal financial management has been completed—if such a certificate is required by Rule 1007(b)(7);

(I) a motion is pending to delay or postpone a discharge under §727(a)(12);

(J) a motion is pending to extend the time to file a reaffirmation agreement under Rule 4008(a);

(K) the court has not concluded a hearing on a presumption—in effect under §524(m)—that a reaffirmation agreement is an undue hardship; or

(L) a motion is pending to delay discharge because the debtor has not filed with the court all tax documents required to be filed under §521(f).

(2) *Delay in Entering a Discharge in General*. On the debtor's motion, the court may delay entering a discharge for 30 days and, on a motion made within that time, delay entry to a date certain.

(3) *Delaying Entry Because of Rule 1007(b)(8)*. If the debtor is required to file a statement under Rule 1007(b)(8), the court must not grant a discharge until at least 30 days after the statement is filed.

(4) *Individual Chapter 11 or Chapter 13 Case*. In a Chapter 11 case in which the debtor is an individual—or in a Chapter 13 case—the court must not grant a discharge if the debtor has not filed a certificate required by Rule 1007(b)(7).

(d) **Applying Part VII Rules and Rule 9014**. The Part VII rules govern an objection to a discharge, except that Rule 9014 governs an objection to a discharge under §727(a)(8) or (9) or §1328(f).

(e) **Form of a Discharge Order**. A discharge order must conform to the appropriate Official Form.

(f) **Registering a Discharge in Another District**. A discharge order that becomes final may be registered in another district by filing a certified copy with the clerk for that district. When registered, the order has the same effect as an order of the court where it is registered.

(g) **Notice of a Final Discharge Order**. The clerk must promptly mail a copy of the final discharge order to those entities listed in (a)(4).

(As amended Mar. 30, 1987, eff. Aug. 1, 1987; Apr. 30, 1991, eff. Aug. 1, 1991; Apr. 23, 1996, eff. Dec. 1, 1996; Apr. 26, 1999, eff. Dec. 1, 1999; Apr. 17, 2000, eff. Dec. 1, 2000; Apr. 29, 2002, eff. Dec. 1, 2002; Apr. 23, 2008, eff. Dec. 1, 2008; Mar. 26, 2009, eff. Dec. 1, 2009; Apr. 28, 2010, eff. Dec. 1, 2010; Apr. 26, 2011, eff. Dec. 1, 2011; Apr. 16, 2013, eff. Dec. 1, 2013; Apr. 2, 2024, eff. Dec. 1, 2024.)

Rule 4005. Burden of Proof in Objecting to a Discharge

At a trial on a complaint objecting to a discharge, the plaintiff has the burden of proof.

(As amended Mar. 30, 1987, eff. Aug. 1, 1987; Apr. 2, 2024, eff. Dec. 1, 2024.)

Rule 4006. Notice When No Discharge Is Granted

The clerk must promptly notify in the manner provided by Rule 2002(f) all parties in interest of an order:

(a) denying a discharge;

(b) revoking a discharge;

(c) approving a waiver of discharge; or

(d) closing an individual debtor's case without entering a discharge.

(As amended Mar. 30, 1987, eff. Aug. 1, 1987; Apr. 23, 2008, eff. Dec. 1, 2008; Apr. 2, 2024, eff. Dec. 1, 2024.)

Rule 4007. Determining Whether a Debt Is Dischargeable

(a) **Who May File a Complaint**. A debtor or any creditor may file a complaint to determine whether a debt is dischargeable.

(b) **Time to File; No Fee for a Reopened Case**. A complaint, except one under §523(c), may be filed at any time. If a case is reopened to permit filing the complaint, no fee for reopening is required.

(c) **Chapter 7, 11, 12, or 13—Time to File a Complaint Under §523(c); Notice of Time; Extension**. Except as (d) provides, a complaint to determine whether a debt is dischargeable under §523(c) must be filed within 60 days after the first date set for the §341(a) meeting of creditors. The clerk must give all creditors at least 30 days' notice of the time to file in the manner provided by Rule 2002. On a party in interest's motion filed before the time expires, the court may, after notice and a hearing and for cause, extend the time to file.

(d) **Chapter 13—Time to File a Complaint Under §523(a)(6); Notice of Time; Extension**. When a debtor files a motion for a discharge under §1328(b), the court must set the time to file a complaint under §523(a)(6) to determine whether a debt is dischargeable. The clerk must give all creditors at least 30 days' notice of the time to file in the manner provided by Rule 2002. On a party in interest's motion filed before the time expires, the court may, after notice and a hearing and for cause, extend the time to file.

(e) **Applying Part VII Rules**. The Part VII rules govern a proceeding on a complaint filed under this Rule 4007.

(As amended Mar. 30, 1987, eff. Aug. 1, 1987; Apr. 30, 1991, eff. Aug. 1, 1991; Apr. 26, 1999, eff. Dec. 1, 1999; Apr. 23, 2008, eff. Dec. 1, 2008; Apr. 2, 2024, eff. Dec. 1, 2024.)

Rule 4008. Reaffirmation Agreement and Supporting Statement

(a) **Time to File; Cover Sheet**. A reaffirmation agreement must be filed within 60 days after the first date set for the §341(a) meeting of creditors. The agreement must have a cover sheet prepared as prescribed by Form 427. At any time, the court may extend the time to file an agreement.

(b) **Supporting Statement**. The debtor's supporting statement required by §524(k)(6)(A) must be accompanied by a statement of the total income and expenses as shown on Schedules I and J. If the income and expenses shown on the supporting statement differ from those shown on the schedules, the supporting statement must explain the difference.

(As amended Apr. 30, 1991, eff. Aug. 1, 1991; Apr. 23, 2008, eff. Dec. 1, 2008; Mar. 26, 2009, eff. Dec. 1, 2009; Apr. 2, 2024, eff. Dec. 1, 2024.)

Part V—Courts and Clerks

Rule 5001. Court Operations; Clerks' Offices

(a) **Courts Always Open**. Bankruptcy courts are considered always open for filing a pleading, motion, or other paper; issuing and returning process; making rules; or entering an order.

(b) **Location for Trials and Hearings; Proceedings in Chambers**. Every trial or hearing must be held in open court—in a regular courtroom if convenient. Except as provided in 28 U.S.C. §152(c), any other act may be performed—or a proceeding held—in chambers anywhere within or outside the district. But unless it is ex parte, a hearing may be held outside the district only if all affected parties consent.

(c) **Clerk's Office Hours**. A clerk's office—with the clerk or a deputy in attendance—must be open during business hours on all days except Saturdays, Sundays, and the legal holidays listed in Rule 9006(a)(6).

(As amended Mar. 30, 1987, eff. Aug. 1, 1987; Apr. 30, 1991, eff. Aug. 1, 1991; Apr. 23, 2008, eff. Dec. 1, 2008; Apr. 2, 2024, eff. Dec. 1, 2024.)

Rule 5002. Restrictions on Approving Court Appointments

(a) **Appointing or Employing Relatives**.
    (1) *Trustee or Examiner*. A bankruptcy judge must not approve appointing an individual as a trustee or examiner under §1104 if the individual is a relative of either the judge or the United States trustee in the region where the case is pending.
    (2) *Attorney, Accountant, Appraiser, Auctioneer, or Other Professional Person*. A bankruptcy judge must not approve employing under §327, §1103, or §1114 an individual as an attorney, accountant, appraiser, auctioneer, or other professional person who is a relative of the judge. The court may approve employing a relative of the United States trustee in the region where the case is pending, unless the relationship makes the employment improper.
    (3) *Related Entities and Associates*. If an appointment under (1) or an employment under (2) is forbidden, so is appointing or employing:
        (A) any entity—including any firm, partnership, or corporation—with which the individual has a business association or relationship; or
        (B) a member, associate, or professional employee of such an entity.
(b) **Other Considerations in Approving Appointments or Employment**. A bankruptcy judge must not approve appointing a person as a trustee or examiner—or employing an attorney, accountant, appraiser, auctioneer, or other professional person—if the person is, or has been, so connected with the judge or the United States trustee as to make the appointment or employment improper.

(As amended Apr. 29, 1985, eff. Aug. 1, 1985; Apr. 30, 1991, eff. Aug. 1, 1991; Apr. 2, 2024, eff. Dec. 1, 2024.)

Rule 5003. Records to Be Kept by the Clerk

(a) **Bankruptcy Docket**. The clerk must keep a docket in each case and must:
    (1) enter on the docket each judgment, order, and activity, as prescribed by the Director of the Administrative Office of the United States Courts; and
    (2) show the date of entry for each judgment or order.
(b) **Claims Register**. When it appears that there will be a distribution to unsecured creditors, the clerk must keep in a claims register a list of the claims filed in the case.

(c) **Judgments and Orders**.

   (1) *In General*. In the form and manner prescribed by the Director of the Administrative Office of the United States Courts, the clerk must keep a copy of:

      (A) every final judgment or order affecting title to, or a lien on, real property;

      (B) every final judgment or order for the recovery of money or property; and

      (C) any other order the court designates.

   (2) *Indexing with the District Court*. On a prevailing party's request, a copy of the following must be kept and indexed with the district court's civil judgments:

      (A) every final judgment or order affecting title to, or a lien on, real or personal property; and

      (B) every final judgment or order for the recovery of money or property.

(d) **Index of Cases; Certificate of Search**.

   (1) *Index of Cases*. The clerk must keep an index of cases and adversary proceedings in the form and manner prescribed by the Director of the Administrative Office of the United States Courts.

   (2) *Searching the Index; Certificate of Search*. On request, the clerk must search the index and papers in the clerk's custody and certify whether:

      (A) a case or proceeding has been filed in or transferred to the court; or

      (B) a discharge has been entered.

(e) **Register of Mailing Addresses of Federal and State Governmental Units and Certain Taxing Authorities**.

   (1) *In General*. The United States—or a state or a territory where the court is located—may file a statement designating its mailing address. A taxing authority (including a local taxing authority) may also file a statement designating an address for serving requests under §505(b). The authority's designation must describe where to find further information about additional requirements for serving a request.

   (2) *Register of Mailing Address*.

      (A) In General. In the form and manner prescribed by the Director of the Administrative Office of the United States Courts, the clerk must keep a register of the mailing addresses of the governmental units listed in the first sentence of (1) and a separate register containing the addresses of taxing authorities for serving requests under §505(b).

      (B) Number of Entries. The clerk need not include in any register more than one mailing address for each department, agency, or instrumentality of the United States or the state or territory. But if more than one mailing address is included, the clerk must also include information that would enable a user to determine when each address applies. Mailing to only one applicable address provides effective notice.

(C) *Keeping the Register Current.* The clerk must update the register annually, as of January 2 of each year.

(D) *Mailing Address Presumed to Be Proper.* A mailing address in the register is conclusively presumed to be proper. But a failure to use that address does not invalidate a notice that is otherwise effective under applicable law.

(f) **Other Books and Records**. The clerk must keep any other books and records required by the Director of the Administrative Office of the United States Courts.

(As amended Mar. 30, 1987, eff. Aug. 1, 1987; Apr. 17, 2000, eff. Dec. 1, 2000; Apr. 23, 2008, eff. Dec. 1, 2008; Apr. 2, 2024, eff. Dec. 1, 2024.)

Rule 5004. Disqualifying a Bankruptcy Judge

(a) **From Presiding Over a Proceeding, Contested Matter, or Case**. A bankruptcy judge's disqualification is governed by 28 U.S.C. §455. The judge is disqualified from presiding over a proceeding or contested matter in which a disqualifying circumstance arises—and, when appropriate, from presiding over the entire case.

(b) **From Allowing Compensation**. The bankruptcy judge is disqualified from allowing compensation to a relative or to a person who is so connected with the judge as to make the judge's allowing it improper.

(As amended Apr. 29, 1985, eff. Aug. 1, 1985; Mar. 30, 1987, eff. Aug. 1, 1987; Apr. 2, 2024, eff. Dec. 1, 2024.)

Rule 5005. Filing Papers and Sending Copies to the United States Trustee

(a) **Filing Papers**.

(1) *With the Clerk.* Except as provided in 28 U.S.C. §1409, the following papers required to be filed by these rules must be filed with the clerk in the district where the case is pending:

- lists;
- schedules;
- statements;
- proofs of claim or interest;
- complaints;
- motions;
- applications;
- objections; and
- other required papers.

The clerk must not refuse to accept for filing any petition or other paper solely because it is not in the form required by these rules or by any local rule or practice.

(2) *With a Judge of the Court.* A judge may personally accept for filing a paper listed in (1). The judge must note on it the date of filing and promptly send it to the clerk.

(3) *Electronic Filing and Signing.*

(A) By a Represented Entity—Generally Required; Exceptions. An entity represented by an attorney must file electronically, unless nonelectronic filing is allowed by the court for cause or is allowed or required by local rule.

(B) By an Unrepresented Individual—When Allowed or Required. An individual not represented by an attorney:

(i) may file electronically only if allowed by court order or local rule; and

(ii) may be required to file electronically only by court order, or by a local rule that includes reasonable exceptions.

(C) Signing. A filing made through a person's electronic-filing account and authorized by that person, together with the person's name on a signature block, constitutes the person's signature.

(D) Same as a Written Paper. A paper filed electronically is a written paper for purposes of these rules, the Federal Rules of Civil Procedure made applicable by these rules, and §107.

(b) **Sending Copies to the United States Trustee**.

(1) *Papers Sent Electronically.* All papers required to be sent to the United States trustee may be sent by using the court's electronic-filing system in accordance with Rule 9036, unless a court order or local rule provides otherwise.

(2) *Papers Not Sent Electronically.* If an entity other than the clerk sends a paper to the United States trustee without using the court's electronic-filing system, the entity must promptly file a statement identifying the paper and stating the manner by which and the date it was sent. The clerk need not send a copy of a paper to a United States trustee who requests in writing that it not be sent.

(c) **When a Paper Is Erroneously Filed or Delivered**.

(1) *Paper Intended for the Clerk.* If a paper intended to be filed with the clerk is erroneously delivered to a person listed below, that person must note on it the date of receipt and promptly send it to the clerk:

- the United States trustee;
- the trustee;
- the trustee's attorney;
- a bankruptcy judge;
- a district judge;

- the clerk of the bankruptcy appellate panel; or
- the clerk of the district court.

(2) *Paper Intended for the United States Trustee.* If a paper intended for the United States trustee is erroneously delivered to the clerk or to another person listed in (1), the clerk or that person must note on it the date of receipt and promptly send it to the United States trustee.

(3) *Applicable Filing Date.* In the interests of justice, the court may order that the original receipt date shown on a paper erroneously delivered under (1) or (2) be deemed the date it was filed with the clerk or sent to the United States trustee.

(As amended Mar. 30, 1987, eff. Aug. 1, 1987; Apr. 30, 1991, eff. Aug. 1, 1991; Apr. 22, 1993, eff. Aug. 1, 1993; Apr. 23, 1996, eff. Dec. 1, 1996; Apr. 12, 2006, eff. Dec. 1, 2006; Apr. 26, 2018, eff. Dec. 1, 2018; Apr. 11, 2022, eff. Dec. 1, 2022; Apr. 2, 2024, eff. Dec. 1, 2024.)

Rule 5006. Providing Certified Copies

Upon payment of the prescribed fee, the clerk must issue a certified copy of the record of any proceeding or any paper filed with the clerk.

(As amended Apr. 30, 1991, eff. Aug. 1, 1991; Apr. 2, 2024, eff. Dec. 1, 2024.)

Rule 5007. Record of Proceedings; Transcripts

(a) **Filing Original Notes, Tape Recordings, and Other Original Records of a Proceeding; Transcripts.**

(1) *Records.* The reporter or operator of a recording device must certify the original notes of testimony, any tape recordings, and other original records of a proceeding and must promptly file them with the clerk.

(2) *Transcripts.* A person who prepares a transcript must promptly file a certified copy with the clerk.

(b) **Fee for a Transcript.** The fee for a copy of a transcript must be charged at the rate prescribed by the Judicial Conference of the United States. No fee may be charged for filing the certified copy

(c) **Sound Recording or Transcript as Prima Facie Evidence.** In any proceeding, a certified sound recording or a transcript of a proceeding is admissible as prima facie evidence of the record.

(As amended Mar. 30, 1987, eff. Aug. 1, 1987; Apr. 30, 1991, eff. Aug. 1, 1991; Apr. 2, 2024, eff. Dec. 1, 2024.)

Rule 5008. Chapter 7—Notice That a Presumption of Abuse Has Arisen Under §707(b)

(a) **Notice to Creditors.** When a presumption of abuse under §707(b) arises in a Chapter 7 case of an individual debtor with primarily consumer debts, the clerk must, within 10 days after the petition is filed, so notify the creditors in accordance with Rule 2002.

(b) **Debtor's Statement**. If the debtor does not file a statement indicating whether a presumption has arisen, the clerk must, within 10 days after the petition is filed, so notify creditors and indicate that further notice will be given if a later-filed statement shows that the presumption has arisen. If the debtor later files such a statement, the clerk must promptly notify the creditors.

(Added Apr. 23, 2008, eff. Dec. 1, 2008; amended Apr. 2, 2024, eff. Dec. 1, 2024.)

Rule 5009. Closing a Chapter 7, 12, 13, or 15 Case; Declaring Liens Satisfied

(a) **Closing a Chapter 7, 12, or 13 Case**. The estate in a Chapter 7, 12, or 13 case is presumed to have been fully administered when:
  (1) the trustee has filed a final report and final account and has certified that the estate has been fully administered; and
  (2) within 30 days after the filing, no objection to the report has been filed by the United States trustee or a party in interest.

(b) **Chapter 7 or 13—Notice of a Failure to File a Certificate of Completion for a Course on Personal Financial Management**. This subdivision (b) applies if an individual debtor in a Chapter 7 or 13 case is required to file a certificate under Rule 1007(b)(7) and fails to do so within 45 days after the first date set for the meeting of creditors under §341(a). The clerk must promptly notify the debtor that the case will be closed without entering a discharge if the certificate is not filed within the time prescribed by Rule 1007(c).

(c) **Closing a Chapter 15 Case**.
  (1) *Foreign Representative's Final Report*. In a proceeding recognized under §1517, when the purpose of a foreign representative's appearance is completed, the representative must file a final report describing the nature and results of the representative's activities in the court.
  (2) *Giving Notice of the Report*. The representative must send a copy of the report to the United States trustee, give notice of its filing, and file a certificate indicating that the notice has been given to:
    (A) the debtor;
    (B) all persons or bodies authorized to administer the debtor's foreign proceedings;
    (C) all parties to litigation pending in the United States in which the debtor was a party when the petition was filed; and
    (D) any other entity the court designates.
  (3) *Presumption of Full Administration*. If the United States trustee or a party in interest does not file an objection within 30 days after the

certificate is filed, the case is presumed to have been fully administered.

(d) **Order Declaring a Lien Satisfied**. This subdivision (d) applies in a Chapter 12 or 13 case when a claim secured by property of the estate is subject to a lien under applicable nonbankruptcy law. The debtor may move for an order declaring that the secured claim has been satisfied and the lien has been released under the terms of the confirmed plan. The motion must be served—in the manner provided by Rule 7004 for serving a summons and complaint—on the claim holder and any other entity the court designates.

(As amended Apr. 30, 1991, eff. Aug. 1, 1991; Apr. 28, 2010, eff. Dec. 1, 2010; Apr. 16, 2013, eff. Dec. 1, 2013; Apr. 27, 2017, eff. Dec. 1, 2017; Apr. 2, 2024, eff. Dec. 1, 2024.)

Rule 5010. Reopening a Case

On the debtor's or another party in interest's motion, the court may, under §350(b), reopen a case. In a reopened Chapter 7, 12, or 13 case, the United States trustee must not appoint a trustee unless the court determines that one is needed to protect the interests of the creditors and the debtor, or to ensure that the reopened case is efficiently administered.

(As amended Mar. 30, 1987, eff. Aug. 1, 1987; Apr. 30, 1991, eff. Aug. 1, 1991; Apr. 2, 2024, eff. Dec. 1, 2024.)

Rule 5011. Motion to Withdraw a Case or Proceeding or to Abstain from Hearing a Proceeding; Staying a Proceeding

(a) **Withdrawing a Case or Proceeding**. A motion to withdraw a case or proceeding under 28 U.S.C. §157(d) must be heard by a district judge.

(b) **Abstaining from Hearing a Proceeding**. Rule 9014 governs a motion asking the court to abstain from hearing a proceeding under 28 U.S.C. §1334(c). The motion must be served on all parties to the proceeding.

(c) **Staying a Proceeding After a Motion to Withdraw or Abstain**. A motion filed under (a) or (b) does not stay proceedings in a case or affect its administration. But a bankruptcy judge may, on proper terms and conditions, stay a proceeding until the motion is decided.

(d) **Motion to Stay a Proceeding**. A motion to stay a proceeding must ordinarily be submitted first to the bankruptcy judge. If it—or a motion for relief from a stay—is filed in the district court, the motion must state why it was not first presented to or obtained from the bankruptcy judge. The district judge may grant relief on proper terms and conditions.

(Added Mar. 30, 1987, eff. Aug. 1, 1987; amended Apr. 30, 1991, eff. Aug. 1, 1991; Apr. 2, 2024, eff. Dec. 1, 2024.)

Rule 5012. Chapter 15—Agreement to Coordinate Proceedings

An agreement to coordinate proceedings under §1527(4) may be approved on motion with an attached copy of the agreement or protocol. Unless the court orders otherwise, the movant must give at least 30 days' notice of any hearing on the motion by sending a copy to the United States trustee and serving it on:

- the debtor;
- all persons or bodies authorized to administer the debtor's foreign proceedings;
- all entities against whom provisional relief is sought under §1519;
- all parties to litigation pending in the United States in which the debtor was a party when the petition was filed; and
- any other entity the court designates.

(Added Apr. 28, 2010, eff. Dec. 1, 2010; amended Apr. 2, 2024, eff. Dec. 1, 2024.)

Part VI—Collecting and Liquidating the Estate

Rule 6001. Burden of Proving the Validity of a Postpetition Transfer

An entity that asserts the validity of a postpetition transfer under §549 has the burden of proof.

(As amended Apr. 2, 2024, eff. Dec. 1, 2024.)

Rule 6002. Custodian's Report to the United States Trustee

(a) **Custodian's Report and Account**. A custodian required by the Code to deliver property to the trustee must promptly file and send to the United States trustee a report and account about the property of the estate and its administration.

(b) **Examining the Administration**. After the custodian's report and account has been filed and the superseded administration has been examined, the court must, after notice and a hearing, determine whether the custodian's administration has been proper, including whether disbursements have been reasonable.

(As amended Mar. 30, 1987, eff. Aug. 1, 1987; Apr. 30, 1991, eff. Aug. 1, 1991; Apr. 22, 1993, eff. Aug. 1, 1993; Apr. 2, 2024, eff. Dec. 1, 2024.)

Rule 6003. Prohibition on Granting Certain Applications and Motions Made Immediately After the Petition Is Filed

(a) **In General**. Unless relief is needed to avoid immediate and irreparable harm, the court must not, within 21 days after the petition is filed, grant an application or motion to:

(1) employ a professional person under Rule 2014;

(2) use, sell, or lease property of the estate, including a motion to pay all or a part of a claim that arose before the petition was filed;

(3) incur any other obligation regarding the property of the estate; or

(4) assume or assign an executory contract or unexpired lease under §365.

(b) **Exception**. This rule does not apply to a motion under Rule 4001.

(Added Apr. 30, 2007, eff. Dec. 1, 2007; amended Mar. 26, 2009, eff. Dec. 1, 2009; Apr. 26, 2011, eff. Dec. 1, 2011; Apr. 2, 2024, eff. Dec. 1, 2024.)

Rule 6004. Use, Sale, or Lease of Property

(a) **Notice**.

(1) *In General*. Notice of a proposed use, sale, or lease of property that is not in the ordinary course of business must be given:

(A) under Rule 2002(a)(2), (c)(1), (i), and (k); and

(B) in accordance with §363(b)(2), if applicable.

(2) *Exceptions*. Notice is not required if (d) applies or the proposal involves cash collateral only.

(b) **Objection**. Except as provided in (c) and (d), an objection to a proposed use, sale, or lease of property must be filed and served at least 7 days before the date set for the proposed action or within the time set by the court. Rule 9014 governs the objection.

(c) **Motion to Sell Property Free and Clear of Liens and Other Interests; Objection**. A motion for authority to sell property free and clear of liens or other interests must be made in accordance with Rule 9014 and served on the parties who have the liens or other interests. The notice required by (a) must include:

(1) the date of the hearing on the motion; and

(2) the time to file and serve an objection on the debtor in possession or trustee.

(d) **Notice of an Intent to Sell Property Valued at Less Than $2,500; Objection**. If all the nonexempt property of the estate—in the aggregate— has a gross value less than $2,500, a notice of an intent to sell the property that is not in the ordinary course of business must be given to:

- all creditors;
- all indenture trustees;
- any committees appointed or elected under the Code;
- the United States trustee; and
- other persons as the court orders.

A party in interest may file and serve an objection within 14 days after the notice is mailed or within the time set by the court. Rule 9014 governs the objection.

(e) **Notice of a Hearing on an Objection**. The date of a hearing on an objection under (b) or (d) may be set in the notice under (a).

(f) **Conducting a Sale That Is Not in the Ordinary Course of Business**.
  (1) *Public Auction or Private Sale.*
    (A) Itemized Statement Required. A sale that is not in the ordinary course of business may be made by public auction or private sale. Unless it is impracticable, when the sale is completed, an itemized statement must be filed that shows:
      • the property sold;
      • the name of each purchaser; and
      • the consideration received for each item or lot or, if sold in bulk, for the entire property.
    (B) If by an Auctioneer. If the property is sold by an auctioneer, the auctioneer must file the itemized statement and send a copy to the United States trustee and to either the trustee, debtor in possession, or Chapter 13 debtor.
    (C) If Not by an Auctioneer. If the property is not sold by an auctioneer, the trustee, debtor in possession, or Chapter 13 debtor must file the itemized statement and send a copy to the United States trustee.
  (2) *Signing the Sale Documents.* When a sale is complete, the debtor, trustee, or debtor in possession must sign any document that is necessary or court-ordered to transfer the property to the purchaser.

(g) **Selling Personally Identifiable Information**.
  (1) *Request for a Consumer-Privacy Ombudsman.* A motion for authority to sell or lease personally identifiable information under §363(b)(1)(B) must include a request for an order directing the United States trustee to appoint a consumer-privacy ombudsman under §332. Rule 9014 governs the motion. It must be sent to the United States trustee and served on:
      • any committee elected under §705 or appointed under §1102;
      • in a Chapter 11 case in which no committee of unsecured creditors has been appointed under §1102, on the creditors included on the list filed under Rule 1007(d); and
      • other entities as the court orders.
  (2) *Notice That an Ombudsman Has Been Appointed.* If a consumer-privacy ombudsman is appointed, the United States trustee must give notice of the appointment at least 7 days before the hearing on any motion under §363(b)(1)(B). The notice must give the name and address of the person appointed and include the person's verified statement that sets forth any connection with:
      • the debtor, creditors, or any other party in interest;
      • their respective attorneys and accountants;
      • the United States trustee; and
      • any person employed in the United States trustee's office.

(h) **Staying an Order Authorizing the Use, Sale, or Lease of Property**. Unless the court orders otherwise, an order authorizing the use, sale, or lease of property (other than cash collateral) is stayed for 14 days after the order is entered.

(As amended Mar. 30, 1987, eff. Aug. 1, 1987; Apr. 30, 1991, eff. Aug. 1, 1991; Apr. 26, 1999, eff. Dec. 1, 1999; Apr. 23, 2008, eff. Dec. 1, 2008; Mar. 26, 2009, eff. Dec. 1, 2009; Apr. 2, 2024, eff. Dec. 1, 2024.)

Rule 6005. Employing an Appraiser or Auctioneer

A court order approving the employment of an appraiser or auctioneer must set the amount or rate of compensation. An officer or employee of the United States judiciary or United States Department of Justice is not eligible to act as an appraiser or auctioneer. No residence or licensing requirement disqualifies a person from being so employed.

(As amended Apr. 30, 1991, eff. Aug. 1, 1991; Apr. 2, 2024, eff. Dec. 1, 2024.)

Rule 6006. Assuming, Rejecting, or Assigning an Executory Contract or Unexpired Lease

(a) **Procedure in General**. Rule 9014 governs a proceeding to assume, reject, or assign an executory contract or unexpired lease, other than as part of a plan.

(b) **Requiring a Trustee, Debtor in Possession, or Debtor to Assume or Reject a Contract or Lease**. In a Chapter 9, 11, 12, or 13 case, Rule 9014 governs a proceeding by a party to an executory contract or unexpired lease to require the trustee, debtor in possession, or debtor to determine whether to assume or reject the contract or lease.

(c) **Notice of a Motion**. Notice of a motion under (a) or (b) must be given to:
- the other party to the contract or lease;
- other parties in interest as the court orders; and
- except in a Chapter 9 case, the United States trustee.

(d) **Staying an Order Authorizing an Assignment**. Unless the court orders otherwise, an order authorizing the trustee to assign an executory contract or unexpired lease under §365(f) is stayed for 14 days after the order is entered.

(e) **Combining in One Motion a Request Involving Multiple Contracts or Leases**.
  (1) *Requests to Assume or Assign*. The trustee must not seek authority to assume or assign multiple executory contracts or unexpired leases in one omnibus motion unless:
    (A) they are all between the same parties or are to be assigned to the same assignee;

(B) the trustee seeks to assume—but not assign to more than one assignee—unexpired leases of real property; or

(C) the court allows the motion to be filed.

(2) *Requests to Reject.* Subject to (f), a trustee may join in one omnibus motion requests for authority to reject multiple executory contracts or unexpired leases.

(f) **Content of an Omnibus Motion.** A motion to reject—or, if permitted under (e), a motion to assume or assign—multiple executory contracts or unexpired leases that are not between the same parties must:

(1) state in a conspicuous place that the parties' names and their contracts or leases are listed in the motion;

(2) list the parties alphabetically and identify the corresponding contract or lease;

(3) specify the terms, including how a default will be cured, for each requested assumption or assignment;

(4) specify the terms, including the assignee's identity and the adequate assurance of future performance by each assignee, for each requested assignment;

(5) be numbered consecutively with other omnibus motions to reject, assume, or assign executory contracts or unexpired leases; and

(6) be limited to no more than 100 executory contracts or unexpired leases.

(g) **Determining the Finality of an Order Regarding an Omnibus Motion.** The finality of an order regarding any executory contract or unexpired lease included in an omnibus motion must be determined as though the contract or lease were the subject of a separate motion.

(As amended Mar. 30, 1987, eff. Aug. 1, 1987; Apr. 30, 1991, eff. Aug. 1, 1991; Apr. 22, 1993, eff. Aug. 1, 1993; Apr. 26, 1999, eff. Dec. 1, 1999; Apr. 30, 2007, eff. Dec. 1, 2007; Mar. 26, 2009, eff. Dec. 1, 2009; Apr. 2, 2024, eff. Dec. 1, 2024.)

Rule 6007. Abandoning or Disposing of Property

(a) **Notice by the Trustee or Debtor in Possession.**

(1) *In General.* Unless the court orders otherwise, the trustee or debtor in possession must give notice of a proposed abandonment or disposition of property to:

• all creditors;

• all indenture trustees;

• any committees appointed or elected under the Code; and

• the United States trustee.

(2) *Objection.* A party in interest may file and serve an objection within 14 days after the notice is mailed or within the time set by the court. If a timely objection is filed, the court must set a hearing on notice to the United States trustee and other entities as the court orders.

(b) **Motion by a Party in Interest.**

(1) *Service.* A party in interest may file and serve a motion to require the trustee or debtor in possession to abandon property of the estate. Unless the court orders otherwise, the motion (and any notice of it) must be served on:

- the trustee or debtor in possession;
- all creditors;
- all indenture trustees;
- any committees appointed or elected under the Code; and
- the United States trustee.

(2) *Objection.* A party in interest may file and serve an objection within 14 days after service or within the time set by the court. If a timely objection is filed, the court must set a hearing on notice to the United States trustee and other entities as the court orders.

(3) *Order.* Unless the court orders otherwise, an order granting the motion to abandon property effects the trustee's or debtor in possession's abandonment without further notice.

(As amended Mar. 30, 1987, eff. Aug. 1, 1987; Apr. 30, 1991, eff. Aug. 1, 1991; Apr. 22, 1993, eff. Aug. 1, 1993; Mar. 26, 2009, eff. Dec. 1, 2009; Apr. 25, 2019, eff. Dec. 1, 2019; Apr. 2, 2024, eff. Dec. 1, 2024.)

Rule 6008. Redeeming Property from a Lien or a Sale to Enforce a Lien

On motion by the debtor, trustee, or debtor in possession and after a hearing on notice as the court may order, the court may authorize property to be redeemed from a lien or from a sale to enforce a lien under applicable law.

(As amended Apr. 2, 2024, eff. Dec. 1, 2024.)

Rule 6009. Right of the Trustee or Debtor in Possession to Prosecute and Defend Proceedings

With or without court approval, the trustee or debtor in possession may:
(a) prosecute—or appear in and defend—any pending action or proceeding by or against the debtor; or
(b) commence and prosecute in any tribunal an action or proceeding on the estate's behalf.

(As amended Apr. 2, 2024, eff. Dec. 1, 2024.)

Rule 6010. Avoiding an Indemnifying Lien or a Transfer to a Surety

This rule applies if a lien voidable under §547 has been dissolved by furnishing a bond or other obligation, and the surety has been indemnified by the transfer of or creation of a lien on the debtor's nonexempt property. The surety must be joined as a defendant in any proceeding to avoid that transfer or lien. Part VII governs the proceeding.

(As amended Apr. 30, 1991, eff. Aug. 1, 1991; Apr. 2, 2024, eff. Dec. 1, 2024.)

Rule 6011. Claiming Patient Records Scheduled for Destruction in a Health-Care-Business Case

(a) **Notice by Publication About the Records**. A notice by publication about destroying or claiming patient records under §351(1)(A) must not identify any patient by name or contain other identifying information. The notice must:
  (1) identify with particularity the health-care facility whose patient records the trustee proposes to destroy;
  (2) state the name, address, telephone number, email address, and website (if any) of the person from whom information about the records may be obtained;
  (3) state how to claim the records and the final date for doing so; and
  (4) state that if they are not claimed by that date, they will be destroyed.

(b) **Notice by Mail About the Records**.
  (1) *Required Information*. Subject to applicable nonbankruptcy law relating to patient privacy, a notice by mail about destroying or claiming patient records under §351(1)(B) must:
    (A) include the information described in (a); and
    (B) direct a family member or other representative who receives the notice to tell the patient about it.
  (2) *Mailing*. The notice must be mailed to:
    • the patient;
    • any family member or other contact person whose name and address have been given to the trustee or debtor for providing information about the patient's health care;
    • the Attorney General of the State where the health-care facility is located; and
    • any insurance company known to have provided health-care insurance to the patient.

(c) **Proof of Compliance with Notice Requirements**. Unless the court orders the trustee to file a proof of compliance with §351(1)(B) under seal, the trustee must keep the proof of compliance for a reasonable time but not file it.

(d) **Report on the Destruction of Unclaimed Records**. Within 30 days after a patient's unclaimed records have been destroyed under §351(3), the trustee must file a report that certifies the destruction and explains the method used. The report must not identify any patient by name or by other identifying information.

(Added Apr. 23, 2008, eff. Dec. 1, 2008; amended Apr. 2, 2024, eff. Dec. 1, 2024.)

Part VII—Adversary Proceedings

Rule 7001. Types of Adversary Proceedings

An adversary proceeding is governed by the rules in this Part VII. The following are adversary proceedings:

(a) a proceeding to recover money or property—except a proceeding to compel the debtor to deliver property to the trustee, a proceeding by an individual debtor to recover tangible personal property under §542(a), or a proceeding under §554(b), §725, Rule 2017, or Rule 6002;

(b) a proceeding to determine the validity, priority, or extent of a lien or other interest in property—except a proceeding under Rule 3012 or Rule 4003(d);

(c) a proceeding to obtain authority under §363(h) to sell both the estate's interest in property and that of a co-owner;

(d) a proceeding to revoke or object to a discharge—except an objection under §727(a)(8) or (a)(9), or §1328(f);

(e) a proceeding to revoke an order confirming a plan in a Chapter 11, 12, or 13 case;

(f) a proceeding to determine whether a debt is dischargeable;

(g) a proceeding to obtain an injunction or other equitable relief—except when the relief is provided in a Chapter 9, 11, 12, or 13 plan;

(h) a proceeding to subordinate an allowed claim or interest—except when subordination is provided in a Chapter 9, 11, 12, or 13 plan;

(i) a proceeding to obtain a declaratory judgment related to any proceeding described in (a)–(h); and

(j) a proceeding to determine a claim or cause of action removed under 28 U.S.C. §1452.

(As amended Mar. 30, 1987, eff. Aug. 1, 1987; Apr. 30, 1991, eff. Aug. 1, 1991; Apr. 26, 1999, eff. Dec. 1, 1999; Apr. 28, 2010, eff. Dec. 1, 2010; Apr. 27, 2017, eff. Dec. 1, 2017; Apr. 2, 2024, eff. Dec. 1, 2024.)

Rule 7002. References to the Federal Rules of Civil Procedure

When a Federal Rule of Civil Procedure applicable to an adversary proceeding refers to another civil rule, that reference is to the civil rule as modified by this Part VII.

(As amended Apr. 2, 2024, eff. Dec. 1, 2024.)

Rule 7003. Commencing an Adversary Proceeding

Fed. R. Civ. P. 3 applies in an adversary proceeding.

(As amended Apr. 2, 2024, eff. Dec. 1, 2024.)

Rule 7004. Process; Issuing and Serving a Summons and Complaint

(a) **Issuing, Delivering, and Personally Serving a Summons and Complaint**.

    (1) *In General*. Except as provided in (2), Fed. R. Civ. P. 4(a), (b), (c)(1), (d)(5), (e)–(j), (l), and (m) applies in an adversary proceeding.

    (2) *Issuing and Delivering a Summons*. The clerk may:

        (A) sign, seal, and issue the summons electronically by placing an "s/" before the clerk's name and adding the court's seal to the summons; and

        (B) deliver the summons to the person who will serve it.

    (3) *Personally Serving a Summons and Complaint*. Any person who is at least 18 years old and not a party may personally serve a summons and complaint under Fed. R. Civ. P. 4(e)–(j).

(b) **Service by Mail as an Alternative**. Except as provided in subdivision (h), in addition to the methods of service authorized by Fed. R. Civ. P. 4(e)–(j), a copy of a summons and complaint may be served by first-class mail, postage prepaid, within the United States on:

    (1) an individual except an infant or an incompetent person—by mailing the copy to the individual's dwelling or usual place of abode or where the individual regularly conducts a business or profession;

    (2) an infant or incompetent person—by mailing the copy:

        (A) to a person who, under the law of the state where service is made, is authorized to receive service on behalf of the infant or incompetent person when an action is brought in that state's courts of general jurisdiction; and

        (B) at that person's dwelling or usual place of abode or where the person regularly conducts a business or profession;

    (3) a domestic or foreign corporation, or a partnership or other unincorporated association—by mailing the copy:

        (A) to an officer, a managing or general agent, or an agent authorized by appointment or by law to receive service; and

        (B) also to the defendant if a statute authorizes an agent to receive service and the statute so requires;

    (4) the United States, with these requirements:

        (A) a copy of the summons and complaint must be mailed to:

            (i) the civil-process clerk in the United States attorney's office in the district where the action is filed;

            (ii) the Attorney General of the United States in Washington, D.C.; and

            (iii) in an action attacking the validity of an order of a United States officer or agency that is not a party, also to that officer or agency; and

    (B) if the plaintiff has mailed a copy of the summons and complaint to a person specified in either (A)(i) or (ii), the court must allow a reasonable time to serve the others that must be served under (A);

(5) an officer or agency of the United States, with these requirements:

    (A) the summons and complaint must be mailed not only to the officer or the agency—as prescribed in (3) if the agency is a corporation—but also to the United States, as prescribed in (4);

    (B) if the plaintiff has mailed a copy of the summons and complaint to a person specified in either (4)(A)(i) or (ii), the court must allow a reasonable time to serve the others that must be served under (A); and

    (C) if a United States trustee is the trustee in the case, service may be made on the United States trustee solely as trustee, as prescribed in (10);

(6) a state or municipal corporation or other governmental organization subject to suit, with these requirements:

    (A) the summons and complaint must be mailed to the person or office that, under the law of the state where service is made, is authorized to receive service in a case filed against that defendant in that state's courts of general jurisdiction; and

    (B) if there is no such authorized person or office, the summons and complaint must be mailed to the defendant's chief executive officer;

(7) a defendant of any class referred to in (1) and (3)—for whom it also suffices to mail the summons and complaint to the entity on which service must be made under a federal statute or under the law of the state where service is made when an action is brought against that defendant in that state's courts of general jurisdiction;

(8) any defendant—for whom it also suffices to mail the summons and complaint to the defendant's agent under these conditions:

    (A) the agent is authorized by appointment or by law to accept service;

    (B) the mail is addressed to the agent's dwelling or usual place of abode or where the agent regularly conducts a business or profession; and

    (C) if the agent's authorization so requires, a copy is also mailed to the defendant as provided in this subdivision (b);

(9) the debtor, after a petition has been filed by or served upon a debtor, and until the case is dismissed or closed—by mailing the copy to the address shown on the debtor's petition or the address the debtor specifies in a filed writing;

(10) a United States trustee who is the trustee in the case and service is made upon the United States trustee solely as trustee—by addressing the mail to the United States trustee's office or other place that the United States trustee designates within the district.

(c) **Service by Publication in an Adversary Proceeding Involving Property Rights**. If a party to an adversary proceeding to determine or protect rights in property in the court's custody cannot be served under (b) or Fed. R. Civ. P. 4(e)–(j), the court may order the summons and complaint to be served by:

    (1) first-class mail, postage prepaid, to the party's last known address; and

    (2) at least one publication in a form and manner as the court orders.

(d) **Nationwide Service of Process**. A summons and complaint (and all other process, except a subpoena) may be served anywhere within the United States.

(e) **Time to Serve a Summons and Complaint**.

    (1) *In General*. A summons and complaint served by delivery under Fed. R. Civ. P. 4(e), (g), (h)(1), (i), or (j)(2) must be served within 7 days after the summons is issued. If served by mail, they must be deposited in the mail within 7 days after the summons is issued. If a summons is not timely delivered or mailed, a new summons must be issued.

    (2) *Exception*. This subdivision (e) does not apply to service in a foreign country.

(f) **Establishing Personal Jurisdiction**. If exercising jurisdiction is consistent with the United States Constitution and laws, serving a summons or filing a waiver of service under this Rule 7004 or the applicable provisions of Fed. R. Civ. P. 4 establishes personal jurisdiction over a defendant:

    (1) in a bankruptcy case; or

    (2) in a civil proceeding arising under the Code, or arising in or related to a case under the Code.

(g) **Serving a Debtor's Attorney**. If, when served, a debtor is represented by an attorney, the attorney must also be served by any means authorized by Fed. R. Civ. P. 5(b).

(h) **Service of Process on an Insured Depository Institution**. Service on an insured depository institution (as defined in section 3 of the Federal Deposit Insurance Act) in a contested matter or adversary proceeding shall be made by certified mail addressed to an officer of the institution unless—

    (1) the institution has appeared by its attorney, in which case the attorney shall be served by first class mail;

    (2) the court orders otherwise after service upon the institution by certified mail of notice of an application to permit service on the institution by first class mail sent to an officer of the institution designated by the institution; or

    (3) the institution has waived in writing its entitlement to service by certified mail by designating an officer to receive service.

        (i) Service of Process by Title. This subdivision (i) applies to service on a domestic or foreign corporation or partnership or other unincorporated association under Rule 7004(b)(3), or on an officer of an insured depository institution under Rule 7004(h). The defendant's officer or agent need not be correctly named in the address—or even be named—if the envelope is addressed to the defendant's proper address and directed to the attention of the officer's or agent's position or title.

(As amended Mar. 30, 1987, eff. Aug. 1, 1987; Apr. 30, 1991, eff. Aug. 1, 1991; Pub. L. 103–394, title I, §114, Oct. 22, 1994, 108 Stat. 4118; Apr. 23, 1996, eff. Dec. 1, 1996; Apr. 26, 1999, eff. Dec. 1, 1999; Apr. 25, 2005, eff. Dec. 1, 2005; Apr. 12, 2006, eff. Dec. 1, 2006; Mar. 26, 2009, eff. Dec. 1, 2009; Apr. 25, 2014, eff. Dec. 1, 2014; Apr. 26, 2018, eff. Dec. 1, 2018; Apr. 11, 2022, eff. Dec. 1, 2022; Apr. 2, 2024, eff. Dec. 1, 2024.)

Rule 7005. Serving and Filing Pleadings and Other Papers

Fed. R. Civ. P. 5 applies in an adversary proceeding.

(As amended Apr. 2, 2024, eff. Dec. 1, 2024.)

Rule 7007. Pleadings Allowed

Fed. R. Civ. P. 7 applies in an adversary proceeding.

(As amended Apr. 2, 2024, eff. Dec. 1, 2024.)

Rule 7007.1. Corporate Ownership Statement

(a) **Required Disclosure**. Any nongovernmental corporation—other than the debtor—that is a party to an adversary proceeding must file a statement identifying any parent corporation and any publicly held corporation that owns 10% or more of its stock or stating that there is no such corporation. The same requirement applies to a nongovernmental corporation that seeks to intervene.

(b) **Time for Filing; Supplemental Filing**. The statement must:
   (1) be filed with the corporation's first appearance, pleading, motion, response, or other request to the court; and
   (2) be supplemented whenever the information required by this rule changes.

(Added Mar. 27, 2003, eff. Dec. 1, 2003; amended Apr. 30, 2007, eff. Dec. 1, 2007; Apr. 14, 2021, eff. Dec. 1, 2021; Apr. 2, 2024, eff. Dec. 1, 2024.)

Rule 7008. General Rules of Pleading

Fed. R. Civ. P. 8 applies in an adversary proceeding. The allegation of jurisdiction required by that rule must include a reference to the name, number, and Code chapter of the case that the adversary proceeding relates to and the district and division where it is pending. In an adversary proceeding before a bankruptcy court, a complaint, counterclaim, crossclaim, or third-party complaint must state whether the pleader does or does not consent to the entry of final orders or judgment by the bankruptcy court.

(As amended Mar. 30, 1987, eff. Aug. 1, 1987; Apr. 25, 2014, eff. Dec. 1, 2014; Apr. 28, 2016, eff. Dec. 1, 2016; Apr. 2, 2024, eff. Dec. 1, 2024.)

Rule 7009. Pleading Special Matters

Fed. R. Civ. P. 9 applies in an adversary proceeding.

(As amended Apr. 2, 2024, eff. Dec. 1, 2024.)

Rule 7010. Form of Pleadings in an Adversary Proceeding

Fed. R. Civ. P. 10 applies in an adversary proceeding—except that a pleading's caption must substantially conform to the appropriate version of Form 416.

(As amended Apr. 30, 1991, eff. Aug. 1, 1991; Apr. 2, 2024, eff. Dec. 1, 2024.)

Rule 7012. Defenses; Effect of a Motion; Motion for Judgment on the Pleadings and Other Procedural Matters

(a) **Time to Serve**. The time to serve a responsive pleading is as follows:
　(1) *Answer to a Complaint in General*. A defendant must serve an answer to a complaint within 30 days after the summons was issued, unless the court sets a different time.
　(2) *Answer to a Complaint Served by Publication or on a Party in a Foreign Country*. The court must set the time to serve an answer to a complaint served by publication or served on a party in a foreign country.
　(3) *Answer to a Crossclaim*. A party served with a pleading that states a crossclaim must serve an answer to the crossclaim within 21 days after being served.
　(4) *Answer to a Counterclaim*. A plaintiff served with an answer that contains a counterclaim must serve an answer to the counterclaim within 21 days after service of:
　　(A) the answer; or
　　(B) a court order requiring an answer, unless the order states otherwise.
　(5) *Answer to a Complaint or Crossclaim—or Answer to a Counterclaim—Served on the United States or an Officer or Agency*. The United States or its officer or agency must serve:
　　(A) an answer to a complaint within 35 days after the summons was issued; and
　　(B) an answer to a crossclaim or a counterclaim within 35 days after the United States attorney is served with the pleading that asserts the claim.
　(6) *Effect of a Motion*. Unless the court sets a different time, serving a motion under this rule alters these times as follows:

(A) if the court denies the motion or postpones disposition until trial, the responsive pleading must be served within 14 days after notice of the court's action; or

(B) if the court grants a motion for a more definite statement, the responsive pleading must be served within 14 days after the statement is served.

(b) **Applicability of Civil Rule 12(b)–(i)**. Fed. R. Civ. P. 12(b)–(i) applies in an adversary proceeding. A responsive pleading must state whether the party does or does not consent to the entry of final orders or judgment by the bankruptcy court.

(As amended Mar. 30, 1987, eff. Aug. 1, 1987; Apr. 23, 2008, eff. Dec. 1, 2008; Mar. 26, 2009, eff. Dec. 1, 2009; Apr. 28, 2016, eff. Dec. 1, 2016; Apr. 2, 2024, eff. Dec. 1, 2024.)

Rule 7013. Counterclaim and Crossclaim

Fed. R. Civ. P. 13 applies in an adversary proceeding. But a party sued by a trustee or debtor in possession need not state as a counterclaim any claim the party has against the debtor, the debtor's property, or the estate, unless the claim arose after the order for relief. If, through oversight, inadvertence, or excusable neglect, a trustee or debtor in possession fails to plead a counterclaim—or when justice so requires—the court may permit the trustee or debtor in possession to:

(a) amend the pleading; or

(b) commence a new adversary proceeding or separate action.

(As amended Mar. 30, 1987, eff. Aug. 1, 1987; Apr. 2, 2024, eff. Dec. 1, 2024.)

Rule 7014. Third-Party Practice

Fed. R. Civ. P. 14 applies in an adversary proceeding.

(As amended Apr. 2, 2024, eff. Dec. 1, 2024.)

Rule 7015. Amended and Supplemental Pleadings

Fed. R. Civ. P. 15 applies in an adversary proceeding.

(As amended Apr. 2, 2024, eff. Dec. 1, 2024.)

Rule 7016. Pretrial Procedures

(a) **Pretrial Conferences; Scheduling; Management**. Fed. R. Civ. P. 16 applies in an adversary proceeding.

(b) **Determining Procedure**. On its own or a party's timely motion, the court must decide whether:

(1) to hear and determine the proceeding;

(2) to hear it and issue proposed findings of fact and conclusions of law; or

(3) to take other action.

(As amended Apr. 28, 2016, eff. Dec. 1, 2016; Apr. 2, 2024, eff. Dec. 1, 2024.)

Rule 7017. Plaintiff and Defendant; Capacity; Public Officers

Fed. R. Civ. P. 17 applies in an adversary proceeding, except as provided in Rule 2010(b).

(As amended Apr. 30, 1991, eff. Aug. 1, 1991; Apr. 2, 2024, eff. Dec. 1, 2024.)

Rule 7018. Joinder of Claims

Fed. R. Civ. P. 18 applies in an adversary proceeding.

(As amended Apr. 2, 2024, eff. Dec. 1, 2024.)

Rule 7019. Required Joinder of Parties

Fed. R. Civ. P. 19 applies in an adversary proceeding. But these exceptions apply:

(a) if an entity joined as a party raises the defense that the court lacks subject-matter jurisdiction and the defense is sustained, the court must dismiss the party; and

(b) if an entity joined as a party properly and timely raises the defense of improper venue, the court must determine under 28 U.S.C. §1412 whether to transfer to another district the entire adversary proceeding or just that part involving the joined party.

(As amended Mar. 30, 1987, eff. Aug. 1, 1987; Apr. 2, 2024, eff. Dec. 1, 2024.)

Rule 7020. Permissive Joinder of Parties

Fed. R. Civ. P. 20 applies in an adversary proceeding.

(As amended Apr. 2, 2024, eff. Dec. 1, 2024.)

Rule 7021. Misjoinder and Nonjoinder of Parties

Fed. R. Civ. P. 21 applies in an adversary proceeding.

(As amended Apr. 2, 2024, eff. Dec. 1, 2024.)

Rule 7022. Interpleader

Fed. R. Civ. P. 22(a) applies in an adversary proceeding. This rule supplements and does not limit the joinder of parties under Rule 7020.

(As amended Apr. 23, 2008, eff. Dec. 1, 2008; Apr. 2, 2024, eff. Dec. 1, 2024.)

Rule 7023. Class Actions

Fed. R. Civ. P. 23 applies in an adversary proceeding.

(As amended Apr. 2, 2024, eff. Dec. 1, 2024.)

Rule 7023.1. Derivative Actions

Fed. R. Civ. P. 23.1 applies in an adversary proceeding.

(As amended Apr. 23, 2008, eff. Dec. 1, 2008; Apr. 2, 2024, eff. Dec. 1, 2024.)

Rule 7023.2. Adversary Proceedings Relating to Unincorporated Associations

Fed. R. Civ. P. 23.2 applies in an adversary proceeding.

(As amended Apr. 2, 2024, eff. Dec. 1, 2024.)

Rule 7024. Intervention

Fed. R. Civ. P. 24 applies in an adversary proceeding.

(As amended Apr. 2, 2024, eff. Dec. 1, 2024.)

Rule 7025. Substitution of Parties

Fed. R. Civ. P. 25 applies in an adversary proceeding—but is subject to Rule 2012.

(As amended Apr. 2, 2024, eff. Dec. 1, 2024.)

Rule 7026. Duty to Disclose; General Provisions Governing Discovery

Fed. R. Civ. P. 26 applies in an adversary proceeding.

(As amended Apr. 2, 2024, eff. Dec. 1, 2024.)

Rule 7027. Depositions to Perpetuate Testimony

Fed. R. Civ. P. 27 applies in an adversary proceeding.

(As amended Apr. 2, 2024, eff. Dec. 1, 2024.)

Rule 7028. Persons Before Whom Depositions May Be Taken

Fed. R. Civ. P. 28 applies in an adversary proceeding.

(As amended Apr. 2, 2024, eff. Dec. 1, 2024.)

Rule 7029. Stipulations About Discovery Procedure

Fed. R. Civ. P. 29 applies in an adversary proceeding.

(As amended Apr. 2, 2024, eff. Dec. 1, 2024.)

Rule 7030. Depositions by Oral Examination

Fed. R. Civ. P. 30 applies in an adversary proceeding.

(As amended Apr. 2, 2024, eff. Dec. 1, 2024.)

Rule 7031. Depositions by Written Questions

Fed. R. Civ. P. 31 applies in an adversary proceeding.

(As amended Apr. 2, 2024, eff. Dec. 1, 2024.)

Rule 7032. Using Depositions in Court Proceedings

Fed. R. Civ. P. 32 applies in an adversary proceeding.

(As amended Apr. 2, 2024, eff. Dec. 1, 2024.)

Rule 7033. Interrogatories to Parties

Fed. R. Civ. P. 33 applies in an adversary proceeding.

(As amended Apr. 2, 2024, eff. Dec. 1, 2024.)

Rule 7034. Producing Documents, Electronically Stored Information, and Tangible Things, or Entering onto Land, for Inspection and Other Purposes

Fed. R. Civ. P. 34 applies in an adversary proceeding.

(As amended Apr. 2, 2024, eff. Dec. 1, 2024.)

Rule 7035. Physical and Mental Examinations

Fed. R. Civ. P. 35 applies in an adversary proceeding.

(As amended Apr. 2, 2024, eff. Dec. 1, 2024.)

Rule 7036. Requests for Admission

Fed. R. Civ. P. 36 applies in an adversary proceeding.

(As amended Apr. 2, 2024, eff. Dec. 1, 2024.)

Rule 7037. Failure to Make Disclosures or to Cooperate in Discovery; Sanctions

Fed. R. Civ. P. 37 applies in an adversary proceeding.

(As amended Apr. 2, 2024, eff. Dec. 1, 2024.)

Rule 7040. Scheduling Cases for Trial

Fed. R. Civ. P. 40 applies in an adversary proceeding.

(As amended Apr. 2, 2024, eff. Dec. 1, 2024.)

Rule 7041. Dismissing Adversary Proceedings

Fed. R. Civ. P. 41 applies in an adversary proceeding. But a complaint objecting to the debtor's discharge may be dismissed on the plaintiff's motion only:

(a) by a court order setting out any terms and conditions for the dismissal; and

(b) with notice to the trustee, the United States trustee, and any other person the court designates.

(As amended Apr. 30, 1991, eff. Aug. 1, 1991; Apr. 2, 2024, eff. Dec. 1, 2024.)

Rule 7042. Consolidating Adversary Proceedings; Separate Trials

Fed. R. Civ. P. 42 applies in an adversary proceeding.

(As amended Apr. 2, 2024, eff. Dec. 1, 2024.)

Rule 7052. Findings and Conclusions by the Court; Judgment on Partial Findings

Fed. R. Civ. P. 52 applies in an adversary proceeding—except that a motion under Fed. R. Civ. P. 52(b) to amend or add findings must be filed within 14 days after the judgment is entered. The reference in Fed. R. Civ. P. 52(a) to entering a judgment under Fed. R. Civ. P. 58 must be read as referring to entering a judgment or order under Rule 5003(a).

(As amended Mar. 26, 2009, eff. Dec. 1, 2009; Apr. 2, 2024, eff. Dec. 1, 2024.)

Rule 7054. Judgments; Costs

(a) **Judgment.** Fed. R. Civ. P. 54(a)–(c) applies in an adversary proceeding.

(b) **Costs and Attorney's Fees.**

    (1) *Costs Other Than Attorney's Fees.* The court may allow costs to the prevailing party, unless a federal statute or these rules provide otherwise. Costs against the United States, its officers, and its agencies may be imposed only to the extent permitted by law. The clerk, on 14

days' notice, may tax costs, and the court, on motion served within the next 7 days, may review the clerk's action.

    (2) *Attorney's Fees.*

        (A) In General. Fed. R. Civ. P. 54(d)(2)(A)–(C) and (E) applies in an adversary proceeding—except for the reference in 54(d)(2)(C) to Civil Rule 78.

        (B) Local Rules for Resolving Issues. By local rule, the court may establish special procedures to resolve fee-related issues without extensive evidentiary hearings.

(As amended Apr. 23, 2012, eff. Dec. 1, 2012; Apr. 25, 2014, eff. Dec. 1, 2014; Apr. 2, 2024, eff. Dec. 1, 2024.)

Rule 7055. Default; Default Judgment

Fed. R. Civ. P. 55 applies in an adversary proceeding.

(As amended Apr. 2, 2024, eff. Dec. 1, 2024.)

Rule 7056. Summary Judgment

Fed. R. Civ. P. 56 applies in an adversary proceeding. But a motion for summary judgment must be filed at least 30 days before the first date set for an evidentiary hearing on any issue that the motion addresses, unless a local rule sets a different time or the court orders otherwise.

(As amended Apr. 23, 2012, eff. Dec. 1 2012; Apr. 2, 2024, eff. Dec. 1, 2024.)

Rule 7058. Entering Judgment

Fed. R. Civ. P. 58 applies in an adversary proceeding. A reference in that rule to the civil docket must be read as referring to the docket maintained by the clerk under Rule 5003(a).

(Added Mar. 26, 2009, eff. Dec. 1, 2009; amended Apr. 2, 2024, eff. Dec. 1, 2024.)

Rule 7062. Stay of Proceedings to Enforce a Judgment

Fed. R. Civ. P. 62 applies in an adversary proceeding—except that a proceeding to enforce a judgment is stayed for 14 days after its entry.

(As amended Apr. 30, 1991, eff. Aug. 1, 1991; Apr. 26, 1999, eff. Dec. 1, 1999; Apr. 26, 2018, eff. Dec. 1, 2018; Apr. 2, 2024, eff. Dec. 1, 2024.)

Rule 7064. Seizing a Person or Property

Fed. R. Civ. P. 64 applies in an adversary proceeding.

(As amended Apr. 2, 2024, eff. Dec. 1, 2024.)

Rule 7065. Injunctions

Fed. R. Civ. P. 65 applies in an adversary proceeding. But on application of a debtor, trustee, or debtor in possession, the court may issue a temporary restraining order or preliminary injunction without complying with subdivision (c) of that rule.

(As amended Apr. 2, 2024, eff. Dec. 1, 2024.)

Rule 7067. Deposit into Court

Fed. R. Civ. P. 67 applies in an adversary proceeding.

(As amended Apr. 2, 2024, eff. Dec. 1, 2024.)

Rule 7068. Offer of Judgment

Fed. R. Civ. P. 68 applies in an adversary proceeding.

(As amended Apr. 2, 2024, eff. Dec. 1, 2024.)

Rule 7069. Execution

Fed. R. Civ. P. 69 applies in an adversary proceeding.

(As amended Apr. 2, 2024, eff. Dec. 1, 2024.)

Rule 7070. Enforcing a Judgment for a Specific Act; Vesting Title

Fed. R. Civ. P. 70 applies in an adversary proceeding. When real or personal property is within the court's jurisdiction, the court may enter a judgment divesting a party's title and vesting it in another person.

(As amended Mar. 30, 1987, eff. Aug. 1, 1987; Apr. 2, 2024, eff. Dec. 1, 2024.)

Rule 7071. Enforcing Relief for or Against a Nonparty

Fed. R. Civ. P. 71 applies in an adversary proceeding.

(As amended Apr. 2, 2024, eff. Dec. 1, 2024.)

Rule 7087. Transferring an Adversary Proceeding

On motion and after a hearing, the court may transfer an adversary proceeding, or any part of it, to another district under 28 U.S.C. §1412—except as provided in Rule 7019(b).

(As amended Mar. 30, 1987, eff. Aug. 1, 1987; Apr. 2, 2024, eff. Dec. 1, 2024.)

Part VIII—Appeal to a District Court or a Bankruptcy Appellate Panel

Rule 8001. Scope; Definition of "BAP"; Sending Documents Electronically

(a) **Scope**. These Part VIII rules govern the procedure in a United States district court and in a bankruptcy appellate panel on appeal from a bankruptcy court's judgment, order, or decree. They also govern certain procedures on appeal to a United States court of appeals under 28 U.S.C. §158(d).

(b) **Definition of "BAP."** "BAP" means a bankruptcy appellate panel established by a circuit judicial council and authorized to hear appeals from a bankruptcy court under 28 U.S.C. §158.

(c) **Requirement to Send Documents Electronically**. Under these Part VIII rules, a document must be sent electronically, unless:

    (1) it is sent by or to an individual who is not represented by counsel; or

    (2) the court's local rules permit or require mailing or delivery by other means.

(Added Apr. 25, 2014, eff. Dec. 1, 2014; amended Apr. 2, 2024, eff. Dec. 1, 2024.)

Rule 8002. Time to File a Notice of Appeal

(a) **In General**.

    (1) *Time to File*. Except as (b) and (c) provide otherwise, a notice of appeal must be filed with the bankruptcy clerk within 14 days after the judgment, order, or decree to be appealed is entered.

    (2) *Filing Before the Entry of Judgment*. A notice of appeal filed after the bankruptcy court announces a decision or order—but before entry of the judgment, order, or decree—is treated as filed on the date of and after the entry.

    (3) *Multiple Appeals*. If one party timely files a notice of appeal, any other party may file a notice of appeal within 14 days after the date when the first notice was filed, or within the time otherwise allowed by this rule—whichever is later.

    (4) *Mistaken Filing in Another Court*. If a notice of appeal is mistakenly filed in a district court, BAP, or court of appeals, that court's clerk must note on it the date when it was received and send it to the bankruptcy clerk. The notice is then considered filed in the bankruptcy court on the date noted.

    (5) *Entry Defined*.

        (A) In General. A judgment, order, or decree is entered for purposes of this subdivision (a):

            (i) when it is entered in the docket under Rule 5003(a); or

(ii) if Rule 7058 applies and Fed. R. Civ. P. 58(a) requires a separate document, when the judgment, order, or decree is entered in the docket under Rule 5003(a) and when the earlier of these events occurs:

- the judgment, order, or decree is set out in a separate document; or
- 150 days have run from entry of the judgment, order, or decree in the docket under Rule 5003(a).

(B) *Failure to Use a Separate Document.* A failure to set out a judgment, order, or decree in a separate document when required by Fed. R. Civ. P. 58(a) does not affect the validity of an appeal from that judgment, order, or decree.

(b) **Effect of a Motion on the Time to Appeal**.

(1) *In General.* If a party files in the bankruptcy court any of the following motions—and does so within the time allowed by these rules—the time to file an appeal runs for all parties from the entry of the order disposing of the last such remaining motion:

(A) to amend or make additional findings under Rule 7052, whether or not granting the motion would alter the judgment;

(B) to alter or amend the judgment under Rule 9023;

(C) for a new trial under Rule 9023; or

(D) for relief under Rule 9024 if the motion is filed within 14 days after the judgment is entered.

(2) *Notice of Appeal Filed Before a Motion Is Decided.* If a party files a notice of appeal after the court announces or enters a judgment, order, or decree—but before it disposes of any motion listed in (1)—the notice becomes effective when the order disposing of the last such remaining motion is entered.

(3) *Appealing a Ruling on a Motion.* A party intending to challenge an order disposing of a motion listed in (1)—or an alteration or amendment of a judgment, order, or decree made by a decision on the motion—must file a notice of appeal or an amended notice of appeal. It must:

(A) comply with Rule 8003 or 8004; and

(B) be filed within the time allowed by this rule, measured from the entry of the order disposing of the last such remaining motion.

(4) *No Additional Fee for an Amended Notice.* No additional fee is required to file an amended notice of appeal.

(c) **Appeal by an Inmate Confined in an Institution**.

(1) *In General.* If an institution has a system designed for legal mail, an inmate confined there must use that system to receive the benefit of this paragraph (1). If an inmate files a notice of appeal from a bankruptcy court's judgment, order, or decree, the notice is timely if it is deposited

in the institution's internal mail system on or before the last day for filing and:

    (A) it is accompanied by:

        (i) a declaration in compliance with 28 U.S.C. §1746—or a notarized statement—setting out the date of deposit and stating that first-class postage is being prepaid; or

        (ii) evidence (such as a postmark or date stamp) showing that the notice was so deposited and that postage was prepaid; or

    (B) the appellate court exercises its discretion to permit the later filing of a declaration or notarized statement that satisfies (A)(i).

  (2) *Multiple Appeals.* If an inmate files under this subdivision (c) the first notice of appeal, the 14-day period provided in (a)(3) for another party to file a notice of appeal runs from the date when the bankruptcy clerk dockets the first notice.

(d) **Extending the Time to File a Notice of Appeal.**

  (1) *When the Time May Be Extended.* Except as (2) provides otherwise, the bankruptcy court may, on motion, extend the time to file a notice of appeal if the motion is filed:

    (A) within the time allowed by this rule; or

    (B) within 21 days after that time expires if the party shows excusable neglect.

  (2) *When the Time Must Not Be Extended.* The bankruptcy court must not extend the time to file the notice if the judgment, order, or decree being appealed:

    (A) grants relief from an automatic stay under §362, 922, 1201, or 1301;

    (B) authorizes the sale or lease of property or the use of cash collateral under §363;

    (C) authorizes obtaining credit under §364;

    (D) authorizes assuming or assigning an executory contract or unexpired lease under §365;

    (E) approves a disclosure statement under §1125; or

    (F) confirms a plan under §943, 1129, 1225, or 1325.

  (3) *Limit on Extending Time.* An extension of time must not exceed 21 days after the time allowed by this rule, or 14 days after the order granting the motion to extend time is entered—whichever is later.

(Added Apr. 25, 2014, eff. Dec. 1, 2014; amended Apr. 26, 2018, eff. Dec. 1, 2018; Apr. 2, 2024, eff. Dec. 1, 2024.)

Rule 8003. Appeal as of Right—How Taken; Docketing the Appeal

(a) **Filing a Notice of Appeal**.

  (1) *Time to File.* An appeal under 28 U.S.C. §158(a)(1) or (2) from a bankruptcy court's judgment, order, or decree to a district court or a

BAP may be taken only by filing a notice of appeal with the bankruptcy clerk within the time allowed by Rule 8002.

(2) *Failure to Take Any Other Step.* An appellant's failure to take any step other than timely filing a notice of appeal does not affect the appeal's validity, but is ground only for the district court or BAP to act as it considers appropriate, including dismissing the appeal.

(3) *Content of the Notice of Appeal.* A notice of appeal must:

    (A) conform substantially to Form 417A;

    (B) be accompanied by the judgment—or the appealable order or decree—from which the appeal is taken; and

    (C) be accompanied by the prescribed filing fee.

(4) *Merger.* The notice of appeal encompasses all orders that, for purposes of appeal, merge into the identified judgment or appealable order or decree. It is not necessary to identify those orders in the notice of appeal.

(5) *Final Judgment.* The notice of appeal encompasses the final judgment, whether or not that judgment is set out in a separate document under Rule 7058, if the notice identifies:

    (A) an order that adjudicates all remaining claims and the rights and liabilities of all remaining parties; or

    (B) an order described in Rule 8002(b)(1).

(6) *Limited Appeal.* An appellant may identify only part of a judgment or appealable order or decree by expressly stating that the notice of appeal is so limited. Without such an express statement, specific identifications do not limit the scope of the notice of appeal.

(7) *Impermissible Ground for Dismissal.* An appeal must not be dismissed for failure to properly identify the judgment or appealable order or decree if the notice of appeal was filed after entry of the judgment or appealable order or decree and identifies an order that merged into that judgment or appealable order or decree.

(8) *Clerk's Request for Additional Copies of the Notice of Appeal.* On the bankruptcy clerk's request, the appellant must provide enough copies of the notice of appeal to enable the clerk to comply with (c).

(b) **Joint or Consolidated Appeals.**

(1) *Joint Notice of Appeal.* When two or more parties are entitled to appeal from a bankruptcy court's judgment, order, or decree and their interests make joinder practicable, they may file a joint notice of appeal. They may then proceed on appeal as a single appellant.

(2) *Consolidating Appeals.* When parties have separately filed timely notices of appeal, the district court or BAP may join or consolidate the appeals.

(c) **Serving the Notice of Appeal.**

(1) *Serving Parties; Sending to the United States Trustee.* The bankruptcy clerk must serve the notice of appeal by sending a copy to counsel of

record for each party to the appeal—excluding the appellant's counsel—and send it to the United States trustee. If a party is proceeding pro se, the clerk must send the notice to the party's last known address. The clerk must note, on each copy, the date when the notice of appeal was filed.

(2) *Failure to Serve the Notice of Appeal.* The bankruptcy clerk's failure to serve notice on a party or send notice to the United States trustee does not affect the appeal's validity.

(3) *Entry of Service on the Docket.* The clerk must note on the docket the names of the parties served and the date and method of service.

(d) **Sending the Notice of Appeal to the District Court or BAP; Docketing the Appeal.**

(1) *Where to Send the Notice of Appeal.* If a BAP has been established to hear appeals from that district—and an appellant has not elected to have the appeal heard in the district court—the bankruptcy clerk must promptly send the notice of appeal to the BAP clerk. Otherwise, the bankruptcy clerk must promptly send it to the district clerk.

(2) *Docketing the Appeal.* Upon receiving the notice of appeal, the district or BAP clerk must:

(A) docket the appeal under the title of the bankruptcy case and the title of any adversary proceeding; and

(B) identify the appellant, adding the appellant's name if necessary.

(Added Apr. 25, 2014, eff. Dec. 1, 2014; amended Apr. 24, 2023, eff. Dec. 1, 2023; Apr. 2, 2024, eff. Dec. 1, 2024.)

Rule 8004. Leave to Appeal from an Interlocutory Order or Decree Under 28 U.S.C. §158(a)(3)

(a) **Notice of Appeal and Accompanying Motion for Leave to Appeal.** To appeal under 28 U.S.C. §158(a)(3) from a bankruptcy court's interlocutory order or decree, a party must file with the bankruptcy clerk a notice of appeal under Rule 8003(a). The notice must:

(1) be filed within the time allowed by Rule 8002;

(2) be accompanied by a motion for leave to appeal prepared in accordance with (b); and

(3) unless served electronically using the court's electronic-filing system, include proof of service in accordance with Rule 8011(d).

(b) **Content of the Motion for Leave to Appeal; Response.**

(1) *Content.* A motion for leave to appeal under 28 U.S.C. §158(a)(3) must include:

(A) the facts needed to understand the question presented;

(B) the question itself;

(C) the relief sought;

(D) the reasons why leave to appeal should be granted; and

(E) a copy of the interlocutory order or decree and any related opinion or memorandum.

(2) *Response.* Within 14 days after the motion for leave is served, a party may file with the district or BAP clerk a response in opposition or a cross-motion.

(c) **Sending the Notice of Appeal and Motion for Leave to Appeal; Docketing the Appeal; Oral Argument Not Required.**

(1) *Sending to the District Court or BAP.* If a BAP has been established to hear appeals from that district—and an appellant has not elected to have the appeal heard in the district court—the bankruptcy clerk must promptly send to the BAP clerk the notice of appeal and the motion for leave to appeal. Otherwise, the bankruptcy clerk must promptly send the notice and motion to the district clerk.

(2) *Docketing the Appeal.* Upon receiving the notice and motion, the district or BAP clerk must docket the appeal as prescribed by Rule 8003(d)(2).

(3) *Oral Argument Not Required.* Unless the district court or BAP orders otherwise, a motion, a cross-motion, and any response will be submitted without oral argument.

(d) **Failure to File a Motion for Leave to Appeal.** If an appellant files a timely notice of appeal under this rule but fails to include a motion for leave to appeal, the district court or BAP may:

(1) treat the notice of appeal as a motion for leave to appeal and grant or deny it; or

(2) order the appellant to file a motion for leave to appeal within 14 days after the order has been entered—unless the order provides otherwise.

(e) **Direct Appeal to a Court of Appeals.** If leave to appeal an interlocutory order or decree is required under 28 U.S.C. §158(a)(3), an authorization by a court of appeals for a direct appeal under 28 U.S.C. §158(d)(2) satisfies the requirement.

(Added Apr. 25, 2014, eff. Dec. 1, 2014; amended Apr. 2, 2024, eff. Dec. 1, 2024.)

Rule 8005. Election to Have an Appeal Heard in the District Court Instead of the BAP

(a) **Filing a Statement of Election.** To elect to have the district court hear an appeal, a party must file a statement of election within the time prescribed by 28 U.S.C. §158(c)(1). The statement must substantially conform to Form 417A.

(b) **Sending Documents Relating to the Appeal.** Upon receiving an appellant's timely statement of election, the bankruptcy clerk must send all documents related to the appeal to the district clerk. A BAP clerk who receives a timely statement of election from a party other than the appellant must:

(1) send those documents to the district clerk; and

(2) notify the bankruptcy clerk that they have been sent.

(c) **Determining the Validity of an Election**. Within 14 days after the statement of election has been filed, a party seeking to determine the election's validity must file a motion in the court where the appeal is pending.

(d) **Effect of Filing a Motion for Leave to Appeal Without Filing a Notice of Appeal**. If an appellant moves for leave to appeal under Rule 8004 but fails to file a notice of appeal with the motion, it must be treated as a notice of appeal in determining whether the statement of election has been timely filed.

(Added Apr. 25, 2014, eff. Dec. 1, 2014; amended Apr. 2, 2024, eff. Dec. 1, 2024.)

Rule 8006. Certifying a Direct Appeal to a Court of Appeals

(a) **Effective Date of a Certification**. A certification of a bankruptcy court's judgment, order, or decree to a court of appeals for direct review under 28 U.S.C. §158(d)(2) becomes effective when:

(1) it is filed;

(2) a timely appeal is taken under Rule 8003 or Rule 8004; and

(3) the notice of appeal becomes effective under Rule 8002.

(b) **Filing the Certification**. The certification must be filed with the clerk of the court where the matter is pending. For purposes of this rule, a matter remains pending in the bankruptcy court for 30 days after the first notice of appeal concerning that matter becomes effective under Rule 8002. After that time, the matter is pending in the district court or BAP.

(c) **Joint Certification by All Appellants and Appellees**.

(1) In General. A joint certification by all appellants and appellees under 28 U.S.C. §158(d)(2)(A) must be made using Form 424. The parties may supplement the certification with a short statement about its basis. The statement may include the information required by (f)(2).

(2) Supplemental Statement by the Court. Within 14 days after the parties file the certification, the bankruptcy court—or the court where the matter is pending—may file a short supplemental statement about the certification's merits.

(d) **Court's Authority to Certify a Direct Appeal**. Only the court where the matter is pending under (b) may certify a direct appeal to a court of appeals. The court may do so on a party's request or on its own.

(e) **Certification by the Court Acting on Its Own**.

(1) *Separate Document Required; Service; Content*. A certification by a court acting on its own must be set forth in a separate document. The clerk of the certifying court must serve the document on the parties to the appeal in the manner required for serving a notice of appeal under

Rule 8003(c)(1). It must be accompanied by an opinion or memorandum that contains the information required by (f)(2)(A)–(D).

(2) *Supplemental Statement by a Party.* Within 14 days after the court's certification, a party may file with the clerk of the certifying court a short supplemental statement about the merits of certification.

(f) **Certification by the Court on Request.**

(1) *How Requested.* A party's request for certification under 28 U.S.C. §158(d)(2)(A)—or a request by a majority of the appellants and of the appellees—must be filed with the clerk of the court where the matter is pending. The request must be filed within 60 days after the judgment, order, or decree is entered.

(2) *Service; Content.* The request must be served on all parties to the appeal in the manner required for serving a notice of appeal under Rule 8003(c)(1). The request must include:

(A) the facts needed to understand the question presented;

(B) the question itself;

(C) the relief sought;

(D) the reasons why a direct appeal should be allowed, including which circumstance specified in 28 U.S.C. §158(d)(2)(A)(i)–(iii) applies; and

(E) the judgment, order, or decree, and any related opinion or memorandum.

(3) *Time to File a Response or a Cross-Request.*

(A) Response. A party may file a response within 14 days after the request has been served, or within such other time as the court where the matter is pending allows.

(B) Cross-Request. A party may file a cross-request for certification within 14 days after the request has been served or within 60 days after the judgment, order, or decree has been entered—whichever occurs first.

(4) *Oral Argument Not Required.* Unless the court where the matter is pending orders otherwise, a request, a cross-request, and any response will be submitted without oral argument.

(5) *Form of a Certification; Service.* The court that certifies a direct appeal in response to a request must do so in a separate document served on all parties to the appeal in the manner required for serving a notice of appeal under Rule 8003(c)(1).

(g) Request for Leave to Take a Direct Appeal to a Court of Appeals After Certification. Within 30 days after the certification has become effective under (a), a request for leave to take a direct appeal to a court of appeals must be filed with the circuit clerk in accordance with Fed. R. App. P. 6(c).

(Added Apr. 25, 2014, eff. Dec. 1, 2014; amended Apr. 26, 2018, eff. Dec. 1, 2018; Apr. 2, 2024, eff. Dec. 1, 2024.)

Rule 8007. Stay Pending Appeal; Bond; Suspending Proceedings

(a) **Initial Motion in the Bankruptcy Court**.

    (1) *In General*. Ordinarily, a party must move first in the bankruptcy court for the following relief:

        (A) a stay of the bankruptcy court's judgment, order, or decree pending appeal;

        (B) the approval of a bond or other security provided to obtain a stay of judgment;

        (C) an order suspending, modifying, restoring, or granting an injunction while an appeal is pending; or

        (D) an order suspending or continuing proceedings or granting other relief permitted by (e).

    (2) *Time to File*. The motion may be filed either before or after the notice of appeal is filed.

(b) **Motion in the District Court, BAP, or Court of Appeals on Direct Appeal**.

    (1) *In General*. A motion for the relief specified in (a)(1)—or to vacate or modify a bankruptcy court's order granting such relief—may be filed in the court where the appeal is pending.

    (2) *Required Showing*. The motion must:

        (A) show that moving first in the bankruptcy court would be impracticable; or

        (B) if a motion has already been made in the bankruptcy court, state whether the court has ruled on it, and if so, state any reasons given for the ruling.

    (3) *Additional Requirements*. The motion must also include:

        (A) the reasons for granting the relief requested and the facts relied on;

        (B) affidavits or other sworn statements supporting facts subject to dispute; and

        (C) relevant parts of the record.

    (4) *Serving Notice*. The movant must give reasonable notice of the motion to all parties.

(c) **Filing a Bond or Other Security as a Condition of Relief**. The district court, BAP, or court of appeals may condition relief on filing a bond or other security with the bankruptcy court.

(d) **Bond or Other Security for a Trustee; Not for the United States**. The court may require a trustee who appeals to file a bond or other security. No bond or security is required when:

    (1) the United States, its officer, or its agency appeals; or

    (2) an appeal is taken by direction of any federal governmental department.

(e) **Continuing Proceedings in the Bankruptcy Court**. Despite Rule 7062—but subject to the authority of the district court, BAP, or court of appeals—while the appeal is pending, the bankruptcy court may:

(1) suspend or order the continuation of other proceedings in the case, or

(2) issue any appropriate order to protect the rights of all parties in interest.

(Added Apr. 25, 2014, eff. Dec. 1, 2014; amended Apr. 26, 2018, eff. Dec. 1, 2018; Apr. 2, 2024, eff. Dec. 1, 2024.)

Rule 8008. Indicative Rulings

(a) **Motion for Relief Filed When an Appeal Is Pending; Bankruptcy Court's Options**. If a party files a timely motion in the bankruptcy court for relief that the court lacks authority to grant because an appeal has been docketed and is pending, the bankruptcy court may:

(1) defer considering the motion;

(2) deny the motion;

(3) state that it would grant the motion if the court where the appeal is pending remands for that purpose; or

(4) state that the motion raises a substantial issue.

(b) **Notice to the Court Where the Appeal Is Pending**. If the bankruptcy court states that it would grant the motion or that the motion raises a substantial issue, the movant must promptly notify the clerk of the court where the appeal is pending.

(c) **Remand After an Indicative Ruling**. If the bankruptcy court states that it would grant the motion or that the motion raises a substantial issue, the district court or BAP may remand for further proceedings but retains jurisdiction unless it expressly dismisses the appeal. If the district court or BAP remands but retains jurisdiction, the parties must promptly notify the clerk of that court when the bankruptcy court has decided the motion on remand.

(Added Apr. 25, 2014, eff. Dec. 1, 2014; amended Apr. 2, 2024, eff. Dec. 1, 2024.)

Rule 8009. Record on Appeal; Sealed Documents

(a) **Designating the Record on Appeal; Statement of the Issues; Content of the Record**.

(1) *Appellant's Designation and Statement of the Issues*. The appellant must:

(A) file with the bankruptcy clerk a designation of the items to be included in the record on appeal and a statement of the issues to be presented; and

(B) file and serve the designation and statement on the appellee within 14 days after:

- the notice of appeal as of right has become effective under Rule 8002; or

- an order granting leave to appeal has been entered.

Premature service is treated as service on the first day on which filing is timely.

(2) *Appellee's and Cross-Appellant's Designation and Statement of the Issues.*

   (A) Appellee. Within 14 days after being served, the appellee may file with the bankruptcy clerk and serve on the appellant a designation of additional items to be included in the record.

   (B) Cross-Appellant. An appellee who files a cross-appeal must file and serve a designation of additional items to be included in the record and a statement of the issues to be presented on the cross-appeal.

(3) *Cross-Appellee's Designation.* Within 14 days after the cross-appellant's designation and statement have been served, the cross-appellee may file with the bankruptcy clerk and serve on the cross-appellant a designation of additional items to be included in the record.

(4) *Record on Appeal.* The record on appeal must include:

   - the docket entries kept by the bankruptcy clerk;
   - items designated by the parties;
   - the notice of appeal;
   - the judgment, order, or decree being appealed;
   - any order granting leave to appeal;
   - any certification required for a direct appeal to the court of appeals;
   - any opinion, findings of fact and conclusions of law relating to the issues on appeal, including transcripts of all oral rulings;
   - any transcript ordered under (b);
   - any statement required by (c); and
   - any other items from the record that the court where the appeal is pending orders to be included.

(5) *Copies for the Bankruptcy Clerk.* If paper copies are needed and the bankruptcy clerk requests copies of designated items, the party filing the designation must provide them. If the party fails to do so, the bankruptcy clerk must prepare them at that party's expense.

(b) **Transcript of Proceedings**.

   (1) *Appellant's Duty to Order.* Within the period prescribed by (a)(1), the appellant must:

      (A) order in writing from the reporter, as defined in Rule 8010(a)(1), a transcript of such parts of the proceedings not already on file as the appellant considers necessary for the appeal, and file a copy of the order with the bankruptcy clerk; or

      (B) file with the bankruptcy clerk a certificate stating that the appellant is not ordering a transcript.

(2) *Appellee's Duty to Order as a Cross-Appellant.* Within 14 days after the appellant has filed a copy of the transcript order—or a certificate stating that the appellant is not ordering a transcript—the appellee as cross-appellant must:

    (A) order in writing from the reporter a transcript of such additional parts of the proceedings as the cross-appellant considers necessary for the appeal, and file a copy of the order with the bankruptcy clerk; or

    (B) file with the bankruptcy clerk a certificate stating that the cross-appellant is not ordering a transcript.

(3) *Appellee's or Cross-Appellee's Right to Order.* Within 14 days after the appellant or cross-appellant has filed a copy of a transcript order—or a certificate stating that the appellant or cross-appellant is not ordering a transcript—the appellee or cross-appellee:

    (A) may order in writing from the reporter a transcript of any additional parts of the proceeding that the appellee or cross-appellee considers necessary for the appeal; and

    (B) must file a copy of the order with the bankruptcy clerk.

(4) *Payment.* At the time of ordering, a party must make satisfactory arrangements with the reporter to pay for the transcript.

(5) *Unsupported Finding or Conclusion.* If the appellant intends to argue on appeal that a finding or conclusion is unsupported by the evidence or is contrary to the evidence, the appellant must include in the record a transcript of all relevant testimony and a copy of all relevant exhibits.

(c) **When a Transcript Is Unavailable.**

(1) *Statement of the Evidence.* If a transcript of a hearing or trial is unavailable, the appellant may prepare a statement of the evidence or proceedings from the best available means, including the appellant's recollection. The statement must be filed within the time prescribed by (a)(1) and served on the appellee.

(2) *Appellee's Response.* The appellee may serve objections or proposed amendments within 14 days after being served.

(3) *Court Approval.* The statement and any objections or proposed amendments must then be submitted to the bankruptcy court for settlement and approval. As settled and approved, the statement must be included by the bankruptcy clerk in the record on appeal.

(d) **Agreed Statement as the Record on Appeal.**

(1) Agreed Statement. Instead of the record on appeal as defined in (a), the parties may prepare, sign, and submit to the bankruptcy court a statement of the case showing how the issues presented by the appeal arose and were decided in the bankruptcy court.

(2) *Content.* The statement must set forth only those facts alleged and proved or sought to be proved that are essential to the court's resolution of the issues. If the statement is accurate, it—together with any

additions that the bankruptcy court considers necessary to a full presentation of the issues on appeal—must be:

(A) approved by the bankruptcy court; and

(B) certified to the court where the appeal is pending as the record on appeal.

(3) *Time to Send the Agreed Statement to the Appellate Court*. The bankruptcy clerk must then send the agreed statement to the clerk of the court where the appeal is pending within the time provided by Rule 8010. A copy may be filed in place of the appendix required by Rule 8018(b) or, in the case of a direct appeal to the court of appeals, by Fed. R. App. P. 30.

(e) **Correcting or Modifying the Record**.

(1) *Differences About Accuracy; Improper Designations*. If any difference arises about whether the record accurately discloses what occurred in the bankruptcy court, the difference must be submitted to and settled by the bankruptcy court and the record conformed accordingly. If an item has been improperly designated as part of the record on appeal, a party may move to strike that item.

(2) *Omissions and Misstatements*. If anything material to either party is omitted from or misstated in the record by error or accident, the omission or misstatement may be corrected, and a supplemental record may be certified and sent:

(A) on stipulation of the parties;

(B) by the bankruptcy court before or after the record has been sent; or

(C) by the court where the appeal is pending.

(3) *Remaining Questions*. All other questions about the form and content of the record must be presented to the court where the appeal is pending.

(f) **Sealed Documents**.

(1) *In General*. A document placed under seal by the bankruptcy court may be designated as a part of the record on appeal. But a document so designated:

(A) must be identified without revealing confidential or secret information; and

(B) may be sent only as (2) prescribes.

(2) *When to Send a Sealed Document*. To have a sealed document sent as part of the record, a party must file in the court where the appeal is pending a motion to accept the document under seal. If the motion is granted, the movant must notify the bankruptcy court, and the bankruptcy clerk must promptly send the sealed document to the clerk of the court where the appeal is pending.

(g) **Duty to Assist the Bankruptcy Clerk**. All parties to an appeal must take any other action needed to enable the bankruptcy clerk to assemble and send the record.

(Added Apr. 25, 2014, eff. Dec. 1, 2014; amended Apr. 2, 2024, eff. Dec. 1, 2024.)

Rule 8010. Transcribing the Proceedings; Filing the Transcript; Sending the Record

(a) **Reporter's Duties.**

(1) *Proceedings Recorded Without a Court Reporter Present.* If proceedings are recorded without a reporter present, the person or service selected under bankruptcy court procedures to transcribe the recording is the reporter for purposes of this rule.

(2) *Preparing and Filing the Transcript.* The reporter must prepare and file a transcript as follows:

(A) Initial Steps. Upon receiving a transcript order under Rule 8009(b), the reporter must file in the bankruptcy court an acknowledgment showing when the order was received and when the reporter expects to have the transcript completed.

(B) Filing the Transcript. After completing the transcript, the reporter must file it with the bankruptcy clerk, who will notify the district, BAP, or circuit clerk of its filing.

(C) Extending the Time to Complete a Transcript. If the transcript cannot be completed within 30 days after the order has been received, the reporter must request an extension from the bankruptcy clerk. The clerk must enter on the docket and notify the parties whether the extension is granted.

(D) Failure to File on Time. If the reporter fails to file the transcript on time, the bankruptcy clerk must notify the bankruptcy judge.

(b) **Clerk's Duties.**

(1) *Sending the Record.* Subject to Rule 8009(f) and (5) below, when the record is complete, the bankruptcy clerk must send to the clerk of the court where the appeal is pending either the record or a notice that it is available electronically.

(2) *Multiple Appeals.* If there are multiple appeals from a judgment, order, or decree, the bankruptcy clerk must send a single record.

(3) *Docketing the Record in the Appellate Court.* Upon receiving the record—or a notice that it is available electronically—the district, BAP, or circuit clerk must enter that information on the docket and promptly notify all parties to the appeal.

(4) *If the Court Orders Paper Copies.* If the court where the appeal is pending orders that paper copies of the record be provided, the clerk of that court must so notify the appellant. If the appellant fails to provide them, the bankruptcy clerk must prepare them at the appellant's expense.

(5) *Motion for Leave to Appeal.* Subject to (c), if a motion for leave to appeal is filed under Rule 8004, the bankruptcy clerk must prepare and send the record only after the motion is granted.

(c) **When a Preliminary Motion Is Filed in the District Court, BAP, or Court of Appeals.**

(1) *In General.* This subdivision (c) applies if, before the record is sent, a party moves in the district court, BAP, or court of appeals for:

(A) leave to appeal;

(B) dismissal;

(C) a stay pending appeal;

(D) approval of a bond or other security provided to obtain a stay of judgment; or

(E) any other intermediate order.

(2) *Sending the Record.* The bankruptcy clerk must send to the clerk of the court where the relief is sought any parts of the record designated by a party to the appeal—or send a notice that they are available electronically.

(Added Apr. 25, 2014, eff. Dec. 1, 2014; amended Apr. 26, 2018, eff. Dec. 1, 2018; Apr. 2, 2024, eff. Dec. 1, 2024.)

Rule 8011. Filing and Service; Signature

(a) **Filing.**

(1) *With the Clerk.* A document required or permitted to be filed in a district court or BAP must be filed with the clerk of that court.

(2) *Method and Timeliness.*

(A) Nonelectronic Filing.

(i) In General. For a document not filed electronically, filing may be accomplished by mail addressed to the district or BAP clerk. Except as provided in (ii) and (iii), filing is timely only if the clerk receives the document within the time set for filing.

(ii) Brief or Appendix. A brief or appendix not filed electronically is also timely filed if, on or before the last day for filing, it is:

- mailed to the clerk by first-class mail—or other class of mail that is at least as expeditious—postage prepaid; or

- dispatched to a third-party commercial carrier for delivery to the clerk within 3 days.

(iii) Inmate Filing. If an institution has a system designed for legal mail, an inmate confined there must use that system to receive the benefit of this item (iii). A document not filed electronically by an inmate confined in an institution is timely if it is deposited in the institution's internal mailing system on or before the last day for filing and:

- it is accompanied by a declaration in compliance with 28 U.S.C. §1746—or a notarized statement—setting out the date of deposit and stating that first-class postage is being prepaid; or by evidence (such as a postmark or date stamp) showing that the notice was so deposited and that postage was prepaid; or

- the appellate court exercises its discretion to permit the later filing of a declaration or notarized statement that satisfies this item (iii).

(B) Electronic Filing.

    (i) By a Represented Person—Generally Required; Exceptions. An entity represented by an attorney must file electronically, unless nonelectronic filing is allowed by the court for cause or is allowed or required by local rule.

    (ii) By an Unrepresented Individual—When Allowed or Required. An individual not represented by an attorney:

- may file electronically only if allowed by court order or by local rule; and

- may be required to file electronically only by court order, or by a local rule that includes reasonable exceptions.

    (iii) Same as a Written Paper. A document filed electronically is a written paper for purposes of these rules.

(C) When Paper Copies Are Required. No paper copies are required when a document is filed electronically. If a document is filed by mail or by delivery to the district court or BAP, no additional copies are required. But the district court or BAP may, by local rule or order in a particular case, require that a specific number of paper copies be filed or furnished.

(3) *Clerk's Refusal of Documents.* The court clerk must not refuse to accept for filing any document solely because it is not presented in proper form as required by these rules or by any local rule or practice.

(b) **Service of All Documents Required**. Unless a rule requires service by the clerk, a party must, at or before the time of the filing of a document, serve it on the other parties to the appeal. Service on a party represented by counsel must be made on the party's counsel.

(c) **Manner of Service**.

(1) *Nonelectronic Service.* Nonelectronic service may be by any of the following:

(A) personal delivery;

(B) mail; or

(C) third-party commercial carrier for delivery within 3 days.

(2) *Service By Electronic Means.* Electronic service may be made by:

      (A) sending a document to a registered user by filing it with the court's electronic-filing system; or

      (B) using other electronic means that the person served consented to in writing.

    (3) *When Service Is Complete.* Service by mail or by third-party commercial carrier is complete on mailing or delivery to the carrier. Service by electronic means is complete on filing or sending, unless the person making service receives notice that the document was not received by the person served.

(d) Proof of Service.

    (1) *Requirements.* A document presented for filing must contain either of the following if it was served other than through the court's electronic-filing system:

      (A) an acknowledgement of service by the person served; or

      (B) proof of service consisting of a statement by the person who made service certifying:

        (i) the date and manner of service;

        (ii) the names of the persons served; and

        (iii) the mail or electronic address, the fax number, or the address of the place of delivery—as appropriate for the manner of service—for each person served.

    (2) *Delayed Proof of Service.* A district or BAP clerk may accept a document for filing without an acknowledgement or proof of service, but must require the acknowledgment or proof of service to be filed promptly thereafter.

    (3) *For a Brief or Appendix.* When a brief or appendix is filed, the proof of service must also state the date and manner by which it was filed.

(e) Signature Always Required.

    (1) *Electronic Filing.* Every document filed electronically must include the electronic signature of the person filing it or, if the person is represented, the counsel's electronic signature. A filing made through a person's electronic-filing account and authorized by that person—together with that person's name on a signature block—constitutes the person's signature.

    (2) *Paper Filing.* Every document filed in paper form must be signed by the person filing it or, if the person is represented, by the person's counsel.

(Added Apr. 25, 2014, eff. Dec. 1, 2014; amended Apr. 26, 2018, eff. Dec. 1, 2018; Apr. 2, 2024, eff. Dec. 1, 2024.)

Rule 8012. Disclosure Statement

(a) **Disclosure by a Nongovernmental Corporation**. Any nongovernmental corporation that is a party to a district-court or BAP proceeding or that seeks to intervene must file a statement that:

    (1) identifies any parent corporation and any publicly held corporation that owns 10% or more of its stock; or

    (2) states that there is no such corporation.

(b) **Disclosure About the Debtor**. The debtor, the trustee, or, if neither is a party, the appellant must file a statement that:

    (1) identifies each debtor not named in the caption; and

    (2) for each debtor that is a corporation, discloses the information required by (a).

(c) **Time to File; Supplemental Filing**. A Rule 8012 statement must:

    (1) be filed with the principal brief or upon filing a motion, response, petition, or answer in the district court or BAP, whichever occurs first—unless a local rule requires earlier filing

    (2) be included before the table of contents in the principal brief; and

    (3) be supplemented whenever the information required by this rule changes.

(Added Apr. 25, 2014, eff. Dec. 1, 2014; amended Apr. 27, 2020, eff. Dec. 1, 2020; Apr. 2, 2024, eff. Dec. 1, 2024.)

Rule 8013. Motions; Interventions

(a) **Content of a Motion; Response; Reply**.

    (1) *Request for Relief*. A request for an order or other relief is made by filing a motion with the district or BAP clerk.

    (2) *Content of a Motion*.

        (A) Grounds, Relief Sought, and Supporting Argument. A motion must state with particularity the grounds for the motion, the relief sought, and the legal argument supporting it.

        (B) Motion to Expedite an Appeal. A motion to expedite an appeal must explain what justifies considering the appeal ahead of other matters. The motion may be filed as an emergency motion under (d). If it is granted, the district court or BAP may accelerate the time to:

            (i) send the record;

            (ii) file briefs and other documents;

            (iii) conduct oral argument; and

            (iv) resolve the appeal.

        (C) Accompanying Documents.

      (i) Supporting Document. Any affidavit or other document necessary to support a motion must be served and filed with the motion.

      (ii) Content of Affidavit. An affidavit must contain only factual information, not legal argument.

      (iii) Motion Seeking Substantive Relief. A motion seeking substantive relief must include a copy of the bankruptcy court's judgment, order, or decree, and any accompanying opinion as a separate exhibit.

    (D) Documents Barred or Not Required.

      (i) No Separate Brief. A separate brief supporting or responding to a motion must not be filed.

      (ii) Notice and Proposed Order Not Required. Unless the court orders otherwise, a notice of motion or a proposed order is not required.

  (3) *Response and Reply; Time to File.* Unless the district court or BAP orders otherwise:

    (A) any party to the appeal may—within 7 days after the motion is served—file a response to the motion; and

    (B) the movant may—within 7 days after the response is served—file a reply that addresses only matters raised in the response.

(b) **Disposition of a Motion for a Procedural Order**. The district court or BAP may rule on a motion for a procedural order—including a motion under Rule 9006(b) or (c)—at any time, without awaiting a response. A party adversely affected by the ruling may move to reconsider, vacate, or modify it within 7 days after the order is served.

(c) **Oral Argument**. A motion will be decided without oral argument unless the district court or BAP orders otherwise.

(d) **Emergency Motion**.

  (1) *Noting the Emergency.* A movant who requests expedited action—because irreparable harm would occur during the time needed to consider a response—must insert "Emergency" before the motion's title.

  (2) *Content.* An emergency motion must:

    (A) be accompanied by an affidavit setting forth the nature of the emergency;

    (B) state whether all grounds for it were previously submitted to the bankruptcy court and, if not, why the motion should not be remanded;

    (C) include:

      (i) the email address, office address, and telephone number of the moving counsel; and

      (ii) when known, the same information as in (i) for opposing counsel and any unrepresented party to the appeal; and

(D) be served as Rule 8011 prescribes.

(3) *Notifying Opposing Parties.* Before filing an emergency motion, the movant must make every practicable effort to notify opposing counsel and any unrepresented party in time for them to respond. The affidavit accompanying the motion must state:

(A) when and how notice was given; or

(B) why giving it was impracticable.

(e) **Motion Considered by a Single BAP Judge.**

(1) *Judge's Authority.* A BAP judge may act alone on any motion but may not:

(A) dismiss or otherwise determine an appeal;

(B) deny a motion for leave to appeal; or

(C) deny a motion for a stay pending appeal if denial would make the appeal moot.

(2) *Reviewing a Single Judge's Action.* The BAP, on its own or on a party's motion, may review a single judge's action.

(f) **Form of Documents; Length Limits; Number of Copies.**

(1) *Document Filed in Paper Form.* Fed. R. App. P. 27(d)(1) applies to a motion, response, or reply filed in paper form in the district court or BAP.

(2) *Document Filed Electronically.* A motion, response, or reply filed electronically must comply with the requirements in (1) for covers, line spacing, margins, typeface, and type style. It must also comply with the length limits in (3).

(3) *Length Limits.* Except by the district court's or BAP's permission, and excluding the accompanying documents authorized by (a)(2)(C):

(A) a motion or a response to a motion produced using a computer must include a certificate under Rule 8015(h) and not exceed 5,200 words;

(B) a handwritten or typewritten motion or a response to a motion must not exceed 20 pages;

(C) a reply produced using a computer must include a certificate under Rule 8015(h) and not exceed 2,600 words; and

(D) a handwritten or typewritten reply must not exceed 10 pages.

(4) *Providing Paper Copies.* Paper copies must be provided only if required by a local rule or by an order in a particular case.

(g) **Motion for Leave to Intervene.**

(1) *Time to File.* Unless a statute provides otherwise, an entity seeking to intervene in an appeal in the district court or BAP must move for leave to intervene and serve a copy of the motion on all parties to the appeal. The motion—or other notice of intervention authorized by statute— must be filed within 30 days after the appeal is docketed.

(2) *Content.* The motion must concisely state:

(A) the movant's interest;

(B) the grounds for intervention;

(C) whether intervention was sought in the bankruptcy court;

(D) why intervention is being sought at this stage of the proceedings; and

(E) why participating as an amicus curiae—rather than intervening— would not be adequate.

(Added Apr. 25, 2014, eff. Dec. 1, 2014; amended Apr. 26, 2018, eff. Dec. 1, 2018; Apr. 27, 2020, eff. Dec. 1, 2020; Apr. 2, 2024, eff. Dec. 1, 2024.)

Rule 8014. Briefs

(a) **Appellant's Brief**. The appellant's brief must contain the following under appropriate headings and in the order indicated:

(1) a disclosure statement, if required by Rule 8012;

(2) a table of contents, with page references;

(3) a table of authorities—cases (alphabetically arranged), statutes, and other authorities—with references to the pages of the brief where they are cited;

(4) a jurisdictional statement, including:

(A) the basis for the bankruptcy court's subject-matter jurisdiction, citing applicable statutory provisions and stating relevant facts establishing jurisdiction;

(B) the basis for the district court's or BAP's jurisdiction, citing applicable statutory provisions and stating relevant facts establishing jurisdiction;

(C) the filing dates establishing the timeliness of the appeal; and

(D) an assertion that the appeal is from a final judgment, order, or decree—or information establishing the district court's or BAP's jurisdiction on another basis;

(5) a statement of the issues presented and, for each one, a concise statement of the applicable standard of appellate review;

(6) a concise statement of the case setting out the facts relevant to the issues submitted for review, describing the relevant procedural history, and identifying the rulings presented for review, with appropriate references to the record;

(7) a summary of the argument, which must contain a succinct, clear, and accurate statement of the arguments made in the body of the brief, and which must not merely repeat the argument headings;

(8) the argument, which must contain the appellant's contentions and the reasons for them, with citations to the authorities and parts of the record on which the appellant relies;

(9) a short conclusion stating the precise relief sought; and

(10) the certificate of compliance, if required by Rule 8015(a)(7) or (b).

(b) **Appellee's Brief**. The appellee's brief must conform to the requirements of (a)(1)–(8) and (10), except that none of the following need appear unless the appellee is dissatisfied with the appellant's statement:

   (1) the jurisdictional statement;

   (2) the statement of the issues and the applicable standard of appellate review; and

   (3) the statement of the case.

(c) **Reply Brief**. The appellant may file a brief in reply to the appellee's brief. A reply brief must comply with (a)(2)–(3).

(d) **Setting Out Statutes, Rules, Regulations, or Similar Authorities**. If the court's determination of the issues presented requires the study of the Code or other statutes, rules, regulations, or similar authority, the relevant parts must be set out in the brief or in an addendum.

(e) **Briefs in a Case Involving Multiple Appellants or Appellees**. In a case involving more than one appellant or appellee, including consolidated cases, any number of appellants or appellees may join in a brief, and any party may adopt by reference a part of another's brief. Parties may also join in reply briefs.

(f) **Citation of Supplemental Authorities**. If pertinent and significant authorities come to a party's attention after the party's brief has been filed— or after oral argument but before a decision—a party may promptly advise the district or BAP clerk by a signed submission, with a copy to all other parties, setting forth the citations. The submission must state the reasons for the supplemental citations, referring either to the pertinent page of a brief or to a point argued orally. The body of the submission must not exceed 350 words. Any response must be similarly limited, and it must be made within 7 days after service unless the court orders otherwise.

(Added Apr. 25, 2014, eff. Dec. 1, 2014; amended Apr. 2, 2024, eff. Dec. 1, 2024.)

Rule 8015. Form and Length of a Brief; Form of an Appendix or Other Paper

(a) **Paper Copies of a Brief**. If a paper copy of a brief may or must be filed, the following provisions apply:

   (1) *Reproduction.*

      (A) Printing. The brief may be reproduced by any process that yields a clear black image on light paper. The paper must be opaque and unglazed. Only one side of the paper may be used.

      (B) Text. Text must be reproduced with a clarity that equals or exceeds the output of a laser printer.

      (C) Other Reproductions. Photographs, illustrations, and tables may be reproduced by any method that results in a good copy of the original. A glossy finish is acceptable if the original is glossy.

   (2) *Cover.* The front cover of the brief must contain:

    (A) the number of the case centered at the top;

    (B) the name of the court;

    (C) the title of the case as prescribed by Rule 8003(d)(2) or 8004(c)(2);

    (D) the nature of the proceeding and the name of the court below;

    (E) the title of the brief, identifying the party or parties for whom the brief is filed; and

    (F) the name, office address, telephone number, and email address of counsel representing the party for whom the brief is filed.

  (3) *Binding.* The brief must be bound in any manner that is secure, does not obscure the text, and permits the brief to lie reasonably flat when open.

  (4) *Paper Size, Line Spacing, and Margins.* The brief must be on 8½"-by-11" paper. The text must be double-spaced, but quotations more than two lines long may be indented and single-spaced. Headings and footnotes may be single-spaced. Margins must be at least one inch on all four sides. Page numbers may be placed in the margins, but no text may appear there.

  (5) *Typeface.* Either a proportionally spaced or monospaced face may be used.

    (A) Proportional Spacing. A proportionally spaced face must include serifs, but sans-serif type may be used in headings and captions. A proportionally spaced face must be 14-point or larger.

    (B) Monospacing. A monospaced face may not contain more than 10½ characters per inch.

  (6) *Type Styles.* The brief must be set in plain, roman style, although italics or boldface may be used for emphasis. Case names must be italicized or underlined.

  (7) *Length.*

    (A) Page Limitation. A principal brief must not exceed 30 pages, or a reply brief 15 pages, unless it complies with (B).

    (B) Type-Volume Limitation.

        (i) Principal Brief. A principal brief is acceptable if it contains a certificate under (h) and:

           • contains no more than 13,000 words; or

           • uses a monospaced face and contains no more than 1,300 lines of text.

        (ii) Reply Brief. A reply brief is acceptable if it includes a certificate under (h) and contains no more than half the type volume specified in item (i).

(b) **Brief Filed Electronically**. A brief filed electronically must comply with (a)—except for (a)(1), (a)(3), and the paper requirement of (a)(4).

(c) **Paper Copies of an Appendix**. A paper copy of an appendix must comply with (a)(1), (2), (3), and (4), with the following exceptions:

(1) an appendix may include a legible photocopy of any document found in the record or of a printed decision; and

(2) when necessary for including odd-sized documents such as technical drawings, an appendix may be a size other than 8½" by 11", and need not lie reasonably flat when opened.

(d) **Appendix Filed Electronically**. An appendix filed electronically must comply with (a)(2) and (4)—except for the paper requirement of (a)(4).

(e) **Other Documents**.

(1) *Motion*. Rule 8013(f) governs the form of a motion, response, or reply.

(2) *Paper Copies of Other Documents*. A paper copy of any other document—except one submitted under Rule 8014(f)—must comply with (a), with the following exceptions:

(A) a cover is not necessary if the caption and signature page together contain the information required by (a)(2); and

(B) the length limits of (a)(7) do not apply.

(3) *Document Filed Electronically*. Any other document filed electronically—except a document submitted under Rule 8014(f)—must comply with the requirements of (2).

(f) **Local Variation**. A district court or BAP must accept documents that comply with the form requirements of this rule and the length limits set by this Part VIII. By local rule or order in a particular case, a district court or BAP may accept documents that do not meet all the form requirements of this rule or the length limits set by this Part VIII.

(g) **Items Excluded from Length**. In computing any length limit, headings, footnotes, and quotations count toward the limit, but the following items do not:

- cover page;
- disclosure statement under Rule 8012;
- table of contents;
- table of citations;
- statement regarding oral argument;
- addendum containing statutes, rules, or regulations;
- certificate of counsel;
- signature block;
- proof of service; and
- any item specifically excluded by these rules or by local rule.

(h) **Certificate of Compliance**.

(1) *Briefs and Documents That Require a Certificate*. A brief submitted under Rule 8015(a)(7)(B), 8016(d)(2), or 8017(b)(4)—and a document submitted under Rule 8013(f)(3)(A), 8013(f)(3)(C), or 8022(b)(1)—must include a certificate by the attorney, or an unrepresented party, that the document complies with the type-volume limitation. The individual preparing the certificate may rely on the word or line count

of the word-processing system used to prepare the document. The certificate must state the number of words—or the number of lines of monospaced type—in the document.

(2) *Using the Official Form.* A certificate of compliance that conforms substantially to Form 417C satisfies the certificate requirement.

(Added Apr. 25, 2014, eff. Dec. 1, 2014; amended Apr. 26, 2018, eff. Dec. 1, 2018; Apr. 27, 2020, eff. Dec. 1, 2020; Apr. 2, 2024, eff. Dec. 1, 2024.)

Rule 8016. Cross-Appeals

(a) **Applicability**. This rule applies to a case in which a cross-appeal is filed. Rules 8014(a)–(c), 8015(a)(7)(A)–(B), and 8018(a)(1)–(3) do not apply to such a case, unless this rule states otherwise.

(b) **Designation of Appellant**. The party who files a notice of appeal first is the appellant for purposes of this rule and Rule 8018(a)(4) and (b) and Rule 8019. If notices are filed on the same day, the plaintiff, petitioner, applicant, or movant in the proceeding below is the appellant. These designations may be modified by the parties' agreement or by court order.

(c) **Briefs**. In a case involving a cross-appeal:

(1) *Appellant's Principal Brief.* The appellant must file a principal brief in the appeal. That brief must comply with Rule 8014(a).

(2) *Appellee's Principal and Response Brief.* The appellee must file a principal brief in the cross-appeal and must, in the same brief, respond to the principal brief in the appeal. That brief must comply with Rule 8014(a), but the brief need not include a statement of the case unless the appellee is dissatisfied with the appellant's statement.

(3) *Appellant's Response and Reply Brief.* The appellant must file a brief that responds to the principal brief in the cross-appeal and may, in the same brief, reply to the response in the appeal. That brief must comply with Rule 8014(a)(2)–(8) and (10), but none of the following need appear unless the appellant is dissatisfied with the appellee's statement in the cross-appeal:

(A) the jurisdictional statement;

(B) the statement of the issues;

(C) the statement of the case; and

(D) the statement of the applicable standard of appellate review.

(4) *Appellee's Reply Brief.* The appellee may file a brief in reply to the response in the cross-appeal. That brief must comply with Rule 8014(a)(2)–(3) and (10) and must be limited to the issues presented by the cross-appeal.

(d) **Length**.

(1) *Page Limitation.* Unless it complies with (2), the appellant's principal brief must not exceed 30 pages; the appellee's principal and response

brief, 35 pages; the appellant's response and reply brief, 30 pages; and the appellee's reply brief, 15 pages.

(2) *Type-Volume Limitation.*

(A) Appellant's Brief. The appellant's principal brief or the appellant's response and reply brief is acceptable if it includes a certificate under Rule 8015(h) and:

(i) contains no more than 13,000 words; or

(ii) uses a monospaced face and contains no more than 1,300 lines of text.

(B) Appellee's Principal and Response Brief. The appellee's principal and response brief is acceptable if it includes a certificate under Rule 8015(h) and:

(i) contains no more than 15,300 words; or

(ii) uses a monospaced face and contains no more than 1,500 lines of text.

(C) Appellee's Reply Brief. The appellee's reply brief is acceptable if it includes a certificate under Rule 8015(h) and contains no more than half the type volume specified in (A).

(e) **Time to Serve and File a Brief**. Briefs must be served and filed as follows, unless the district court or BAP by order in a particular case excuses the filing of briefs or sets different time limits:

(1) the appellant's principal brief, within 30 days after the docketing of a notice that the record has been sent or is available electronically;

(2) the appellee's principal and response brief, within 30 days after the appellant's principal brief is served;

(3) the appellant's response and reply brief, within 30 days after the appellee's principal and response brief is served; and

(4) the appellee's reply brief, within 14 days after the appellant's response and reply brief is served but at least 7 days before scheduled argument—unless the district court or BAP, for cause, allows a later filing.

(Added Apr. 25, 2014, eff. Dec. 1, 2014; amended Apr. 26, 2018, eff. Dec. 1, 2018; Apr. 2, 2024, eff. Dec. 1, 2024.)

Rule 8017. Brief of an Amicus Curiae

(a) **During the Initial Consideration of a Case on the Merits**.

(1) *Applicability.* This subdivision (a) governs amicus filings during a court's initial consideration of a case on the merits.

(2) *When Permitted.* The United States, its officer or agency, or a state may file an amicus brief without the parties' consent or leave of court. Any other amicus curiae may file a brief only by leave of court or if the brief states that all parties have consented to its filing, but a district court or BAP may prohibit the filing of or may strike an amicus brief that would

result in a judge's disqualification. On its own, and with notice to all parties to an appeal, the district court or BAP may request a brief by an amicus curiae.

(3) *Motion for Leave to File.* A motion for leave must be accompanied by the proposed brief and state:

    (A) the movant's interest; and

    (B) the reason why an amicus brief is desirable and why the matters asserted are relevant to the disposition of the appeal.

(4) *Content and Form.* An amicus brief must comply with Rule 8015. In addition, the cover must identify the party or parties supported and indicate whether the brief supports affirmance or reversal. If an amicus curiae is a corporation, the brief must include a disclosure statement like that required of parties by Rule 8012. An amicus brief need not comply with Rule 8014, but must include the following:

    (A) a table of contents, with page references;

    (B) a table of authorities—cases (alphabetically arranged), statutes, and other authorities—with references to the pages of the brief where they are cited;

    (C) a concise statement of the identity of the amicus curiae, its interest in the case, and the source of its authority to file;

    (D) unless the amicus curiae is one listed in the first sentence of (2), a statement that indicates whether:

        (i) a party's counsel authored the brief in whole or in part;

        (ii) a party or a party's counsel contributed money that was intended to fund preparing or submitting the brief; and

        (iii) a person—other than the amicus curiae, its members, or its counsel—contributed money that was intended to fund preparing or submitting the brief and, if so, identifies each such person;

    (E) an argument, which may be preceded by a summary and need not include a statement of the applicable standard of review; and

    (F) a certificate of compliance, if required by Rule 8015(h).

(5) *Length.* Except by the district court's or BAP's permission, an amicus brief must be no more than one-half the maximum length authorized by these rules for a party's principal brief. If the court grants a party permission to file a longer brief, that extension does not affect the length of an amicus brief.

(6) *Time for Filing.* An amicus curiae must file its brief—accompanied by a motion for leave to file when required—within 7 days after the principal brief of the party being supported is filed. An amicus curiae that does not support either party must file its brief within 7 days after the appellant's principal brief is filed. The district court or BAP may grant leave for later filing, specifying the time within which an opposing party may answer.

(7) *Reply Brief.* Except by the district court's or BAP's permission, an amicus curiae may not file a reply brief.

(8) *Oral Argument.* An amicus curiae may participate in oral argument only with the district court's or BAP's permission.

(b) **During Consideration of Whether to Grant Rehearing**.

(1) *Applicability.* This subdivision (b) governs amicus filings during a district court's or BAP's consideration of whether to grant rehearing, unless a local rule or order in a particular case provides otherwise.

(2) *When Permitted.* The United States, its officer or agency, or a state may file an amicus brief without the parties' consent or leave of court. Any other amicus curiae may file a brief only by leave of court.

(3) *Motion for Leave to File.* Paragraph (a)(3) applies to a motion for leave to file.

(4) *Content, Form, and Length.* Paragraph (a)(4) applies to the amicus brief. The brief must include a certificate under Rule 8015(h) and not exceed 2,600 words.

(5) *Time to File.* An amicus curiae supporting a motion for rehearing or supporting neither party must file its brief—accompanied by a motion for leave to file when required—within 7 days after the motion is filed. An amicus curiae opposing the motion for rehearing must file its brief—accompanied by a motion for leave to file when required—no later than the date set by the court for the response.

(Added Apr. 25, 2014, eff. Dec. 1, 2014; amended Apr. 26, 2018, eff. Dec. 1, 2018; Apr. 2, 2024, eff. Dec. 1, 2024.)

Rule 8018. Serving and Filing Briefs and Appendices

(a) **Time to Serve and File a Brief**. Unless the district court or BAP by order in a particular case excuses the filing of briefs or sets a different time, the following time limits apply:

(1) *Appellant's Brief.* The appellant must serve and file a brief within 30 days after the docketing of notice that the record has been sent or that it is available electronically.

(2) *Appellee's Brief.* The appellee must serve and file a brief within 30 days after the appellant's brief is served.

(3) *Appellant's Reply Brief.* The appellant may serve and file a reply brief within 14 days after service of the appellee's brief but at least 7 days before scheduled argument—unless the district court or BAP, for cause, allows a later filing.

(4) *Consequence of Failure to File.* If an appellant fails to file a brief on time or within an extended time authorized under (a)(3), the district court or BAP may—on its own after notice or on the appellee's motion—dismiss the appeal. An appellee who fails to file a brief will

not be heard at oral argument unless the district court or BAP grants permission.

(b) **Duty to Serve and File an Appendix**.

    (1) *Appellant's Duty*. Subject to (e) and Rule 8009(d), the appellant must serve and file with its principal brief an appendix containing excerpts from the record. It must contain:

        (A) the relevant docket entries;

        (B) the complaint and answer, or equivalent filings;

        (C) the judgment, order, or decree from which the appeal is taken;

        (D) any other orders, pleadings, jury instructions, findings, conclusions, or opinions relevant to the appeal;

        (E) the notice of appeal; and

        (F) any relevant transcript or portion of it.

    (2) *Appellee's Appendix*. The appellee may serve and file with its brief an appendix containing any material that is required to be included or is relevant to the appeal or cross-appeal but that is omitted from the appellant's appendix.

    (3) *Cross-Appellee's Appendix*. The appellant—as cross-appellee—may also serve and file with its response an appendix containing material that is relevant to matters raised initially by the cross-appeal but that is omitted by the cross-appellant.

(c) **Format of the Appendix**.

    (1) *Content*. The appendix must:

        (A) begin with a table of contents identifying the page at which each part begins;

        (B) put the relevant docket entries after the table of contents;

        (C) then put other parts of the record chronologically;

        (D) when transcript pages are included, show the transcript page numbers in brackets immediately before the included pages; and

        (E) indicate omissions from the text of a document or of the transcript by asterisks.

    (2) *Immaterial Formal Matters*. The appendix should not include immaterial formal matters, such as captions, subscriptions, and acknowledgments.

(d) **Reproducing Exhibits**. Exhibits designated for inclusion in the appendix may be reproduced in a separate volume or volumes, suitably indexed.

(e) **Appeal on the Original Record Without an Appendix**. The district court or BAP may, either by rule for all cases or classes of cases or by order in a particular case:

    (1) dispense with the appendix; and

    (2) permit an appeal to proceed on the original record with the submission of any relevant parts that the district court or BAP orders the parties to file.

Rule 8018.1. Reviewing a Judgment That the Bankruptcy Court Lacked Authority to Enter

(Added Apr. 25, 2014, eff. Dec. 1, 2014; amended Apr. 2, 2024, eff. Dec. 1, 2024.)

Rule 8018.1. Reviewing a Judgment That the Bankruptcy Court Lacked Authority to Enter

If, on appeal, a district court determines that the bankruptcy court did not have authority under Article III of the Constitution to enter the judgment, order, or decree being appealed, the district court may treat it as proposed findings of fact and conclusions of law.

(Added Apr. 26, 2018, eff. Dec. 1, 2018; amended Apr. 2, 2024, eff. Dec. 1, 2024.)

Rule 8019. Oral Argument

(a) **Party's Statement**. Any party may file, or a district court or BAP may require, a statement explaining why oral argument should, or need not, be permitted.

(b) **Presumption of Oral Argument; Exceptions**. Oral argument must be allowed in every case unless the district judge—or each BAP judge assigned to hear the appeal—examines the briefs and record and determines that oral argument is unnecessary because:

    (1) the appeal is frivolous;

    (2) the dispositive issue or issues have been authoritatively decided; or

    (3) the facts and legal arguments are adequately presented in the briefs and record, and the decisional process would not be significantly aided by oral argument.

(c) **Notice of Oral Argument; Motion to Postpone**. The district court or BAP must advise all parties of the date, time, and place for oral argument and the time allowed for each side. A motion to postpone the argument or to allow longer argument must be filed reasonably before the hearing date.

(d) **Order and Content of the Argument**. The appellant opens and concludes the argument. Counsel must not read at length from briefs, the record, or authorities.

(e) **Cross-Appeals and Separate Appeals**. If there is a cross-appeal, Rule 8016(b) determines which party is the appellant and which is the appellee for the purposes of oral argument. Unless the district court or BAP orders otherwise, a cross-appeal or separate appeal must be argued when the initial appeal is argued. Separate parties should avoid duplicative argument.

(f) **Nonappearance of a Party**. If the appellee fails to appear for argument, the district court or BAP may hear the appellant's argument. If the appellant fails to appear for argument, the district court or BAP may hear the appellee's argument. If neither party appears, the case will be decided on the briefs unless the district court or BAP orders otherwise.

(g) **Submission on Briefs**. The parties may agree to submit a case for decision on the briefs, but the district court or BAP may order that the case be argued.

(h) **Use of Physical Exhibits at Argument; Removal**. An attorney intending to use physical exhibits other than documents at the argument must arrange to place them in the courtroom on the day of the argument before the court convenes. After the argument, the attorney must remove the exhibits from the courtroom unless the district court or BAP orders otherwise. The clerk may destroy or dispose of them if the attorney does not reclaim them within a reasonable time after the clerk gives notice to do so.

(Added Apr. 25, 2014, eff. Dec. 1, 2014; amended Apr. 2, 2024, eff. Dec. 1, 2024.)

Rule 8020. Frivolous Appeal; Other Misconduct

(a) **Frivolous Appeal; Damages and Costs**. If the district court or BAP determines that an appeal is frivolous, then after a separate motion is filed or the court gives notice and a reasonable opportunity to respond, it may award just damages and single or double costs to the appellee.

(b) **Other Misconduct; Sanctions**. The district court or BAP may discipline or sanction an attorney or party appearing before it for other misconduct, including a failure to comply with a court order. But the court must first give the attorney or party reasonable notice and an opportunity to show cause to the contrary—and if requested, grant a hearing.

(Added Apr. 25, 2014, eff. Dec. 1, 2014; amended Apr. 2, 2024, eff. Dec. 1, 2024.)

Rule 8021. Costs

(a) **Against Whom Assessed**. The following rules apply unless the law provides or the district court or BAP orders otherwise:

    (1) if an appeal is dismissed, costs are taxed against the appellant, unless the parties agree otherwise;

    (2) if a judgment is affirmed, costs are taxed against the appellant;

    (3) if a judgment is reversed, costs are taxed against the appellee;

    (4) if a judgment is affirmed or reversed in part, modified, or vacated, costs are taxed only as the district court or BAP orders.

(b) **Costs for and Against the United States**. Costs for or against the United States, its agency, or its officer may be assessed under (a) only if authorized by law.

(c) **Costs on Appeal Taxable in the Bankruptcy Court**. The following costs on appeal are taxable in the bankruptcy court for the benefit of the party entitled to costs under this rule:

    (1) producing any required copies of a brief, appendix, exhibit, or the record;

   (2) preparing and sending the record;

   (3) the reporter's transcript, if needed to determine the appeal;

   (4) premiums paid for a bond or other security to preserve rights pending appeal; and

   (5) the fee for filing the notice of appeal.

(d) **Bill of Costs; Objections**. A party who wants costs taxed must, within 14 days after a judgment on appeal is entered, file with the bankruptcy clerk and serve an itemized and verified bill of costs. Objections must be filed within 14 days after the bill of costs is served, unless the bankruptcy court extends the time.

(Added Apr. 25, 2014, eff. Dec. 1, 2014; amended Apr. 26, 2018, eff. Dec. 1, 2018; Apr. 27, 2020, eff. Dec. 1, 2020; Apr. 2, 2024, eff. Dec. 1, 2024.)

Rule 8022. Motion for Rehearing

(a) **Time to File; Content; Response; Action by the District Court or BAP If Granted**.

   (1) *Time*. Unless the time is shortened or extended by order or local rule, any motion for rehearing by the district court or BAP must be filed within 14 days after a judgment on appeal is entered.

   (2) *Content*. The motion must state with particularity each point of law or fact that the movant believes the district court or BAP has overlooked or misapprehended and must argue in support of the motion.

   (3) *Response*. Unless the district court or BAP requests, no response to a motion for rehearing is permitted. But ordinarily, rehearing will not be granted without such a request.

   (4) *No Oral Argument*. Oral argument is not permitted.

   (5) *Action by the District Court or BAP*. If a motion for rehearing is granted, the district court or BAP may do any of the following:

     (A) make a final disposition of the appeal without reargument;

     (B) restore the case to the calendar for reargument or resubmission; or

     (C) issue any other appropriate order.

(b) **Form; Length**. A motion for rehearing must comply in form with Rule 8013(f)(1) and (2). Copies must be served and filed as Rule 8011 provides. Except by the district court's or BAP's permission:

   (1) a motion produced using a computer must include a certificate under Rule 8015(h) and not exceed 3,900 words; and

   (2) a handwritten or typewritten motion must not exceed 15 pages.

(Added Apr. 25, 2014, eff. Dec. 1, 2014; amended Apr. 26, 2018, eff. Dec. 1, 2018; Apr. 2, 2024, eff. Dec. 1, 2024.)

Rule 8023. Voluntary Dismissal

(a) **Stipulated Dismissal**. The clerk of the district court or BAP must dismiss an appeal if the parties file a signed dismissal agreement specifying how costs are to be paid and pay any court fees that are due.

(b) **Appellant's Motion to Dismiss**. An appeal may be dismissed on the appellant's motion on terms agreed to by the parties or fixed by the district court or BAP.

(c) **Other Relief**. A court order is required for any relief beyond the dismissal of an appeal—including approving a settlement, vacating an action of the bankruptcy court, or remanding the case to it.

(d) **Court Approval**. This rule does not alter the legal requirements governing court approval of a settlement, payment, or other consideration.

(Added Apr. 25, 2014, eff. Dec. 1, 2014; amended Apr. 11, 2022, eff. Dec. 1, 2022; Apr. 2, 2024, eff. Dec. 1, 2024.)

Rule 8023.1. Substitution of Parties

(a) **Death of a Party**.

(1) *After a Notice of Appeal Is Filed*. If a party dies after a notice of appeal has been filed or while a proceeding is pending on appeal in the district court or BAP, the decedent's personal representative may be substituted as a party on motion filed with that court's clerk by the representative or by any party. A party's motion must be served on the representative in accordance with Rule 8011. If the decedent has no representative, any party may suggest the death on the record, and the appellate court may then direct appropriate proceedings.

(2) *Before a Notice of Appeal Is Filed—Potential Appellant*. If a party entitled to appeal dies before filing a notice of appeal, the decedent's personal representative—or, if there is no personal representative, the decedent's attorney of record—may file a notice of appeal within the time prescribed by these rules. After the notice of appeal is filed, substitution must be in accordance with (1).

(3) *Before a Notice of Appeal Is Filed—Potential Appellee*. If a party against whom an appeal may be taken dies after entry of a judgment or order in the bankruptcy court, but before a notice of appeal is filed, an appellant may proceed as if the death had not occurred. After the notice of appeal is filed, substitution must be in accordance with (1).

(b) **Substitution for a Reason Other Than Death**. If a party needs to be substituted for any reason other than death, the procedure prescribed in (a) applies.

(c) **Public Officer: Identification; Substitution**.

(1) *Identification of a Party*. A public officer who is a party to an appeal or other proceeding in an official capacity may be described as a party by

the public officer's official title rather than by name. But the appellate court may require the public officer's name to be added.

(2) *Automatic Substitution of an Officeholder.* When a public officer who is a party to an appeal or other proceeding in an official capacity dies, resigns, or otherwise ceases to hold office, the action does not abate. Subject to Rule 2012, the public officer's successor is automatically substituted as a party. Proceedings after the substitution are to be in the name of the substituted party, but any misnomer that does not affect the parties' substantial rights may be disregarded. An order of substitution may be entered at any time, but failure to enter an order does not affect the substitution.

(Added Apr. 2, 2024, eff. Dec. 1, 2024.)

Rule 8024. Clerk's Duties on Disposition of the Appeal

(a) **Preparing the Judgment**. After receiving the court's opinion—or instructions if there is no opinion—the district or BAP clerk must:
   (1) prepare and sign the judgment; and
   (2) note it on the docket, which act constitutes entry of judgment.
(b) **Giving Notice of the Judgment**. Immediately after a judgment is entered, the district or BAP clerk must:
   (1) send notice of its entry, together with a copy of any opinion, to:
   • the parties to the appeal;
   • the United States trustee; and
   • the bankruptcy clerk; and
   (2) note on the docket the date the notice was sent.
(c) **Returning Physical Items**. On disposition of the appeal, the district or BAP clerk must return to the bankruptcy clerk any physical items sent as the record on appeal.

(Added Apr. 25, 2014, eff. Dec. 1, 2014; amended Apr. 2, 2024, eff. Dec. 1, 2024.)

Rule 8025. Staying a District Court or BAP Judgment

(a) **Automatic Stay of a Judgment on Appeal**. Unless the district court or BAP orders otherwise, its judgment is stayed for 14 days after its entry.
(b) **Stay Pending an Appeal to the United States Court of Appeals**.
   (1) *In General*. On a party's motion with notice to all other parties to the appeal, the district court or BAP may stay its judgment pending an appeal to the court of appeals.
   (2) *Time Limit*. Except for cause, the stay must not exceed 30 days after the judgment is entered.

(3) *Stay Continued When an Appeal Is Filed*. If, before a stay expires, the party who obtained it appeals to a court of appeals, the stay continues until final disposition by the court of appeals.

(4) *Bond or Other Security*. A bond or other security may be required as a condition for granting or continuing a stay. If a trustee obtains a stay, a bond or other security may be required. But neither is required if a stay is obtained by the United States or its officer or agency, or by direction of any department of the United States government.

(c) **Automatic Stay of the Bankruptcy Court's Order, Judgment, or Decree**. If the district court or BAP enters a judgment affirming the bankruptcy court's order, judgment, or decree, a stay of the district court's or BAP's judgment automatically stays the bankruptcy court's order, judgment, or decree while the appellate stay is in effect.

(d) **Power of a Court of Appeals or Its Judges Not Limited**. This rule does not limit the power of a court of appeals or any of its judges to:

(1) stay a judgment pending appeal;

(2) stay proceedings while an appeal is pending;

(3) suspend, modify, restore, vacate, or grant a stay or injunction while an appeal is pending; or

(4) issue any order appropriate to preserve the status quo or the effectiveness of any judgment that might be entered.

(Added Apr. 25, 2014, eff. Dec. 1, 2014; amended Apr. 2, 2024, eff. Dec. 1, 2024.)

Rule 8026. Making and Amending Local Rules; Procedure When There Is No Controlling Law

(a) **Local Rules**.

(1) *Making and Amending Local Rules*.

(A) BAP Local Rules. A circuit council that has authorized a BAP under 28 U.S.C. §158(b) may make and amend local rules governing the practice and procedure on appeal to the BAP from a bankruptcy court's judgment, order, or decree.

(B) District-Court Local Rules. A district court may make and amend local rules governing the practice and procedure on appeal to the district court from a bankruptcy court's judgment, order, or decree.

(C) Procedure. Fed. R. Civ. P. 83 governs the procedure for making and amending local rules. A local rule must be consistent with— but not duplicate—an Act of Congress and these Part VIII rules.

(2) *Numbering*. Local rules must conform to any uniform numbering system prescribed by the Judicial Conference of the United States.

(3) *Limitation on Enforcing a Local Rule Relating to Form*. A local rule imposing a requirement of form must not be enforced in a way that causes a party to lose any right because of a nonwillful failure to comply.

(b) **Procedure When There Is No Controlling Law**. A judge may regulate practice in any manner consistent with federal law, these rules, the Official Forms, and the district's local rules. For any requirement set out elsewhere, a sanction or other disadvantage may be imposed for noncompliance only if the alleged violator was given actual notice of the requirement in the particular case.

(Added Apr. 25, 2014, eff. Dec. 1, 2014; amended Apr. 2, 2024, eff. Dec. 1, 2024.)

Rule 8027. Notice of a Mediation Procedure

If the district court or BAP has a mediation procedure applicable to bankruptcy appeals, the clerk must, after docketing the appeal, promptly notify the parties of:
(a) the requirements of the mediation procedure; and
(b) any effect it has on the time to file briefs.

(Added Apr. 25, 2014, eff. Dec. 1, 2014; amended Apr. 2, 2024, eff. Dec. 1, 2024.)

Rule 8028. Suspending These Part VIII Rules

To expedite a decision or for other cause, a district court or BAP—or when appropriate, the court of appeals—may, in a particular case, suspend the requirements of these Part VIII rules, except Rules 8001–8007, 8012, 8020, 8024–8026, and 8028.

(Added Apr. 25, 2014, eff. Dec. 1, 2014; amended Apr. 2, 2024, eff. Dec. 1, 2024.)

Part IX—General Provisions

Rule 9001. Definitions

(a) **In the Code**. The definitions of words and phrases in §§101, 902, 1101, and 1502 and the rules of construction in §102 apply in these rules.
(b) **In These Rules**. In these rules, the following words and phrases have these meanings:
  (1) "Bankruptcy clerk" means a clerk appointed under 28 U.S.C. §156(b).
  (2) "Clerk" means a bankruptcy clerk if one has been appointed; otherwise, it means the district-court clerk.
  (3) "Code" means Title 11 of the United States Code.
  (4) "Court" or "judge" means the judicial officer who presides over the case or proceeding.
  (5) "Debtor," when the debtor is not a natural person and either is required by these rules to perform an act or must appear for examination, includes:
    (A) if the debtor is a corporation and if the court so designates:

- any or all of its officers, directors, trustees, or members of a similar controlling body;
- a controlling stockholder or member; or
- any other person in control; or

(B) if the debtor is a partnership:

- any or all of its general partners; or
- if the court so designates, any other person in control.

(6) "Firm" includes a partnership or professional corporation of attorneys or accountants.

(7) "Judgment" means any appealable order.

(8) "Mail" means first-class mail, postage prepaid.

(9) "Notice provider" means an entity approved by the Administrative Office of the United States Courts to give notice to creditors under Rule 2002(g)(4).

(10) "Regular associate" means an attorney regularly employed by, associated with, or counsel to an individual or firm.

(11) "Trustee" includes a debtor in possession in a Chapter 11 case.

(12) "United States trustee" includes an assistant United States trustee and a United States trustee's designee.

(As amended Mar. 30, 1987, eff. Aug. 1, 1987; Apr. 30, 1991, eff. Aug. 1, 1991; Apr. 25, 2005, eff. Dec. 1, 2005; Apr. 28, 2010, eff. Dec. 1, 2010; Apr. 2, 2024, eff. Dec. 1, 2024.)

Rule 9002. Meaning of Words in the Federal Rules of Civil Procedure

Unless they are inconsistent with the context, the following words and phrases in the Federal Rules of Civil Procedure—when made applicable by these rules—have these meanings:

(a) "Action" or "civil action" means an adversary proceeding or, when appropriate:

(1) a contested petition;

(2) a proceeding to vacate an order for relief; or

(3) a proceeding to determine any other contested matter.

(b) "Appeal" means an appeal under 28 U.S.C. §158.

(c) "Clerk" or "clerk of the district court" means the officer responsible for maintaining the district's bankruptcy records.

(d) "District court," "trial court," "court," "district judge," or "judge" means bankruptcy judge if the case or proceeding is pending before a bankruptcy judge.

(e) "Judgment" includes any appealable order.

(As amended Mar. 30, 1987, eff. Aug. 1, 1987; Apr. 22, 1993, eff. Aug. 1, 1993; Apr. 2, 2024, eff. Dec. 1, 2024.)

Rule 9003. Ex Parte Contacts Prohibited

(a) **In General**. Unless permitted by applicable law, the following persons must refrain from ex parte meetings and communications with the court about matters affecting a particular case or proceeding:

- an examiner;
- a party in interest;
- a party in interest's attorney, accountant, or employee; and
- the United States trustee and any of its assistants, agents, or employees.

(b) **Exception for a United States Trustee**. A United States trustee and any of its assistants, agents, or employees are not prohibited from communicating with the court about general administrative problems and improving bankruptcy administration—including the operation of the United States trustee system.

(As amended Mar. 30, 1987, eff. Aug. 1, 1987; Apr. 30, 1991, eff. Aug. 1, 1991; Apr. 2, 2024, eff. Dec. 1, 2024.)

Rule 9004. General Requirements of Form

(a) **Legibility; Abbreviations**. A petition, pleading, schedule, or other document must be clearly legible. Commonly used English abbreviations are acceptable.

(b) **Caption**. A document presented for filing must contain a caption that sets forth:

(1) the court's name;

(2) the case's title;

(3) the case number and, if appropriate, adversary-proceeding number; and

(4) a brief designation of the document's character.

(As amended Apr. 2, 2024, eff. Dec. 1, 2024.)

Rule 9005. Harmless Error

Fed. R. Civ. P. 61 applies in a bankruptcy case. When appropriate, the court may order the correction of any error or defect—or the cure of any omission—that does not affect a substantial right.

(As amended Apr. 2, 2024, eff. Dec. 1, 2024.)

Rule 9005.1. Constitutional Challenge to a Statute—Notice, Certification, and Intervention

Fed. R. Civ. P. 5.1 applies in a bankruptcy case.

(Added Apr. 30, 2007, eff. Dec. 1, 2007; amended Apr. 2, 2024, eff. Dec. 1, 2024.)

Rule 9006. Computing and Extending Time; Motions

(a) **Computing Time**. The following rules apply in computing any time period specified in these rules, in the Federal Rules of Civil Procedure, in any local rule or court order, or in any statute that does not specify a method of computing time.

    (1) *Period Stated in Days or a Longer Unit.* When the period is stated in days or a longer unit of time:

        (A) exclude the day of the event that triggers the period;

        (B) count every day, including intermediate Saturdays, Sundays, and legal holidays; and

        (C) include the last day of the period, but if the last day is a Saturday, Sunday, or legal holiday, the period continues to run until the end of the next day that is not a Saturday, Sunday, or legal holiday.

    (2) *Period Stated in Hours.* When the period is stated in hours:

        (A) begin counting immediately on the occurrence of the event that triggers the period;

        (B) count every hour, including hours during intermediate Saturdays, Sundays, and legal holidays; and

        (C) if the period would end on a Saturday, Sunday, or legal holiday, then continue the period until the same time on the next day that is not a Saturday, Sunday, or legal holiday.

    (3) *Inaccessibility of the Clerk's Office When a Filing Is Due.* Unless the court orders otherwise, if the clerk's office is inaccessible:

        (A) on the last day for filing under (1), then the time for filing is extended to the first accessible day that is not a Saturday, Sunday, or legal holiday; or

        (B) during the last hour for filing under (2), then the time for filing is extended to the same time on the first accessible day that is not a Saturday, Sunday, or legal holiday.

    (4) "Last Day" Defined. Unless a different time is set by statute, local rule, or order in a case, the last day ends:

        (A) for electronic filing, at midnight in the court's time zone; and

        (B) for filing by other means, when the clerk's office is scheduled to close.

    (5) "Next Day" Defined. The "next day" is determined by continuing to count forward when the period is measured after an event, and backward when measured before an event.

    (6) "Legal Holiday" Defined. "Legal holiday" means:

        (A) the day set aside by statute for observing New Year's Day, Birthday of Martin Luther King Jr., Washington's Birthday, Memorial Day, Juneteenth National Independence Day, Independence Day, Labor Day, Columbus Day, Veteran's Day, Thanksgiving Day, or Christmas Day;

    (B) any day declared a holiday by the President or Congress; and

    (C) for periods that are measured after an event, any other day declared a holiday by the state where the district court is located. (In this rule, "state" includes the District of Columbia and any United States commonwealth or territory.)

(b) **Extending Time**.

  (1) *In General*. This paragraph (1) applies when these rules, a notice given under these rules, or a court order requires or allows an act to be performed at or within a specified period. Except as provided in (2) and (3), the court may—at any time and for cause—extend the time to act if:

    (A) with or without a motion or notice, a request to extend is made before the period (or a previously extended period) expires; or

    (B) on motion made after the specified period expires, the failure to act within that period resulted from excusable neglect.

  (2) *Exceptions*. The court must not extend the time to act under Rules 1007(d), 2003(a) and (d), 7052, 9023, and 9024.

  (3) *Extensions Governed by Other Rules*. The court may extend the time to:

    (A) act under Rules 1006(b)(2), 1017(e), 3002(c), 4003(b), 4004(a), 4007(c), 4008(a), 8002, and 9033—but only as permitted by those rules; and

    (B) file the certificate required by Rule 1007(b)(7), and the schedules and statements in a small business case under §1116(3)—but only as permitted by Rule 1007(c).

(c) **Reducing Time**.

  (1) *When Permitted*. When a rule, notice given under a rule, or court order requires or allows an act to be done within a specified time, the court may—for cause and with or without a motion or notice—reduce the time.

  (2) *When Not Permitted*. The court may not reduce the time to act under Rule 2002(a)(7), 2003(a), 3002(c), 3014, 3015, 4001(b)(2) or (c)(2), 4003(a), 4004(a), 4007(c), 4008(a), 8002, or 9033(b). Also, the court may not reduce the time set by Rule 1007(c) to file the certificate required by Rule 1007(b)(7).

(d) **Time to Serve a Motion and a Response**.

  (1) *In General*. A written motion (other than one that may be heard ex parte) and notice of any hearing must be served at least 7 days before the hearing date, unless the court or these rules set a different period. Any affidavit supporting the motion must be served with it. An order to change the period may be granted for cause on ex parte application.

  (2) *Response*. Except as provided in Rule 9023, any written response must be served at least 1 day before the hearing, unless the court allows otherwise.

(e) **Service Complete on Mailing**. Service by mail of process, any other document, or notice is complete upon mailing.

(f) **Additional Time After Certain Service**. When a party may or must act within a specified time after being served and service is made by mail or under Fed. R. Civ. P. 5(b)(2)(D) (leaving with the clerk) or (F) (other means consented to), 3 days are added after the period would otherwise expire under (a).

(g) **Grain-Storage Facility**. This rule does not limit the court's authority under §557 to issue an order governing procedures in a case in which the debtor owns or operates a grain-storage facility.

(As amended Mar. 30, 1987, eff. Aug. 1, 1987; Apr. 25, 1989, eff. Aug. 1, 1989; Apr. 30, 1991, eff. Aug. 1, 1991; Apr. 23, 1996, eff. Dec. 1, 1996; Apr. 26, 1999, eff. Dec. 1, 1999; Apr. 23, 2001, eff. Dec. 1, 2001; Apr. 25, 2005, eff. Dec. 1, 2005; Apr. 23, 2008, eff. Dec. 1, 2008; Mar. 26, 2009, eff. Dec. 1, 2009; Apr. 16, 2013, eff. Dec. 1, 2013; Apr. 28, 2016, eff. Dec. 1, 2016; Apr. 24, 2023, eff. Dec. 1, 2023; Apr. 2, 2024, eff. Dec. 1, 2024.)

Rule 9007. Authority to Regulate Notices

(a) **In General**. Unless these rules provide otherwise, when notice is to be given, the court must designate:
   (1) the deadline for giving it;
   (2) the entities to whom it must be given; and
   (3) the form and manner of giving it.

(b) **Combined Notices**. When feasible, the court may order notices under these rules to be combined.

(As amended Mar. 30, 1987, eff. Aug. 1, 1987; Apr. 2, 2024, eff. Dec. 1, 2024.)

Rule 9008. Service or Notice by Publication

When these rules require or authorize service or notice by publication, and to the extent that they do not provide otherwise, the court must determine the form and manner of publication—including the newspaper or other medium to be used and the number of publications.

(As amended Apr. 2, 2024, eff. Dec. 1, 2024.)

Rule 9009. Using Official Forms; Director's Forms

(a) **Official Forms**. The Official Forms prescribed by the Judicial Conference of the United States must be used without alteration—unless alteration is authorized by these rules, the form itself, or the national instructions for a particular form. A form may be modified to permit minor changes not affecting wording or the order of presentation, including a change that:
   (1) expands the prescribed response area to permit a complete response;
   (2) deletes space not needed for a response; or

(3) deletes items requiring detail in a question or category if the filer indicates—either by checking "no" or "none," or by stating in words—that there is nothing to report on that item.

(b) **Director's Forms**. The Director of the Administrative Office of the United States Courts may issue additional forms.

(c) **Construing Forms**. The forms must be construed to be consistent with these rules and the Code.

(As amended Apr. 30, 1991, eff. Aug. 1, 1991; Apr. 23, 2008, eff. Dec. 1, 2008; Apr. 27, 2017, eff. Dec. 1, 2017; Apr. 2, 2024, eff. Dec. 1, 2024.)

Rule 9010. Authority to Act Personally or by an Attorney; Power of Attorney

(a) **In General**. A debtor, creditor, equity security holder, indenture trustee, committee, or other party may:

(1) appear in a case and act either on the entity's own behalf or through an attorney authorized to practice in the court; and

(2) perform any act not constituting the practice of law, by an authorized agent, attorney-in-fact, or proxy.

(b) **Attorney's Notice of Appearance**. An attorney appearing for a party in a case must file a notice of appearance containing the attorney's name, office address, and telephone number—unless the appearance is already noted in the record.

(c) **Power of Attorney to Represent a Creditor**. The authority of an agent, attorney-in-fact, or proxy to represent a creditor—for any purpose other than executing and filing a proof of claim or accepting or rejecting a plan—must be evidenced by a power of attorney that substantially conforms to the appropriate version of Form 411. A power of attorney must be acknowledged before:

(1) an officer listed in 28 U.S.C. §459 or §953 or in Rule 9012; or

(2) a person authorized to administer oaths under the state law where the oath is administered.

(As amended Mar. 30, 1987, eff. Aug. 1, 1987; Apr. 30, 1991, eff. Aug. 1, 1991; Apr. 2, 2024, eff. Dec. 1, 2024.)

Rule 9011. Signing Documents; Representations to the Court; Sanctions; Verifying and Providing Copies

(a) **Signature**. Every petition, pleading, written motion, and other document—except a list, schedule, or statement, or an amendment to one of them—must be signed by at least one attorney of record in the attorney's individual name. A party not represented by an attorney must sign all documents. Each document must state the signer's address and telephone number, if any. The court must strike an unsigned document unless the omission is promptly corrected after being called to the attorney's or party's attention.

(b) **Representations to the Court**. By presenting to the court a petition, pleading, written motion, or other document—whether by signing, filing, submitting, or later advocating it—an attorney or unrepresented party certifies that, to the best of the person's knowledge, information, and belief formed after an inquiry reasonable under the circumstances:

    (1) it is not presented for any improper purpose, such as to harass, cause unnecessary delay, or needlessly increase litigation costs;

    (2) the claims, defenses, and other legal contentions are warranted by existing law or by a nonfrivolous argument to extend, modify, or reverse existing law, or to establish new law;

    (3) the allegations and factual contentions have evidentiary support—or if specifically so identified, are likely to have evidentiary support after a reasonable opportunity for further investigation or discovery; and

    (4) the denials of factual contentions are warranted on the evidence—or if specifically so identified, are reasonably based on a lack of information or belief.

(c) **Sanctions**.

    (1) *In General*. If, after notice and a reasonable opportunity to respond, the court determines that (b) has been violated, the court may, subject to the conditions in this subdivision (c), impose an appropriate sanction on any attorney, law firm, or party that committed the violation or is responsible for it. Absent exceptional circumstances, a law firm must be held jointly responsible for a violation committed by its partner, associate, or employee.

    (2) *By Motion*.

        (A) In General. A motion for sanctions must be made separately from any other motion or request, describe the specific conduct alleged to violate (b), and be served under Rule 7004.

        (B) When to File. The motion for sanctions must not be filed or presented to the court if the challenged document, claim, defense, contention, allegation, or denial is withdrawn or appropriately corrected within 21 days after the motion was served (or within another period as the court may order). This limitation does not apply if the conduct alleged is filing a petition in violation of (b).

        (C) Awarding Damages. If warranted, the court may award to the prevailing party the reasonable expenses and attorney's fees incurred in presenting or opposing the motion.

    (3) *By the Court*. On its own, the court may enter an order describing the specific conduct that appears to violate (b) and directing an attorney, law firm, or party to show cause why it has not violated (b).

    (4) *Nature of a Sanction; Limitations*.

(A) In General. A sanction imposed under this rule must be limited to what suffices to deter repetition of the conduct or deter comparable conduct by others similarly situated. The sanction may include:

    (i) a nonmonetary directive;

    (ii) an order to pay a penalty into court; or

    (iii) if imposed on motion and warranted for effective deterrence, an order directing payment to the movant of all or part of the reasonable attorney's fees and other expenses directly resulting from the violation.

(B) Limitations on a Monetary Sanction. The court must not impose a monetary sanction:

    (i) against a represented party for violating (b)(2); or

    (ii) on its own, unless it issued the show-cause order under (c)(3) before voluntary dismissal or settlement of the claims made by or against the party that is, or whose attorneys are, to be sanctioned.

(5) *Content of a Court Order*. An order imposing a sanction must describe the sanctioned conduct and explain the basis for the sanction.

(d) **Inapplicability to Discovery**. Subdivisions (a)–(c) do not apply to disclosures and discovery requests, responses, objections, and motions that are subject to Rules 7026–7037.

(e) **Verifying a Document**. A document filed in a bankruptcy case need not be verified unless these rules provide otherwise. When these rules require verification, an unsworn declaration under 28 U.S.C. §1746 suffices.

(f) **Copies of Signed or Verified Documents**. When these rules require copies of a signed or verified document, if the original is signed or verified, a copy that conforms to the original suffices.

(As amended Mar. 30, 1987, eff. Aug. 1, 1987; Apr. 30, 1991, eff. Aug. 1, 1991; Apr. 11, 1997, eff. Dec. 1, 1997; Apr. 2, 2024, eff. Dec. 1, 2024.)

Rule 9012. Oaths and Affirmations

(a) **Who May Administer an Oath**. These persons may administer an oath or affirmation or take an acknowledgment:

- a bankruptcy judge;
- a clerk;
- a deputy clerk;
- a United States trustee;
- an officer authorized to administer oaths in a proceeding before a federal court or by state law in the state where the oath is taken; or
- a United States diplomatic or consular officer in a foreign country.

(b) **Affirmation as an Alternative**. If an oath is required, a solemn affirmation suffices.

(As amended Mar. 30, 1987, eff. Aug. 1, 1987; Apr. 30, 1991, eff. Aug. 1, 1991; Apr. 2, 2024, eff. Dec. 1, 2024.)

Rule 9013. Motions; Form and Service

(a) **Request for an Order**. A request for an order must be made by written motion unless:

    (1) an application is authorized by these rules; or

    (2) the request is made during a hearing.

(b) **Form and Service of a Motion**. A motion must state its grounds with particularity and set forth the relief or order requested. Unless a written motion may be considered ex parte, the movant must, within the time prescribed by Rule 9006(d), serve the motion on:

- the trustee or debtor in possession and those entities specified by these rules; or
- if these rules do not require service or specify the entities to be served, the entities designated by the court.

(As amended Mar. 30, 1987, eff. Aug. 1, 1987; Apr. 16, 2013, eff. Dec. 1, 2013; Apr. 2, 2024, eff. Dec. 1, 2024.)

Rule 9014. Contested Matters

(a) **Motion Required**. In a contested matter not otherwise governed by these rules, relief must be requested by motion. Reasonable notice and an opportunity to be heard must be given to the party against whom relief is sought. No response is required unless the court orders otherwise.

(b) **Service**.

    (1) *Motion*. The motion must be served within the time prescribed by Rule 9006(d) and in the manner for serving a summons and complaint provided by Rule 7004.

    (2) *Response*. Any written response must be served within the time prescribed by Rule 9006(d).

    (3) *Later Filings*. After a motion is served, any other document must be served in the manner prescribed by Fed. R. Civ. P. 5(b).

(c) **Applying Part VII Rules**.

    (1) *In General*. Unless this rule or a court order provides otherwise, the following rules apply in a contested matter: 7009, 7017, 7021, 7025–7026, 7028–7037, 7041–7042, 7052, 7054–7056, 7064, 7069, and 7071. At any stage of a contested matter, the court may order that one or more other Part VII rules apply.

    (2) *Exception*. Unless the court orders otherwise, the following subdivisions of Fed. R. Civ. P. 26, as incorporated by Rule 7026, do not apply in a contested matter:

- (a)(1), mandatory disclosure;

- (a)(2), disclosures about expert testimony;
- (a)(3), other pretrial disclosures; and
- (f), mandatory meeting before a scheduling conference.

(3) *Procedural Order*. In issuing any procedural order under this subdivision (c), the court must give the parties notice and a reasonable opportunity to comply.

(4) *Perpetuating Testimony*. An entity desiring to perpetuate testimony may do so in the manner provided by Rule 7027 for taking a deposition before an adversary proceeding.

(d) **Taking Testimony on a Disputed Factual Issue**. A witness's testimony on a disputed material factual issue must be taken in the same manner as testimony in an adversary proceeding.

(e) **Determining Whether a Hearing Will Be an Evidentiary Hearing**. The court must provide procedures that allow parties—at a reasonable time before a scheduled hearing—to determine whether it will be an evidentiary hearing at which witnesses may testify.

(As amended Mar. 30, 1987, eff. Aug. 1, 1987; Apr. 26, 1999, eff. Dec. 1, 1999; Apr. 29, 2002, eff. Dec. 1, 2002; Apr. 26, 2004, eff. Dec. 1, 2004; Apr. 16, 2013, eff. Dec. 1, 2013; Apr. 2, 2024, eff. Dec. 1, 2024.)

Rule 9015. Jury Trial

(a) **In General**. In a bankruptcy case or proceeding, Fed. R. Civ. P. 38–39, 47–49, 51, and 81(c) (insofar as it applies to jury trials) apply. But a demand for a jury trial under Fed. R. Civ. P. 38(b) must be filed in accordance with Rule 5005.

(b) **Jury Trial Before a Bankruptcy Judge**. The parties may—jointly or separately—file a statement consenting to a jury trial conducted by a bankruptcy judge under 28 U.S.C. §157(e) if:

(1) the right to a jury trial applies;

(2) a timely demand has been filed under Fed. R. Civ. P. 38(b);

(3) the bankruptcy judge has been specially designated to conduct the jury trial; and

(4) the statement is filed within any time specified by local rule.

(c) **Judgment as a Matter of Law; Motion for a New Trial**. Fed. R. Civ. P. 50 applies in a bankruptcy case or proceeding—except that a renewed motion for judgment, or a request for a new trial, must be filed within 14 days after the judgment is entered.

(Added Apr. 11, 1997, eff. Dec. 1, 1997; amended Mar. 26, 2009, eff. Dec. 1, 2009; Apr. 2, 2024, eff. Dec. 1, 2024.)

Rule 9016. Subpoena

Fed. R. Civ. P. 45 applies in a bankruptcy case.

(As amended Mar. 30, 1987, eff. Aug. 1, 1987; Apr. 2, 2024, eff. Dec. 1, 2024.)

Rule 9017. Evidence

The Federal Rules of Evidence and Fed. R. Civ. P. 43, 44, and 44.1 apply in a bankruptcy case.

(As amended Apr. 2, 2024, eff. Dec. 1, 2024.)

Rule 9018. Secret, Confidential, Scandalous, or Defamatory Matter

(a) **In General**. On motion or on its own, the court may, with or without notice, issue any order that justice requires to:
  (1) protect the estate or any entity regarding a trade secret or other confidential research, development, or commercial information;
  (2) protect an entity from scandalous or defamatory matter in any document filed in a bankruptcy case; or
  (3) protect governmental matters made confidential by statute or regulation.

(b) **Motion to Vacate or Modify an Order Issued Without Notice**. An entity affected by an order issued under (a) without notice may move to vacate or modify it. After notice and a hearing, the court must rule on the motion.

(As amended Mar. 30, 1987, eff. Aug. 1, 1987; Apr. 2, 2024, eff. Dec. 1, 2024.)

Rule 9019. Compromise or Settlement; Arbitration

(a) Approving a Compromise or Settlement. On the trustee's motion and after notice and a hearing, the court may approve a compromise or settlement. Notice must be given to:
  • all creditors;
  • the United States trustee;
  • the debtor;
  • all indenture trustees as provided in Rule 2002; and
  • any other entity the court designates.

(b) **Compromising or Settling Controversies in Classes**. After a hearing on such notice as the court may order, the court may:
  (1) designate a class or classes of controversies; and
  (2) authorize the trustee to compromise or settle controversies within the class or classes without further hearing or notice.

(c) **Arbitration of Controversies Affecting an Estate**. If the parties so stipulate, the court may authorize a controversy affecting an estate to be submitted to final and binding arbitration.

(As amended Mar. 30, 1987, eff. Aug. 1, 1987; Apr. 30, 1991, eff. Aug. 1, 1991; Apr. 22, 1993, eff. Aug. 1, 1993; Apr. 2, 2024, eff. Dec. 1, 2024.)

Rule 9020. Contempt Proceedings

Rule 9014 governs a motion for a contempt order made by the United States trustee or a party in interest.

(As amended Mar. 30, 1987, eff. Aug. 1, 1987; Apr. 30, 1991, eff. Aug. 1, 1991; Apr. 23, 2001, eff. Dec. 1, 2001; Apr. 2, 2024, eff. Dec. 1, 2024.)

Rule 9021. When a Judgment or Order Becomes Effective

A judgment or order becomes effective when it is entered under Rule 5003.

(As amended Mar. 30, 1987, eff. Aug. 1, 1987; Mar. 26, 2009, eff. Dec. 1, 2009; Apr. 2, 2024, eff. Dec. 1, 2024.)

Rule 9022. Notice of a Judgment or Order

(a) **Issued by a Bankruptcy Judge**.
  (1) *In General*. Upon entering a judgment or order, the clerk must:
    (A) promptly serve notice of the entry on the contesting parties and other entities the court designates;
    (B) do so in the manner provided by Fed. R. Civ. P. 5(b);
    (C) except in a Chapter 9 case, promptly send a copy of the judgment or order to the United States trustee; and
    (D) note service on the docket.
  (2) *Lack of Notice; Time to Appeal*. Except as permitted by Rule 8002, lack of notice of the entry does not affect the time to appeal or relieve—or authorize the court to relieve—a party for failing to appeal within the time allowed.
(b) **Issued by a District Judge**. Notice of a district judge's judgment or order is governed by Fed. R. Civ. P. 77(d). Except in a Chapter 9 case, the clerk must promptly send a copy of the judgment or order to the United States trustee.

(As amended Mar. 30, 1987, eff. Aug. 1, 1987; Apr. 30, 1991, eff. Aug. 1, 1991; Apr. 23, 2001, eff. Dec. 1, 2001; Apr. 2, 2024, eff. Dec. 1, 2024.)

Rule 9023. New Trial; Altering or Amending a Judgment

(a) **Application of Civil Rule 59**. Except as this rule and Rule 3008 provide otherwise, Fed. R. Civ. P. 59 applies in a bankruptcy case.
(b) **By Motion**. A motion for a new trial or to alter or amend a judgment must be filed within 14 days after the judgment is entered. In some instances, Rule 8008 governs postjudgment motion practice after an appeal has been docketed and is pending.
(c) **By the Court**. Within 14 days after judgment is entered, the court may, on its own, order a new trial.

(As amended Mar. 26, 2009, eff. Dec. 1, 2009; Apr. 25, 2014, eff. Dec. 1, 2014; Apr. 2, 2024, eff. Dec. 1, 2024.)

Rule 9024. Relief from a Judgment or Order

(a) **In General**. Fed. R. Civ. P. 60 applies in a bankruptcy case—except that:

    (1) the one-year limitation in Fed. R. Civ. P. 60(c) does not apply to a motion to reopen a case or to reconsider an uncontested order allowing or disallowing a claim against the estate;

    (2) a complaint to revoke a discharge in a Chapter 7 case must be filed within the time allowed by §727(e); and

    (3) a complaint to revoke an order confirming a plan must be filed within the time allowed by §1144, 1230, or 1330.

(b) **Indicative Ruling**. In some instances, Rule 8008 governs postjudgment motion practice after an appeal has been docketed and is pending.

(As amended Apr. 30, 1991, eff. Aug. 1, 1991; Apr. 23, 2008, eff. Dec. 1, 2008; Apr. 25, 2014, eff. Dec. 1, 2014; Apr. 2, 2024, eff. Dec. 1, 2024.)

Rule 9025. Security; Proceeding Against a Security Provider

When the Code or these rules require or permit a party to give security and the party gives security with one or more security providers, each provider submits to the court's jurisdiction. Liability may be determined in an adversary proceeding governed by the Part VII rules.

(As amended Apr. 26, 2018, eff. Dec. 1, 2018; Apr. 2, 2024, eff. Dec. 1, 2024.)

Rule 9026. Objecting to a Ruling or Order

Fed. R. Civ. P. 46 applies in a bankruptcy case.

(As amended Apr. 2, 2024, eff. Dec. 1, 2024.)

Rule 9027. Removing a Claim or Cause of Action from Another Court

(a) **Notice of Removal**.

    (1) *Where Filed; Form and Content*. A notice of removal must be filed with the clerk for the district and division where the state or federal civil action is pending. The notice must be signed under Rule 9011 and must:

        (A) contain a short and plain statement of the facts that entitle the party to remove;

        (B) contain a statement that the party filing the notice does or does not consent to the bankruptcy court's entry of a final judgment or order; and

(C) be accompanied by a copy of all process and pleadings.

(2) *Time to File When the Claim Was Filed Before the Bankruptcy Case Is Commenced.* If the claim or cause of action in a civil action is pending when a bankruptcy case is commenced, the notice of removal must be filed within the longest of these periods:

(A) 90 days after the order for relief in the bankruptcy case;

(B) if the claim or cause of action has been stayed under §362, 30 days after an order terminating the stay is entered; or

(C) in a Chapter 11 case, 30 days after a trustee qualifies—but no later than 180 days after the order for relief.

(3) *Time to File When the Claim Is Filed After the Bankruptcy Case Was Commenced.* If a claim or cause of action is asserted in another court after the bankruptcy case was commenced, a party filing a notice of removal must do so within the shorter of these periods:

(A) 30 days after receiving (by service or otherwise) the initial pleading setting forth the claim or cause of action sought to be removed; or

(B) 30 days after receiving the summons if the initial pleading has been filed but not served with the summons.

(b) **Notice to Other Parties and to the Court from Which the Claim Was Removed**. A party filing a notice of removal must promptly:

(1) serve a copy on all other parties to the removed claim or cause of action; and

(2) file a copy with the clerk of the court from which it was removed.

(c) **Effective Date of Removal**. Removal becomes effective when the notice is filed under (b)(2). The parties must proceed no further in the court from which the claim or cause of action was removed, unless it is remanded.

(d) **Remand After Removal**. A motion to remand is governed by Rule 9014. The party filing the motion must serve a copy on all parties to the removed claim or cause of action.

(e) **Procedure After Removal**.

(1) *Bringing Proper Parties Before the Court.* After removal, the district court—or the bankruptcy judge to whom the bankruptcy case has been referred—may issue all necessary orders and process to bring before it all proper parties. It does not matter whether they were served by process issued by the court from which the claim or cause of action was removed, or otherwise.

(2) *Records of Prior Proceedings.* The judge may require the party filing the notice of removal to file with the clerk copies of all records and proceedings relating to the claim or cause of action that were filed in the court from which the removal occurred.

(3) *Statement by a Party Other Than the Removing Party.* A party who has filed a pleading regarding a removed claim or cause of action—except the party filing the notice of removal—must:

      (A) file a statement that the party does or does not consent to the bankruptcy court's entry of a final order or judgment;

      (B) sign the statement under Rule 9011;

      (C) file it within 14 days after the notice of removal is filed; and

      (D) mail a copy to every other party to the removed claim or cause of action.

(f) **Process Regarding a Defendant After Removal**. If a defendant has not been served—or service has not been completed before removal or has been proved defective—then process or service may be completed or new process issued under the Part VII rules. A defendant served after removal may move to remand the claim or cause of action.

(g) **Applying Part VII Rules**.

    (1) *In General*. The Part VII rules apply to a claim or cause of action removed to a district court from a federal or state court, and they govern the procedure after removal. Repleading is not necessary unless the court orders otherwise.

    (2) *Time to File an Answer*. In a removed action, a defendant that has not previously done so must file an answer—or present other defenses or objections available under the Part VII rules. The defendant must do so within the longest of these periods:

      (A) 21 days after receiving—by service or otherwise—a copy of the initial pleading that sets forth the claim for relief;

      (B) 21 days after a summons on the original pleading was served; or

      (C) 7 days after the notice of removal was filed.

(h) **Clerk's Failure to Supply Certified Records of Court Proceedings**. If a party is entitled to copies of the records and proceedings in a civil action or proceeding in a federal or state court for use in the removed action or proceeding, the party may demand certified copies from that court's clerk. After the party pays for them or tenders the fees, if the clerk fails to provide them, the court to which the action or proceeding is removed may—after receiving an affidavit stating these facts—order that the record be supplied by affidavit or otherwise. The court may then proceed to trial and judgment, and may award all process, as if certified copies had been filed.

(i) **Property Attached or Sequestered; Security; Injunction**.

    (1) *Property Attached or Sequestered*. The court from which a claim or cause of action has been removed must hold attached or sequestered property to answer the final judgment or decree in the same way it would have been held had there been no removal.

    (2) *Security*. Any bond, undertaking, or security given by either party before the removal remains valid.

    (3) *Injunction*. Any injunction or order issued, or other proceeding had, before the removal remains in effect until dissolved or modified by the court.

(As amended Mar. 30, 1987, eff. Aug. 1, 1987; Apr. 30, 1991, eff. Aug. 1, 1991; Apr. 29, 2002, eff. Dec. 1, 2002; Mar. 26, 2009, eff. Dec. 1, 2009; Apr. 28, 2016, eff. Dec. 1, 2016; Apr. 2, 2024, eff. Dec. 1, 2024.)

Rule 9028. Judge's Disability

Fed. R. Civ. P. 63 applies in a bankruptcy case.

(As amended Mar. 30, 1987, eff. Aug. 1, 1987; Apr. 2, 2024, eff. Dec. 1, 2024.)

Rule 9029. Adopting Local Rules; Limit on Enforcing a Local Rule; Absence of Controlling Law

(a) **Adopting Local Rules**.
   (1) *By District Courts.* Each district court, acting by a majority of its judges, may make and amend rules governing practice and procedure in all cases and proceedings within its bankruptcy jurisdiction. Fed. R. Civ. P. 83 governs the procedure for adopting local rules. The rules must:
      (A) be consistent with—but not duplicate—Acts of Congress and these rules;
      (B) not prohibit or limit using Official Forms; and
      (C) conform to any uniform numbering system prescribed by the Judicial Conference of the United States.
   (2) *Delegating Authority to the Bankruptcy Judges.* A district court may— subject to any limitation or condition it may prescribe and Fed. R. Civ. P. 83—authorize the district's bankruptcy judges to make and amend local bankruptcy rules.
(b) **Limit on Enforcing a Local Rule Regarding Form**. A local rule imposing a requirement of form must not be enforced in a way that causes a party to lose any right because of a nonwillful failure to comply.
(c) **Procedure When There Is No Controlling Law**. A judge may regulate practice in any manner consistent with federal law, these rules, the Official Forms, and the district's local rules. For any requirement set out elsewhere, a sanction or other disadvantage may be imposed for noncompliance only if the alleged violator was given actual notice of the requirement in the particular case.

(As amended Mar. 30, 1987, eff. Aug. 1, 1987; Apr. 30, 1991, eff. Aug. 1, 1991; Apr. 27, 1995, eff. Dec. 1, 1995; Apr. 2, 2024, eff. Dec. 1, 2024.)

Rule 9030. Jurisdiction and Venue Not Extended or Limited

These rules must not be construed to extend or limit the courts' jurisdiction or the venue of any matters.

(As amended Mar. 30, 1987, eff. Aug. 1, 1987; Apr. 2, 2024, eff. Dec. 1, 2024.)

Rule 9031. Using Masters Not Authorized

Fed. R. Civ. P. 53 does not apply in a bankruptcy case.

(As amended Apr. 2, 2024, eff. Dec. 1, 2024.)

Rule 9032. Effect of an Amendment to the Federal Rules of Civil Procedure

To the extent these rules incorporate by reference the Federal Rules of Civil Procedure, an amendment to those rules is also effective under these rules, unless the amendment or these rules provide otherwise.

(As amended Apr. 30, 1991, eff. Aug. 1, 1991; Apr. 2, 2024, eff. Dec. 1, 2024.)

Rule 9033. Proposed Findings of Fact and Conclusions of Law

(a) **Service**. When a bankruptcy court issues proposed findings of fact and conclusions of law, the clerk must promptly serve a copy, by mail, on every party and must note the date of mailing on the docket.

(b) **Objections; Time to File**.
  (1) *Time to File*. Within 14 days after being served, a party may file and serve objections. They must identify each proposed finding or conclusion objected to and state the grounds for objecting. A party may respond to another party's objections within 14 days after being served with a copy.
  (2) *Ordering a Transcript*. Unless the district judge orders otherwise, a party filing objections must promptly order a transcript of the record, or the parts of it that all parties agree are—or the bankruptcy judge considers to be—sufficient.
  (3) *Extending the Time*. On request made before the time to file objections expires, the bankruptcy judge may, for cause, extend any party's time to file for no more than 21 days after the time otherwise expires. But a request made within 21 days after that time expires may be granted upon a showing of excusable neglect.

(c) **Review by the District Judge**. The district judge:
  (1) must review de novo—on the record or after receiving additional evidence—any part of the bankruptcy judge's findings of fact or conclusions of law to which specific written objection has been made under (b); and
  (2) may accept, reject, or modify the proposed findings of fact or conclusions of law, take additional evidence, or remand the matter to the bankruptcy judge with instructions.

(Added Mar. 30, 1987, eff. Aug. 1, 1987; amended Mar. 26, 2009, eff. Dec. 1, 2009; Apr. 28, 2016, eff. Dec. 1, 2016; Apr. 2, 2024, eff. Dec. 1, 2024.)

Rule 9034. Sending Copies to the United States Trustee

Except in a Chapter 9 case or when the United States trustee requests otherwise, an entity filing a pleading, motion, objection, or similar document relating to any of the following must send a copy to the United States trustee within the time required for service:

(a) a proposed use, sale, or lease of property of the estate other than in the ordinary course of business;

(b) the approval of a compromise or settlement of a controversy;

(c) the dismissal or conversion of a case to another chapter;

(d) the employment of a professional person;

(e) an application for compensation or reimbursement of expenses;

(f) a motion for, or the approval of an agreement regarding, the use of cash collateral or authority to obtain credit;

(g) the appointment of a trustee or examiner in a Chapter 11 case;

(h) the approval of a disclosure statement;

(i) the confirmation of a plan;

(j) an objection to, or waiver or revocation of, the debtor's discharge; or

(k) any other matter in which the United States trustee requests copies of filed documents or the court orders copies sent to the United States trustee.

(Added Apr. 30, 1991, eff. Aug. 1, 1991; amended Apr. 2, 2024, eff. Dec. 1, 2024.)

Rule 9035. Applying These Rules in a Judicial District in Alabama or North Carolina

In a bankruptcy case filed in or transferred to a district in Alabama or North Carolina and in which a United States trustee is not authorized to act, these rules apply to the extent they are not inconsistent with any applicable federal statute.

(Added Apr. 30, 1991, eff. Aug. 1, 1991; amended Apr. 11, 1997, eff. Dec. 1, 1997; Apr. 2, 2024, eff. Dec. 1, 2024.)

Rule 9036. Electronic Notice and Service

(a) **In General.** This rule applies whenever these rules require or permit sending a notice or serving a document by mail or other means.

(b) **Notices from and Service by the Court.**

(1) *To Registered Users.* The clerk may send notice to or serve a registered user by filing the notice or document with the court's electronic-filing system.

(2) *To All Recipients.* For any recipient, the clerk may send notice or serve a document by electronic means that the recipient consented to in writing, including by designating an electronic address for receiving notices. But these exceptions apply:

    (A) if the recipient has registered an electronic address with the Administrative Office of the United States Courts' bankruptcy-noticing program, the clerk must use that address; and

    (B) if an entity has been designated by the Director of the Administrative Office of the United States Courts as a high-volume paper-notice recipient, the clerk may send the notice to or serve the document electronically at an address designated by the Director, unless the entity has designated an address under §342(e) or (f).

(c) **Notices from and Service by an Entity**. An entity may send notice or serve a document in the same manner that the clerk does under (b), excluding (b)(2)(A) and (B).

(d) **When Notice or Service Is Complete; Keeping an Address Current**. Electronic notice or service is complete upon filing or sending but is not effective if the filer or sender receives notice that it did not reach the person to be notified or served. The recipient must keep its electronic address current with the clerk.

(e) **Inapplicability**. This rule does not apply to any document required to be served in accordance with Rule 7004.

(Added Apr. 22, 1993, eff. Aug. 1, 1993; amended Apr. 25, 2005, eff. Dec. 1, 2005; Apr. 25, 2019, eff. Dec. 1, 2019; Apr. 14, 2021, eff. Dec. 1, 2021; Apr. 2, 2024, eff. Dec. 1, 2024.)

Rule 9037. Protecting Privacy for Filings;

(a) **Redacted Filings**. Unless the court orders otherwise, in an electronic or paper filing with the court that contains an individual's social-security number, taxpayer-identification number, or birth date, the name of an individual other than the debtor known to be and identified as a minor, or a financial-account number, a party or nonparty making the filing may include only:

    (1) the last four digits of a social-security and taxpayer-identification number;

    (2) the year of the individual's birth;

    (3) the minor's initials; and

    (4) the last four digits of the financial-account number.

(b) **Exemptions from the Redaction Requirement**. The redaction requirement does not apply to the following:

    (1) a financial-account number that identifies the property allegedly subject to forfeiture in a forfeiture proceeding;

    (2) the record of an administrative or agency proceeding, unless filed with a proof of claim;

    (3) the official record of a state-court proceeding;

    (4) the record of a court or tribunal, if that record was not subject to the redaction requirement when originally filed;

    (5) a filing covered by (c); and

    (6) a filing subject to §110.

(c) **Filings Made Under Seal**. The court may order that a filing be made under seal without redaction. The court may later unseal the filing or order the entity that made it to file a redacted version for the public record.

(d) **Protective Orders**. For cause, the court may by order in a case:

    (1) require redaction of additional information; or

    (2) limit or prohibit a nonparty's remote electronic access to a document filed with the court.

(e) **Option for Additional Unredacted Document Under Seal**. An entity filing a redacted document may also file an unredacted copy under seal. The court must retain the unredacted copy as part of the record.

(f) **Option for Filing a Reference List**. A filing that contains redacted information may be filed together with a reference list that identifies each item of redacted information and specifies an appropriate identifier that uniquely corresponds to each item listed. The list must be filed under seal and may be amended as of right. A reference in the case to a listed identifier will be construed to refer to the corresponding item of information.

(g) **Waiver of Protection of Identifiers**. An entity waives the protection of (a) for the entity's own information by filing it without redaction and not under seal.

(h) **Motion to Redact a Previously Filed Document**.

    (1) *Content; Service*. Unless the court orders otherwise, an entity seeking to redact from a previously filed document information that is protected under (a) must:

        (A) file a motion that identifies the proposed redactions;

        (B) attach to it the proposed redacted document;

        (C) include the docket number—or proof-of-claim number—of the previously filed document; and

        (D) serve the motion and attachment on:

- the debtor;
- the debtor's attorney;
- any trustee;
- the United States trustee;
- the entity that filed the unredacted document; and
- any individual whose personal identifying information is to be redacted.

    (2) *Restricting Public Access to the Unredacted Document; Docketing the Redacted Document*. Pending its ruling, the court must promptly restrict access to the motion and the unredacted document. If the court grants the motion, the clerk must docket the redacted document. The

restrictions on public access to the motion and unredacted document remain in effect until a further court order. If the court denies the motion, the restrictions must be lifted, unless the court orders otherwise.

(Added Apr. 30, 2007, eff. Dec. 1, 2007; amended Apr. 25, 2019, eff. Dec. 1, 2019; Apr. 2, 2024, eff. Dec. 1, 2024.)

Rule 9038. Bankruptcy Rules Emergency

(a) **Conditions for an Emergency.** The Judicial Conference of the United States may declare a Bankruptcy Rules emergency if it determines that extraordinary circumstances relating to public health or safety, or affecting physical or electronic access to a bankruptcy court, substantially impair the court's ability to perform its functions in compliance with these rules.

(b) **Declaring an Emergency.**
   (1) *Content.* The declaration must:
      (A) designate the bankruptcy court or courts affected;
      (B) state any restrictions on the authority granted in (c); and
      (C) be limited to a stated period of no more than 90 days.
   (2) *Early Termination.* The Judicial Conference may terminate a declaration for one or more bankruptcy courts before the termination date.
   (3) *Additional Declarations.* The Judicial Conference may issue additional declarations under this rule.

(c) **Tolling and Extending Time Limits.**
   (1) *In an Entire District or Division.* When an emergency is in effect for a bankruptcy court, the chief bankruptcy judge may, for all cases and proceedings in the district or in a division:
      (A) order the extension or tolling of a Bankruptcy Rule, local rule, or order that requires or allows a court, a clerk, a party in interest, or the United States trustee, by a specified deadline, to commence a proceeding, file or send a document, hold or conclude a hearing, or take any other action, despite any other Bankruptcy Rule, local rule, or order; or
      (B) order that, when a Bankruptcy Rule, local rule, or order requires that an action be taken "promptly," "forthwith," "immediately," or "without delay," it be taken as soon as is practicable or by a date set by the court in a specific case or proceeding.
   (2) *In a Specific Case or Proceeding.* When an emergency is in effect for a bankruptcy court, a presiding judge may take the action described in (1) in a specific case or proceeding.
   (3) *When an Extension or Tolling Ends.* A period extended or tolled under (1) or (2) terminates on the later of:

(A) the last day of the time period as extended or tolled or 30 days after the emergency declaration terminates, whichever is earlier; or

(B) the last day of the time period originally required, imposed, or allowed by the relevant Bankruptcy Rule, local rule, or order that was extended or tolled.

(4) *Further Extensions or Shortenings.* A presiding judge may lengthen or shorten an extension or tolling in a specific case or proceeding. The judge may do so only for good cause after notice and a hearing and only on the judge's own motion or on motion of a party in interest or the United States trustee.

(5) *Exception.* A time period imposed by statute may not be extended or tolled.

(Added Apr. 24, 2023, eff. Dec. 1, 2023; amended Apr. 2, 2024, eff. Dec. 1, 2024.)

United States Code
Title 28 Provisions Relating to Bankruptcy

Title 28 U.S.C. – Judiciary and Judicial Procedure

Chapter 6 – Bankruptcy Judges

§151 - Designation of bankruptcy courts

In each judicial district, the bankruptcy judges in regular active service shall constitute a unit of the district court to be known as the bankruptcy court for that district. Each bankruptcy judge, as a judicial officer of the district court, may exercise the authority conferred under this chapter with respect to any action, suit, or proceeding and may preside alone and hold a regular or special session of the court, except as otherwise provided by law or by rule or order of the district court.

§152 - Appointment of bankruptcy judges

(a)

(1) Each bankruptcy judge to be appointed for a judicial district, as provided in paragraph (2), shall be appointed by the court of appeals of the United States for the circuit in which such district is located. Such appointments shall be made after considering the recommendations of the Judicial Conference submitted pursuant to subsection (b). Each bankruptcy judge shall be appointed for a term of fourteen years, subject to the provisions of subsection (e). However, upon the expiration of the term, a bankruptcy judge may, with the approval of the judicial council of the circuit, continue to perform the duties of the office until the earlier of the date which is 180 days after the expiration of the term or the date of the appointment of a successor. Bankruptcy judges shall serve as judicial officers of the United States district court established under Article III of the Constitution.

(2) The bankruptcy judges appointed pursuant to this section shall be appointed for the several judicial districts as follows:

Districts	Judges
Alabama:	
Northern	5
Middle	2
Southern	2
Alaska	2
Arizona	7
Arkansas:	
Eastern and Western	3
California:	

Districts	Judges
Northern	9
Eastern	6
Central	21
Southern	4
Colorado	5
Connecticut	3
Delaware	1
District of Columbia	1
Florida:	
Northern	1
Middle	8
Southern	5
Georgia:	
Northern	8
Middle	3
Southern	2
Hawaii	1
Idaho	2
Illinois:	
Northern	10
Central	3
Southern	1
Indiana:	
Northern	3
Southern	4
Iowa:	
Northern	2
Southern	2
Kansas	4
Kentucky:	
Eastern	2
Western	3

Districts	Judges
Louisiana:	
Eastern	2
Middle	1
Western	3
Maine	2
Maryland	4
Massachusetts	5
Michigan:	
Eastern	4
Western	3
Minnesota	4
Mississippi:	
Northern	1
Southern	2
Missouri:	
Eastern	3
Western	3
Montana	1
Nebraska	2
Nevada	3
New Hampshire	1
New Jersey	8
New Mexico	2
New York:	
Northern	2
Southern	9
Eastern	6
Western	3
North Carolina:	
Eastern	2
Middle	2
Western	2

Districts	Judges
North Dakota	1
Ohio:	
Northern	8
Southern	7
Oklahoma:	
Northern	2
Eastern	1
Western	3
Oregon	5
Pennsylvania:	
Eastern	5
Middle	2
Western	4
Puerto Rico	2
Rhode Island	1
South Carolina	2
South Dakota	2
Tennessee:	
Eastern	3
Middle	3
Western	4
Texas:	
Northern	6
Eastern	2
Southern	6
Western	4
Utah	3
Vermont	1
Virginia:	
Eastern	5
Western	3
Washington:	

Districts	Judges
Eastern	2
Western	5
West Virginia:	
Northern	1
Southern	1
Wisconsin:	
Eastern	4
Western	2
Wyoming	1.

(1) Whenever a majority of the judges of any court of appeals cannot agree upon the appointment of a bankruptcy judge, the chief judge of such court shall make such appointment.

(2) The judges of the district courts for the territories shall serve as the bankruptcy judges for such courts. The United States court of appeals for the circuit within which such a territorial district court is located may appoint bankruptcy judges under this chapter for such district if authorized to do so by the Congress of the United States under this section.

(b)

(1) The Judicial Conference of the United States shall, from time to time, and after considering the recommendations submitted by the Director of the Administrative Office of the United States Courts after such Director has consulted with the judicial council of the circuit involved, determine the official duty stations of bankruptcy judges and places of holding court.

(2) The Judicial Conference shall, from time to time, submit recommendations to the Congress regarding the number of bankruptcy judges needed and the districts in which such judges are needed.

(3) Not later than December 31, 1994, and not later than the end of each 2-year period thereafter, the Judicial Conference of the United States shall conduct a comprehensive review of all judicial districts to assess the continuing need for the bankruptcy judges authorized by this section, and shall report to the Congress its findings and any recommendations for the elimination of any authorized position which can be eliminated when a vacancy exists by reason of resignation, retirement, removal, or death.

(c)

(1) Each bankruptcy judge may hold court at such places within the judicial district, in addition to the official duty station of such judge, as the business of the court may require.

(2)

    (A) Bankruptcy judges may hold court at such places within the United States outside the judicial district as the nature of the business of the court may require, and upon such notice as the court orders, upon a finding by either the chief judge of the bankruptcy court (or, if the chief judge is unavailable, the most senior available bankruptcy judge) or by the judicial council of the circuit that, because of emergency conditions, no location within the district is reasonably available where the bankruptcy judges could hold court.

    (B) Bankruptcy judges may transact any business at special sessions of court held outside the district pursuant to this paragraph that might be transacted at a regular session.

    (C) If a bankruptcy court issues an order exercising its authority under subparagraph (A), the court—

        (i) through the Administrative Office of the United States Courts, shall—

            (I) send notice of such order, including the reasons for the issuance of such order, to the Committee on the Judiciary of the Senate and the Committee on the Judiciary of the House of Representatives; and

            (II) not later than 180 days after the expiration of such court order submit a brief report to the Committee on the Judiciary of the Senate and the Committee on the Judiciary of the House of Representatives describing the impact of such order, including—

                (aa) the reasons for the issuance of such order;

                (bb) the duration of such order;

                (cc) the impact of such order on litigants; and

                (dd) the costs to the judiciary resulting from such order; and

        (ii) shall provide reasonable notice to the United States Marshals Service before the commencement of any special session held pursuant to such order.

(d) With the approval of the Judicial Conference and of each of the judicial councils involved, a bankruptcy judge may be designated to serve in any district adjacent to or near the district for which such bankruptcy judge was appointed.

(e) A bankruptcy judge may be removed during the term for which such bankruptcy judge is appointed, only for incompetence, misconduct, neglect of duty, or physical or mental disability and only by the judicial council of the circuit in which the judge's official duty station is located. Removal may not occur unless a majority of all of the judges of such council concur in the order of removal. Before any order of removal may be entered, a full specification of charges shall be furnished to such bankruptcy judge who shall be accorded an opportunity to be heard on such charges.

§153 - Salaries; character of service

(a) Each bankruptcy judge shall serve on a full-time basis and shall receive as full compensation for his services, a salary at an annual rate that is equal to 92 percent of the salary of a judge of the district court of the United States as determined pursuant to section 135, to be paid at such times as the Judicial Conference of the United States determines.

(b) A bankruptcy judge may not engage in the practice of law and may not engage in any other practice, business, occupation, or employment inconsistent with the expeditious, proper, and impartial performance of such bankruptcy judge's duties as a judicial officer. The Conference may promulgate appropriate rules and regulations to implement this subsection.

(c) Each individual appointed under this chapter shall take the oath or affirmation prescribed by section 453 of this title before performing the duties of the office of bankruptcy judge.

(d) A bankruptcy judge appointed under this chapter shall be exempt from the provisions of subchapter I of chapter 63 of title 5.

§154 - Division of businesses; chief judge

(a) Each bankruptcy court for a district having more than one bankruptcy judge shall by majority vote promulgate rules for the division of business among the bankruptcy judges to the extent that the division of business is not otherwise provided for by the rules of the district court.

(b) In each district court having more than one bankruptcy judge the district court shall designate one judge to serve as chief judge of such bankruptcy court. Whenever a majority of the judges of such district court cannot agree upon the designation as chief judge, the chief judge of such district court shall make such designation. The chief judge of the bankruptcy court shall ensure that the rules of the bankruptcy court and of the district court are observed and that the business of the bankruptcy court is handled effectively and expeditiously.

§155 - Temporary transfer of bankruptcy judges

(a) A bankruptcy judge may be transferred to serve temporarily as a bankruptcy judge in any judicial district other than the judicial district for which such bankruptcy judge was appointed upon the approval of the judicial council of each of the circuits involved.

(b) A bankruptcy judge who has retired may, upon consent, be recalled to serve as a bankruptcy judge in any judicial district by the judicial council of the circuit within which such district is located. Upon recall, a bankruptcy judge may receive a salary for such service in accordance with regulations promulgated by the Judicial Conference of the United States, subject to the restrictions on the payment of an annuity in section 377 of this title or in subchapter III of chapter 83, and chapter 84, of title 5 which are applicable to such judge.

§156 - Staff; expenses

(a) Each bankruptcy judge may appoint a secretary, a law clerk, and such additional assistants as the Director of the Administrative Office of the United States Courts determines to be necessary. A law clerk appointed under this section shall be exempt from the provisions of subchapter I of chapter 63 of title 5, unless specifically included by the appointing judge or by local rule of court.

(b) Upon certification to the judicial council of the circuit involved and to the Director of the Administrative Office of the United States Courts that the number of cases and proceedings pending within the jurisdiction under section 1334 of this title within a judicial district so warrants, the bankruptcy judges for such district may appoint an individual to serve as clerk of such bankruptcy court. The clerk may appoint, with the approval of such bankruptcy judges, and in such number as may be approved by the Director, necessary deputies, and may remove such deputies with the approval of such bankruptcy judges.

(c) Any court may utilize facilities or services, either on or off the court's premises, which pertain to the provision of notices, dockets, calendars, and other administrative information to parties in cases filed under the provisions of title 11, United States Code, where the costs of such facilities or services are paid for out of the assets of the estate and are not charged to the United States. The utilization of such facilities or services shall be subject to such conditions and limitations as the pertinent circuit council may prescribe.

(d) No office of the bankruptcy clerk of court may be consolidated with the district clerk of court office without the prior approval of the Judicial Conference and the Congress.

(e) In a judicial district where a bankruptcy clerk has been appointed pursuant to subsection (b), the bankruptcy clerk shall be the official custodian of the records and dockets of the bankruptcy court.

(f) For purposes of financial accountability in a district where a bankruptcy clerk has been certified, such clerk shall be accountable for and pay into the Treasury all fees, costs, and other monies collected by such clerk except uncollected fees not required by an Act of Congress to be prepaid. Such clerk shall make returns thereof to the Director of the Administrative Office of the United States Courts and the Director of the Executive Office For United States Trustees, under regulations prescribed by such Directors.

§157 – Procedures

(a) Each district court may provide that any or all cases under title 11 and any or all proceedings arising under title 11 or arising in or related to a case under title 11 shall be referred to the bankruptcy judges for the district.

(b)

(1) Bankruptcy judges may hear and determine all cases under title 11 and all core proceedings arising under title 11, or arising in a case under title 11, referred under subsection (a) of this section, and may enter appropriate orders and judgments, subject to review under section 158 of this title.

(2) Core proceedings include, but are not limited to—

    (A) matters concerning the administration of the estate;

    (B) allowance or disallowance of claims against the estate or exemptions from property of the estate, and estimation of claims or interests for the purposes of confirming a plan under chapter 11, 12, or 13 of title 11but not the liquidation or estimation of contingent or unliquidated personal injury tort or wrongful death claims against the estate for purposes of distribution in a case under title 11;

    (C) counterclaims by the estate against persons filing claims against the estate;

    (D) orders in respect to obtaining credit;

    (E) orders to turn over property of the estate;

    (F) proceedings to determine, avoid, or recover preferences;

    (G) motions to terminate, annul, or modify the automatic stay;

    (H) proceedings to determine, avoid, or recover fraudulent conveyances;

    (I) determinations as to the dischargeability of particular debts;

    (J) objections to discharges;

    (K) determinations of the validity, extent, or priority of liens;

    (L) confirmations of plans;

    (M) orders approving the use or lease of property, including the use of cash collateral;

    (N) orders approving the sale of property other than property resulting from claims brought by the estate against persons who have not filed claims against the estate;

    (O) other proceedings affecting the liquidation of the assets of the estate or the adjustment of the debtor-creditor or the equity security holder relationship, except personal injury tort or wrongful death claims; and

    (P) recognition of foreign proceedings and other matters under chapter 15 of title 11.

(3) The bankruptcy judge shall determine, on the judge's own motion or on timely motion of a party, whether a proceeding is a core proceeding under this subsection or is a proceeding that is otherwise related to a case under title 11. A determination that a proceeding is not a core proceeding shall not be made solely on the basis that its resolution may be affected by State law.

(4) Non-core proceedings under section 157(b)(2)(B) of title 28, United States Code, shall not be subject to the mandatory abstention provisions of section 1334(c)(2).

(5) The district court shall order that personal injury tort and wrongful death claims shall be tried in the district court in which the bankruptcy case is pending, or in the district court in the district in which the claim arose, as determined by the district court in which the bankruptcy case is pending.

(c)

(1) A bankruptcy judge may hear a proceeding that is not a core proceeding but that is otherwise related to a case under title 11. In such proceeding, the bankruptcy judge shall submit proposed findings of fact and conclusions of law to the district court, and any final order or judgment shall be entered by the district judge after considering the bankruptcy judge's proposed findings and conclusions and after reviewing de novo those matters to which any party has timely and specifically objected.

(2) Notwithstanding the provisions of paragraph (1) of this subsection, the district court, with the consent of all the parties to the proceeding, may refer a proceeding related to a case under title 11 to a bankruptcy judge to hear and determine and to enter appropriate orders and judgments, subject to review under section 158 of this title.

(d) The district court may withdraw, in whole or in part, any case or proceeding referred under this section, on its own motion or on timely motion of any party, for cause shown. The district court shall, on timely motion of a party, so withdraw a proceeding if the court determines that resolution of the proceeding requires consideration of both title 11 and other laws of the United States regulating organizations or activities affecting interstate commerce.

(e) If the right to a jury trial applies in a proceeding that may be heard under this section by a bankruptcy judge, the bankruptcy judge may conduct the jury trial if specially designated to exercise such jurisdiction by the district court and with the express consent of all the parties.

§158 – Appeals

(a) The district courts of the United States shall have jurisdiction to hear appeals

(1) from final judgments, orders, and decrees;

(2) from interlocutory orders and decrees issued under section 1121(d) of title 11 increasing or reducing the time periods referred to in section 1121 of such title; and

(3) with leave of the court, from other interlocutory orders and decrees; and, with leave of the court, from interlocutory orders and decrees, of bankruptcy judges entered in cases and proceedings referred to the bankruptcy judges under section 157 of this title. An appeal under this subsection shall be taken only to the district court for the judicial district in which the bankruptcy judge is serving.

(b)

(1) The judicial council of a circuit shall establish a bankruptcy appellate panel service composed of bankruptcy judges of the districts in the circuit who are appointed by the judicial council in accordance with paragraph (3), to hear and determine, with the consent of all the parties, appeals under subsection (a) unless the judicial council finds that—
   (A) there are insufficient judicial resources available in the circuit; or
   (B) establishment of such service would result in undue delay or increased cost to parties in cases under title 11.
   Not later than 90 days after making the finding, the judicial council shall submit to the Judicial Conference of the United States a report containing the factual basis of such finding.

(2)
   (A) A judicial council may reconsider, at any time, the finding described in paragraph (1).
   (B) On the request of a majority of the district judges in a circuit for which a bankruptcy appellate panel service is established under paragraph (1), made after the expiration of the 1-year period beginning on the date such service is established, the judicial council of the circuit shall determine whether a circumstance specified in subparagraph (A) or (B) of such paragraph exists.
   (C) On its own motion, after the expiration of the 3-year period beginning on the date a bankruptcy appellate panel service is established under paragraph (1), the judicial council of the circuit may determine whether a circumstance specified in subparagraph (A) or (B) of such paragraph exists.
   (D) If the judicial council finds that either of such circumstances exists, the judicial council may provide for the completion of the appeals then pending before such service and the orderly termination of such service.

(3) Bankruptcy judges appointed under paragraph (1) shall be appointed and may be reappointed under such paragraph.

(4) If authorized by the Judicial Conference of the United States, the judicial councils of 2 or more circuits may establish a joint bankruptcy appellate panel comprised of bankruptcy judges from the districts within the circuits for which such panel is established, to hear and determine, upon the consent of all the parties, appeals under subsection (a) of this section.

(5) An appeal to be heard under this subsection shall be heard by a panel of 3 members of the bankruptcy appellate panel service, except that a member of such service may not hear an appeal originating in the district for which such member is appointed or designated under section 152 of this title.

(6) Appeals may not be heard under this subsection by a panel of the bankruptcy appellate panel service unless the district judges for the district in which the appeals occur, by majority vote, have authorized such service to hear and determine appeals originating in such district.

(c)

    (1) Subject to subsections (b) and (d)(2), each appeal under subsection (a) shall be heard by a 3-judge panel of the bankruptcy appellate panel service established under subsection (b)(1) unless—

        (A) the appellant elects at the time of filing the appeal; or

        (B) any other party elects, not later than 30 days after service of notice of the appeal;

    to have such appeal heard by the district court.

    (2) An appeal under subsections (a) and (b) of this section shall be taken in the same manner as appeals in civil proceedings generally are taken to the courts of appeals from the district courts and in the time provided by Rule 8002 of the Bankruptcy Rules.

(d)

    (1) The courts of appeals shall have jurisdiction of appeals from all final decisions, judgments, orders, and decrees entered under subsections (a) and (b) of this section.

    (2)

        (A) The appropriate court of appeals shall have jurisdiction of appeals described in the first sentence of subsection (a) if the bankruptcy court, the district court, or the bankruptcy appellate panel involved, acting on its own motion or on the request of a party to the judgment, order, or decree described in such first sentence, or all the appellants and appellees (if any) acting jointly, certify that—

            (i) the judgment, order, or decree involves a question of law as to which there is no controlling decision of the court of appeals for the circuit or of the Supreme Court of the United States, or involves a matter of public importance;

            (ii) the judgment, order, or decree involves a question of law requiring resolution of conflicting decisions; or

            (iii) an immediate appeal from the judgment, order, or decree may materially advance the progress of the case or proceeding in which the appeal is taken;

        and if the court of appeals authorizes the direct appeal of the judgment, order, or decree.

        (B) If the bankruptcy court, the district court, or the bankruptcy appellate panel—

            (i) on its own motion or on the request of a party, determines that a circumstance specified in clause (i), (ii), or (iii) of subparagraph (A) exists; or

            (ii) receives a request made by a majority of the appellants and a majority of appellees (if any) to make the certification described in subparagraph (A);

        then the bankruptcy court, the district court, or the bankruptcy appellate panel shall make the certification described in subparagraph (A).

(C) The parties may supplement the certification with a short statement of the basis for the certification.

(D) An appeal under this paragraph does not stay any proceeding of the bankruptcy court, the district court, or the bankruptcy appellate panel from which the appeal is taken, unless the respective bankruptcy court, district court, or bankruptcy appellate panel, or the court of appeals in which the appeal is pending, issues a stay of such proceeding pending the appeal.

(E) Any request under subparagraph (B) for certification shall be made not later than 60 days after the entry of the judgment, order, or decree.

§159 - Bankruptcy statistics

(a) The clerk of the district court, or the clerk of the bankruptcy court if one is certified pursuant to section 156(b) of this title, shall collect statistics regarding debtors who are individuals with primarily consumer debts seeking relief under chapters 7, 11, and 13 of title 11. Those statistics shall be in a standardized format prescribed by the Director of the Administrative Office of the United States Courts (referred to in this section as the "Director").

(b) The Director shall—
   (1) compile the statistics referred to in subsection (a);
   (2) make the statistics available to the public; and
   (3) not later than July 1, 2008, and annually thereafter, prepare, and submit to Congress a report concerning the information collected under subsection (a) that contains an analysis of the information.

(c) The compilation required under subsection (b) shall—
   (1) be itemized, by chapter, with respect to title 11;
   (2) be presented in the aggregate and for each district; and
   (3) include information concerning—
      (A) the total assets and total liabilities of the debtors described in subsection (a), and in each category of assets and liabilities, as reported in the schedules prescribed pursuant to section 2075 of this title and filed by debtors;
      (B) the current monthly income, average income, and average expenses of debtors as reported on the schedules and statements that each such debtor files under sections 521 and 1322 of title 11;
      (C) the aggregate amount of debt discharged in cases filed during the reporting period, determined as the difference between the total amount of debt and obligations of a debtor reported on the schedules and the amount of such debt reported in categories which are predominantly nondischargeable;
      (D) the average period of time between the date of the filing of the petition and the closing of the case for cases closed during the reporting period;
      (E) for cases closed during the reporting period—

> (i) the number of cases in which a reaffirmation agreement was filed; and
> (ii)
>> (I) the total number of reaffirmation agreements filed;
>> (II) of those cases in which a reaffirmation agreement was filed, the number of cases in which the debtor was not represented by an attorney; and
>> (III) of those cases in which a reaffirmation agreement was filed, the number of cases in which the reaffirmation agreement was approved by the court;

(F) with respect to cases filed under chapter 13 of title 11, for the reporting period—
> (i)
>> (I) the number of cases in which a final order was entered determining the value of property securing a claim in an amount less than the amount of the claim; and
>> (II) the number of final orders entered determining the value of property securing a claim;
> (ii) the number of cases dismissed, the number of cases dismissed for failure to make payments under the plan, the number of cases refiled after dismissal, and the number of cases in which the plan was completed, separately itemized with respect to the number of modifications made before completion of the plan, if any; and
> (iii) the number of cases in which the debtor filed another case during the 6-year period preceding the filing;

(G) the number of cases in which creditors were fined for misconduct and any amount of punitive damages awarded by the court for creditor misconduct; and

(H) the number of cases in which sanctions under rule 9011 of the Federal Rules of Bankruptcy Procedure were imposed against the debtor's attorney or damages awarded under such Rule.

Chapter 39 – United States Trustees

§581 - United States trustees

(a) The Attorney General shall appoint one United States trustee for each of the following regions composed of Federal judicial districts (without regard to section 451):
  (1) The judicial districts established for the States of Maine, Massachusetts, New Hampshire, and Rhode Island.
  (2) The judicial districts established for the States of Connecticut, New York, and Vermont.
  (3) The judicial districts established for the States of Delaware, New Jersey, and Pennsylvania.

(4) The judicial districts established for the States of Maryland, North Carolina, South Carolina, Virginia, and West Virginia and for the District of Columbia.

(5) The judicial districts established for the States of Louisiana and Mississippi.

(6) The Northern District of Texas and the Eastern District of Texas.

(7) The Southern District of Texas and the Western District of Texas.

(8) The judicial districts established for the States of Kentucky and Tennessee.

(9) The judicial districts established for the States of Michigan and Ohio.

(10) The Central District of Illinois and the Southern District of Illinois; and the judicial districts established for the State of Indiana.

(11) The Northern District of Illinois; and the judicial districts established for the State of Wisconsin.

(12) The judicial districts established for the States of Minnesota, Iowa, North Dakota, and South Dakota.

(13) The judicial districts established for the States of Arkansas, Nebraska, and Missouri.

(14) The District of Arizona.

(15) The Southern District of California; and the judicial districts established for the State of Hawaii, and for Guam and the Commonwealth of the Northern Mariana Islands.

(16) The Central District of California.

(17) The Eastern District of California and the Northern District of California; and the judicial district established for the State of Nevada.

(18) The judicial districts established for the States of Alaska, Idaho (exclusive of Yellowstone National Park), Montana (exclusive of Yellowstone National Park), Oregon, and Washington.

(19) The judicial districts established for the States of Colorado, Utah, and Wyoming (including those portions of Yellowstone National Park situated in the States of Montana and Idaho).

(20) The judicial districts established for the States of Kansas, New Mexico, and Oklahoma.

(21) The judicial districts established for the States of Alabama, Florida, and Georgia and for the Commonwealth of Puerto Rico and the Virgin Islands of the United States.

(b) Each United States trustee shall be appointed for a term of five years. On the expiration of his term, a United States trustee shall continue to perform the duties of his office until his successor is appointed and qualifies.

(c) Each United States trustee is subject to removal by the Attorney General.

§582 - Assistant United States trustees

(a) The Attorney General may appoint one or more assistant United States trustees in any region when the public interest so requires.

(b) Each assistant United States trustee is subject to removal by the Attorney General.

§583 - Oath of office

Each United States trustee and assistant United States trustee, before taking office, shall take an oath to execute faithfully his duties.

§584 - Official stations

The Attorney General may determine the official stations of the United States trustees and assistant United States trustees within the regions for which they were appointed.

§585 – Vacancies

(a) The Attorney General may appoint an acting United States trustee for a region in which the office of the United States trustee is vacant. The individual so appointed may serve until the date on which the vacancy is filled by appointment under section 581 of this title or by designation under subsection (b) of this section.

(b) The Attorney General may designate a United States trustee to serve in not more than two regions for such time as the public interest requires.

§586 - Duties; supervision by Attorney General

(a) Each United States trustee, within the region for which such United States trustee is appointed, shall—

(1) establish, maintain, and supervise a panel of private trustees that are eligible and available to serve as trustees in cases under chapter 7 of title 11;

(2) serve as and perform the duties of a trustee in a case under title 11 when required under title 11 to serve as trustee in such a case;

(3) supervise the administration of cases and trustees in cases under chapter 7, 11 (including subchapter V of chapter 11), 12, 13, or 15 of title 11 by, whenever the United States trustee considers it to be appropriate—

(A)

(i) reviewing, in accordance with procedural guidelines adopted by the Executive Office of the United States Trustee (which guidelines shall be applied uniformly by the United States trustee except when circumstances warrant different treatment), applications filed for compensation and reimbursement under section 330 of title 11; and

(ii) filing with the court comments with respect to such application and, if the United States Trustee considers it to be appropriate, objections to such application;

(B) monitoring plans and disclosure statements filed in cases under chapter 11 of title 11 and filing with the court, in connection with hearings under sections 1125 and 1128 of such title, comments with respect to such plans and disclosure statements;

(C) monitoring plans filed under chapters 12 and 13 of title 11 and filing with the court, in connection with hearings under sections 1224, 1229, 1324, and 1329 of such title, comments with respect to such plans;

(D) taking such action as the United States trustee deems to be appropriate to ensure that all reports, schedules, and fees required to be filed under title 11 and this title by the debtor are properly and timely filed;

(E) monitoring creditors' committees appointed under title 11;

(F) notifying the appropriate United States attorney of matters which relate to the occurrence of any action which may constitute a crime under the laws of the United States and, on the request of the United States attorney, assisting the United States attorney in carrying out prosecutions based on such action;

(G) monitoring the progress of cases under title 11 and taking such actions as the United States trustee deems to be appropriate to prevent undue delay in such progress;

(H) in small business cases (as defined in section 101 of title 11), performing the additional duties specified in title 11 pertaining to such cases; and

(I) monitoring applications filed under section 327 of title 11 and, whenever the United States trustee deems it to be appropriate, filing with the court comments with respect to the approval of such applications;

(4) deposit or invest under section 345 of title 11 money received as trustee in cases under title 11;

(5) perform the duties prescribed for the United States trustee under title 11 and this title, and such duties consistent with title 11 and this title as the Attorney General may prescribe;

(6) make such reports as the Attorney General directs, including the results of audits performed under section 603(a) of the Bankruptcy Abuse Prevention and Consumer Protection Act of 2005;

(7) in each of such small business cases—

(A) conduct an initial debtor interview as soon as practicable after the date of the order for relief but before the first meeting scheduled under section 341(a) of title 11, at which time the United States trustee shall—

(i) begin to investigate the debtor's viability;

(ii) inquire about the debtor's business plan;

(iii) explain the debtor's obligations to file monthly operating reports and other required reports;

(iv) attempt to develop an agreed scheduling order; and

(v) inform the debtor of other obligations;

(B) if determined to be appropriate and advisable, visit the appropriate business premises of the debtor, ascertain the state of the debtor's books and records, and verify that the debtor has filed its tax returns; and

(C) review and monitor diligently the debtor's activities, to determine as promptly as possible whether the debtor will be unable to confirm a plan; and

(8) in any case in which the United States trustee finds material grounds for any relief under section 1112 of title 11, apply promptly after making that finding to the court for relief.

(b) If the number of cases under subchapter V of chapter 11 or chapter 12 or 13 of title 11 commenced in a particular region so warrants, the United States trustee for such region may, subject to the approval of the Attorney General, appoint one or more individuals to serve as standing trustee, or designate one or more assistant United States trustees to serve in cases under such chapter. The United States trustee for such region shall supervise any such individual appointed as standing trustee in the performance of the duties of standing trustee.

(c) Each United States trustee shall be under the general supervision of the Attorney General, who shall provide general coordination and assistance to the United States trustees.

(d)

(1) The Attorney General shall prescribe by rule qualifications for membership on the panels established by United States trustees under paragraph (a)(1) of this section, and qualifications for appointment under subsection (b) of this section to serve as standing trustee in cases under subchapter V of chapter 11 or chapter 12 or 13 of title 11. The Attorney General may not require that an individual be an attorney in order to qualify for appointment under subsection (b) of this section to serve as standing trustee in cases under subchapter V of chapter 11 or chapter 12 or 13 of title 11.

(2) A trustee whose appointment under subsection (a)(1) or under subsection (b) is terminated or who ceases to be assigned to cases filed under title 11, United States Code, may obtain judicial review of the final agency decision by commencing an action in the district court of the United States for the district for which the panel to which the trustee is appointed under subsection (a)(1), or in the district court of the United States for the district in which the trustee is appointed under subsection (b) resides, after first exhausting all available administrative remedies, which if the trustee so elects, shall also include an administrative hearing on the record. Unless the trustee elects to have an administrative hearing on the record, the trustee shall be deemed to have exhausted all administrative remedies for purposes of this paragraph if the agency fails to make a final agency decision within 90 days after the trustee requests administrative remedies. The Attorney General shall prescribe procedures to implement this paragraph. The decision of the agency shall be affirmed by the district court unless it is

unreasonable and without cause based on the administrative record before the agency.

(e)

(1) The Attorney General, after consultation with a United States trustee that has appointed an individual under subsection (b) of this section to serve as standing trustee in cases under subchapter V of chapter 11 or chapter 12 or 13 of title 11, shall fix—

(A) a maximum annual compensation for such individual consisting of—

(i) an amount not to exceed the highest annual rate of basic pay in effect for level V of the Executive Schedule; and

(ii) the cash value of employment benefits comparable to the employment benefits provided by the United States to individuals who are employed by the United States at the same rate of basic pay to perform similar services during the same period of time; and

(B) a percentage fee not to exceed—

(i) in the case of a debtor who is not a family farmer, ten percent; or

(ii) in the case of a debtor who is a family farmer, the sum of—

(I) not to exceed ten percent of the payments made under the plan of such debtor, with respect to payments in an aggregate amount not to exceed $450,000; and

(II) three percent of payments made under the plan of such debtor, with respect to payments made after the aggregate amount of payments made under the plan exceeds $450,000;

based on such maximum annual compensation and the actual, necessary expenses incurred by such individual as standing trustee.

(2) Such individual shall collect such percentage fee from all payments received by such individual under plans in the cases under subchapter V of chapter 11 or chapter 12 or 13 of title 11 for which such individual serves as standing trustee. Such individual shall pay to the United States trustee, and the United States trustee shall deposit in the United States Trustee System Fund—

(A) any amount by which the actual compensation of such individual exceeds 5 per centum upon all payments received under plans in cases under subchapter V of chapter 11 or chapter 12 or 13 of title 11 for which such individual serves as standing trustee; and

(B) any amount by which the percentage for all such cases exceeds—

(i) such individual's actual compensation for such cases, as adjusted under subparagraph (A) of paragraph (1); plus

(ii) the actual, necessary expenses incurred by such individual as standing trustee in such cases. Subject to the approval of the Attorney General, any or all of the interest earned from the deposit of payments under plans by such individual may be utilized to pay actual, necessary expenses without regard to the percentage limitation contained in subparagraph (d)(1)(B) of this section.

(3) After first exhausting all available administrative remedies, an individual appointed under subsection (b) may obtain judicial review of final agency action to deny a claim of actual, necessary expenses under this subsection by commencing an action in the district court of the United States for the district where the individual resides. The decision of the agency shall be affirmed by the district court unless it is unreasonable and without cause based upon the administrative record before the agency.

(4) The Attorney General shall prescribe procedures to implement this subsection.

(5) In the event that the services of the trustee in a case under subchapter V of chapter 11 of title 11 are terminated by dismissal or conversion of the case, or upon substantial consummation of a plan under section 1183(c)(1) of that title, the court shall award compensation to the trustee consistent with services performed by the trustee and the limits on the compensation of the trustee established pursuant to paragraph (1) of this subsection.

(f)

(1) The United States trustee for each district is authorized to contract with auditors to perform audits in cases designated by the United States trustee, in accordance with the procedures established under section 603(a) of the Bankruptcy Abuse Prevention and Consumer Protection Act of 2005.

(2)

(A) The report of each audit referred to in paragraph (1) shall be filed with the court and transmitted to the United States trustee. Each report shall clearly and conspicuously specify any material misstatement of income or expenditures or of assets identified by the person performing the audit. In any case in which a material misstatement of income or expenditures or of assets has been reported, the clerk of the district court (or the clerk of the bankruptcy court if one is certified under section 156(b) of this title) shall give notice of the misstatement to the creditors in the case.

(B) If a material misstatement of income or expenditures or of assets is reported, the United States trustee shall—

    (i) report the material misstatement, if appropriate, to the United States Attorney pursuant to section 3057 of title 18; and

    (ii) if advisable, take appropriate action, including but not limited to commencing an adversary proceeding to revoke the debtor's discharge pursuant to section 727(d) of title 11.

§587 – Salaries
Subject to sections 5315 through 5317 of title 5, the Attorney General shall fix the annual salaries of United States trustees and assistant United States trustees at rates of compensation not in excess of the rate of basic compensation provided for Executive Level IV of the Executive Schedule set forth in section 5315 of title 5, United States Code.

§588 – Expenses
Necessary office expenses of the United States trustee shall be allowed when authorized by the Attorney General.

§589 - Staff and other employees
The United States trustee may employ staff and other employees on approval of the Attorney General.

§589a - United States Trustee System Fund
(a) There is hereby established in the Treasury of the United States a special fund to be known as the "United States Trustee System Fund" (hereinafter in this section referred to as the "Fund"). Monies in the Fund shall be available to the Attorney General without fiscal year limitation in such amounts as may be specified in appropriations Acts for the following purposes in connection with the operations of United States trustees—
  (1) salaries and related employee benefits;
  (2) travel and transportation;
  (3) rental of space;
  (4) communication, utilities, and miscellaneous computer charges;
  (5) security investigations and audits;
  (6) supplies, books, and other materials for legal research;
  (7) furniture and equipment;
  (8) miscellaneous services, including those obtained by contract; and
  (9) printing.
(b) For the purpose of recovering the cost of services of the United States Trustee System, there shall be deposited as offsetting collections to the appropriation "United States Trustee System Fund", to remain available until expended, the following—
  (1)
    (A) 40.46 percent of the fees collected under section 1930(a)(1)(A); and
    (B) 28.33 percent of the fees collected under section 1930(a)(1)(B);
  (2) 48.89 percent of the fees collected under section 1930(a)(3) of this title;
  (3) one-half of the fees collected under section 1930(a)(4) of this title;
  (4) one-half of the fees collected under section 1930(a)(5) of this title;
  (5) 100 percent of the fees collected under section 1930(a)(6) of this title;
  (6) three-fourths of the fees collected under the last sentence of section 1930(a) of this title;

(7) the compensation of trustees received under section 330(d) of title 11 by the clerks of the bankruptcy courts;

(8) excess fees collected under section 586(e)(2) of this title;

(9) interest earned on Fund investment; and

(10) fines imposed under section 110(l) of title 11, United States Code.

(c) Amounts in the Fund which are not currently needed for the purposes specified in subsection (a) shall be kept on deposit or invested in obligations of, or guaranteed by, the United States.

(d) The Attorney General shall transmit to the Congress, not later than 120 days after the end of each fiscal year, a detailed report on the amounts deposited in the Fund and a description of expenditures made under this section.

(e) There are authorized to be appropriated to the Fund for any fiscal year such sums as may be necessary to supplement amounts deposited under subsection (b) for the purposes specified in subsection (a).

§589b - Bankruptcy data

(a) Rules.—The Attorney General shall, within a reasonable time after the effective date of this section, issue rules requiring uniform forms for (and from time to time thereafter to appropriately modify and approve)—

(1) final reports by trustees in cases under subchapter V of chapter 11 and chapters 7, 12, and 13 of title 11; and

(2) periodic reports by debtors in possession or trustees in cases under chapter 11 of title 11.

(b) Reports.—Each report referred to in subsection (a) shall be designed (and the requirements as to place and manner of filing shall be established) so as to facilitate compilation of data and maximum possible access of the public, both by physical inspection at one or more central filing locations, and by electronic access through the Internet or other appropriate media.

(c) Required Information.—The information required to be filed in the reports referred to in subsection (b) shall be that which is in the best interests of debtors and creditors, and in the public interest in reasonable and adequate information to evaluate the efficiency and practicality of the Federal bankruptcy system. In issuing rules proposing the forms referred to in subsection (a), the Attorney General shall strike the best achievable practical balance between—

(1) the reasonable needs of the public for information about the operational results of the Federal bankruptcy system;

(2) economy, simplicity, and lack of undue burden on persons with a duty to file reports; and

(3) appropriate privacy concerns and safeguards.

(d) Final Reports.—The uniform forms for final reports required under subsection (a) for use by trustees under subchapter V of chapter 11 and chapters 7, 12, and 13 of title 11 shall, in addition to such other matters as are required by law or as the Attorney General in the discretion of the Attorney General shall propose, include with respect to a case under such title—

(1) information about the length of time the case was pending;

(2) assets abandoned;

(3) assets exempted;

(4) receipts and disbursements of the estate;

(5) expenses of administration, including for use under section 707(b), actual costs of administering cases under chapter 13 of title 11;

(6) claims asserted;

(7) claims allowed; and

(8) distributions to claimants and claims discharged without payment,

in each case by appropriate category and, in cases under subchapter V of chapter 11 and chapters 12 and 13 of title 11, date of confirmation of the plan, each modification thereto, and defaults by the debtor in performance under the plan.

(e) Periodic Reports.—The uniform forms for periodic reports required under subsection (a) for use by trustees or debtors in possession under chapter 11 of title 11 shall, in addition to such other matters as are required by law or as the Attorney General in the discretion of the Attorney General shall propose, include—

(1) information about the industry classification, published by the Department of Commerce, for the businesses conducted by the debtor;

(2) length of time the case has been pending;

(3) number of full-time employees as of the date of the order for relief and at the end of each reporting period since the case was filed;

(4) cash receipts, cash disbursements and profitability of the debtor for the most recent period and cumulatively since the date of the order for relief;

(5) compliance with title 11, whether or not tax returns and tax payments since the date of the order for relief have been timely filed and made;

(6) all professional fees approved by the court in the case for the most recent period and cumulatively since the date of the order for relief (separately reported, for the professional fees incurred by or on behalf of the debtor, between those that would have been incurred absent a bankruptcy case and those not); and

(7) plans of reorganization filed and confirmed and, with respect thereto, by class, the recoveries of the holders, expressed in aggregate dollar values and, in the case of claims, as a percentage of total claims of the class allowed.

Chapter 57 – General Provisions Applicable to Court Officers and Employees (Excerpt)

§959 - Trustees and receivers suable; management; State laws

(a) Trustees, receivers or managers of any property, including debtors in possession, may be sued, without leave of the court appointing them, with respect to any of their acts or transactions in carrying on business connected with such property. Such actions shall be subject to the general equity power of such court so far as the same may be necessary to the ends of justice, but this shall not deprive a litigant of his right to trial by jury.

(b) Except as provided in section 1166 of title 11, a trustee, receiver or manager appointed in any cause pending in any court of the United States, including a debtor in possession, shall manage and operate the property in his possession as such trustee, receiver or manager according to the requirements of the valid laws of the State in which such property is situated, in the same manner that the owner or possessor thereof would be bound to do if in possession thereof.

Chapter 85 – District Courts; Jurisdiction (Excerpt)

§1334. Bankruptcy cases and proceedings

(a) Except as provided in subsection (b) of this section, the district courts shall have original and exclusive jurisdiction of all cases under title 11.

(b) Except as provided in subsection (e)(2), and notwithstanding any Act of Congress that confers exclusive jurisdiction on a court or courts other than the district courts, the district courts shall have original but not exclusive jurisdiction of all civil proceedings arising under title 11, or arising in or related to cases under title 11.

(c)

    (1) Except with respect to a case under chapter 15 of title 11, nothing in this section prevents a district court in the interest of justice, or in the interest of comity with State courts or respect for State law, from abstaining from hearing a particular proceeding arising under title 11 or arising in or related to a case under title 11.

    (2) Upon timely motion of a party in a proceeding based upon a State law claim or State law cause of action, related to a case under title 11 but not arising under title 11 or arising in a case under title 11, with respect to which an action could not have been commenced in a court of the United States absent jurisdiction under this section, the district court shall abstain from hearing such proceeding if an action is commenced, and can be timely adjudicated, in a State forum of appropriate jurisdiction.

(d) Any decision to abstain or not to abstain made under subsection (c) (other than a decision not to abstain in a proceeding described in subsection (c)(2)) is not reviewable by appeal or otherwise by the court of appeals under section 158(d), 1291, or 1292 of this title or by the Supreme Court of the United States under section 1254 of this title. Subsection (c) and this subsection shall not be construed to limit the applicability of the stay provided for by section 362 of title 11, United States Code, as such section applies to an action affecting the property of the estate in bankruptcy.

(e) The district court in which a case under title 11 is commenced or is pending shall have exclusive jurisdiction—

    (1) of all the property, wherever located, of the debtor as of the commencement of such case, and of property of the estate; and

(2) over all claims or causes of action that involve construction of section 327 of title 11, United States Code, or rules relating to disclosure requirements under section 327.

Chapter 87 – District Courts; Venue (Excerpt)

§1408 - Venue of cases under title 11

Except as provided in section 1410 of this title, a case under title 11 may be commenced in the district court for the district—

(1) in which the domicile, residence, principal place of business in the United States, or principal assets in the United States, of the person or entity that is the subject of such case have been located for the one hundred and eighty days immediately preceding such commencement, or for a longer portion of such one-hundred-and-eighty-day period than the domicile, residence, or principal place of business, in the United States, or principal assets in the United States, of such person were located in any other district; or

(2) in which there is pending a case under title 11 concerning such person's affiliate, general partner, or partnership.

§1409 - Venue of proceedings arising under title 11 or arising in or related to cases under title 11

(a) Except as otherwise provided in subsections (b) and (d), a proceeding arising under title 11 or arising in or related to a case under title 11 may be commenced in the district court in which such case is pending.

(b) Except as provided in subsection (d) of this section, a trustee in a case under title 11 may commence a proceeding arising in or related to such case to recover a money judgment of or property worth less than $1,000 [1] or a consumer debt of less than $15,000,[1] or a debt (excluding a consumer debt) against a noninsider of less than $25,000, only in the district court for the district in which the defendant resides.

(c) Except as provided in subsection (b) of this section, a trustee in a case under title 11 may commence a proceeding arising in or related to such case as statutory successor to the debtor or creditors under section 541 or 544(b) of title 11 in the district court for the district where the State or Federal court sits in which, under applicable nonbankruptcy venue provisions, the debtor or creditors, as the case may be, may have commenced an action on which such proceeding is based if the case under title 11 had not been commenced.

(d) A trustee may commence a proceeding arising under title 11 or arising in or related to a case under title 11 based on a claim arising after the commencement of such case from the operation of the business of the debtor only in the district court for the district where a State or Federal court sits in which, under applicable nonbankruptcy venue provisions, an action on such claim may have been brought.

(e) A proceeding arising under title 11 or arising in or related to a case under title 11, based on a claim arising after the commencement of such case from the operation of the business of the debtor, may be commenced against the representative of the estate in such case in the district court for the district where the State or Federal court sits in which the party commencing such proceeding may, under applicable nonbankruptcy venue provisions, have brought an action on such claim, or in the district court in which such case is pending.

§1410 - Venue of cases ancillary to foreign proceedings

A case under chapter 15 of title 11 may be commenced in the district court of the United States for the district—

(1) in which the debtor has its principal place of business or principal assets in the United States;

(2) if the debtor does not have a place of business or assets in the United States, in which there is pending against the debtor an action or proceeding in a Federal or State court; or

(3) in a case other than those specified in paragraph (1) or (2), in which venue will be consistent with the interests of justice and the convenience of the parties, having regard to the relief sought by the foreign representative.

§1411 - Jury trials

(a) Except as provided in subsection (b) of this section, this chapter and title 11 do not affect any right to trial by jury that an individual has under applicable nonbankruptcy law with regard to a personal injury or wrongful death tort claim.

(b) The district court may order the issues arising under section 303 of title 11 to be tried without a jury.

§1412 - Change of venue

A district court may transfer a case or proceeding under title 11 to a district court for another district, in the interest of justice or for the convenience of the parties.

Chapter 89 – District Courts; Removal of Cases from State Courts (Excerpt)

§1452 - Removal of claims related to bankruptcy cases

(a) A party may remove any claim or cause of action in a civil action other than a proceeding before the United States Tax Court or a civil action by a governmental unit to enforce such governmental unit's police or regulatory power, to the district court for the district where such civil action is pending, if such district court has jurisdiction of such claim or cause of action under section 1334 of this title.

(b) The court to which such claim or cause of action is removed may remand such claim or cause of action on any equitable ground. An order entered under this subsection remanding a claim or cause of action, or a decision to not remand, is not reviewable by appeal or otherwise by the court of appeals under section 158(d), 1291, or 1292 of this title or by the Supreme Court of the United States under section 1254 of this title.

Chapter 111 – General Provisions (Excerpt)

§1655 - Lien enforcement; absent defendants

In an action in a district court to enforce any lien upon or claim to, or to remove any incumbrance or lien or cloud upon the title to, real or personal property within the district, where any defendant cannot be served within the State, or does not voluntarily appear, the court may order the absent defendant to appear or plead by a day certain.

Such order shall be served on the absent defendant personally if practicable, wherever found, and also upon the person or persons in possession or charge of such property, if any. Where personal service is not practicable, the order shall be published as the court may direct, not less than once a week for six consecutive weeks.

If an absent defendant does not appear or plead within the time allowed, the court may proceed as if the absent defendant had been served with process within the State, but any adjudication shall, as regards the absent defendant without appearance, affect only the property which is the subject of the action. When a part of the property is within another district, but within the same state, such action may be brought in either district.

Any defendant not so personally notified may, at any time within one year after final judgment, enter his appearance, and thereupon the court shall set aside the judgment and permit such defendant to plead on payment of such costs as the court deems just.

Chapter 123 – Fees and Costs (Excerpt)

§1930 - Bankruptcy fees

(a) The parties commencing a case under title 11 shall pay to the clerk of the district court or the clerk of the bankruptcy court, if one has been certified pursuant to section 156(b) of this title, the following filing fees:
   (1) For a case commenced under—
      (A) chapter 7 of title 11, $245, and
      (B) chapter 13 of title 11, $235.
   (2) For a case commenced under chapter 9 of title 11, equal to the fee specified in paragraph (3) for filing a case under chapter 11 of title 11. The amount by which the fee payable under this paragraph exceeds

$300 shall be deposited in the fund established under section 1931 of this title.

(3) For a case commenced under chapter 11 of title 11 that does not concern a railroad, as defined in section 101 of title 11, $1,167.

(4) For a case commenced under chapter 11 of title 11 concerning a railroad, as so defined, $1,000.

(5) For a case commenced under chapter 12 of title 11, $200.

(6)

    (A) Except as provided in subparagraph (B), in addition to the filing fee paid to the clerk, a quarterly fee shall be paid to the United States trustee, for deposit in the Treasury, in each case under chapter 11 of title 11, other than under subchapter V, for each quarter (including any fraction thereof) until the case is converted or dismissed, whichever occurs first. The fee shall be $325 for each quarter in which disbursements total less than $15,000; $650 for each quarter in which disbursements total $15,000 or more but less than $75,000; $975 for each quarter in which disbursements total $75,000 or more but less than $150,000; $1,625 for each quarter in which disbursements total $150,000 or more but less than $225,000; $1,950 for each quarter in which disbursements total $225,000 or more but less than $300,000; $4,875 for each quarter in which disbursements total $300,000 or more but less than $1,000,000; $6,500 for each quarter in which disbursements total $1,000,000 or more but less than $2,000,000; $9,750 for each quarter in which disbursements total $2,000,000 or more but less than $3,000,000; $10,400 for each quarter in which disbursements total $3,000,000 or more but less than $5,000,000; $13,000 for each quarter in which disbursements total $5,000,000 or more but less than $15,000,000; $20,000 for each quarter in which disbursements total $15,000,000 or more but less than $30,000,000; $30,000 for each quarter in which disbursements total more than $30,000,000. The fee shall be payable on the last day of the calendar month following the calendar quarter for which the fee is owed.

    (B) During each of fiscal years 2018 through 2022, if the balance in the United States Trustee System Fund as of September 30 of the most recent full fiscal year is less than $200,000,000,[1] the quarterly fee payable for a quarter in which disbursements equal or exceed $1,000,000 shall be the lesser of 1 percent of such disbursements or $250,000.

(7) In districts that are not part of a United States trustee region as defined in section 581 of this title, the Judicial Conference of the United States may require the debtor in a case under chapter 11 of title 11 to pay fees equal to those imposed by paragraph (6) of this subsection. Such fees shall be deposited as offsetting receipts to the fund established under section 1931 of this title and shall remain available until expended.

An individual commencing a voluntary case or a joint case under title 11 may pay such fee in installments. For converting, on request of the debtor, a case under chapter 7, or 13 of title 11, to a case under chapter 11 of title 11, the debtor shall pay to the clerk of the district court or the clerk of the bankruptcy court, if one has been certified pursuant to section 156(b) of this title, a fee of the amount equal to the difference between the fee specified in paragraph (3) and the fee specified in paragraph (1).

(b) The Judicial Conference of the United States may prescribe additional fees in cases under title 11 of the same kind as the Judicial Conference prescribes under section 1914(b) of this title.

(c) Upon the filing of any separate or joint notice of appeal or application for appeal or upon the receipt of any order allowing, or notice of the allowance of, an appeal or a writ of certiorari $5 shall be paid to the clerk of the court, by the appellant or petitioner.

(d) Whenever any case or proceeding is dismissed in any bankruptcy court for want of jurisdiction, such court may order the payment of just costs.

(e) The clerk of the court may collect only the fees prescribed under this section.

(f)

(1) Under the procedures prescribed by the Judicial Conference of the United States, the district court or the bankruptcy court may waive the filing fee in a case under chapter 7 of title 11 for an individual if the court determines that such individual has income less than 150 percent of the income official poverty line (as defined by the Office of Management and Budget, and revised annually in accordance with section 673(2) of the Omnibus Budget Reconciliation Act of 1981) applicable to a family of the size involved and is unable to pay that fee in installments. For purposes of this paragraph, the term "filing fee" means the filing fee required by subsection (a), or any other fee prescribed by the Judicial Conference under subsections (b) and (c) that is payable to the clerk upon the commencement of a case under chapter 7.

(2) The district court or the bankruptcy court may waive for such debtors other fees prescribed under subsections (b) and (c).

(3) This subsection does not restrict the district court or the bankruptcy court from waiving, in accordance with Judicial Conference policy, fees prescribed under this section for other debtors and creditors.

Chapter 131 – Rules of Courts (Excerpt)

§2075 - Bankruptcy rules

The Supreme Court shall have the power to prescribe by general rules, the forms of process, writs, pleadings, and motions, and the practice and procedure in cases under title 11.

Such rules shall not abridge, enlarge, or modify any substantive right.

The Supreme Court shall transmit to Congress not later than May 1 of the year in which a rule prescribed under this section is to become effective a copy of the proposed rule. The rule shall take effect no earlier than December 1 of the year in which it is transmitted to Congress unless otherwise provided by law.

The bankruptcy rules promulgated under this section shall prescribe a form for the statement required under section 707(b)(2)(C) of title 11 and may provide general rules on the content of such statement.